Imogen Edwards-Jones is the co-author of the bestselling *Hotel Babylon* (now a major TV series), *Air Babylon* and *Fashion Babylon* as well as author of *The Stork Club* and *The Taming of Eagles*. Her fiction includes *My Canapé Hell*, *Shagpile*, *The Wendy House* and *Tuscany for Beginners*. Her new book, *Beach Babylon*, is now available from Bantam Press. Imogen lives in west London with her husband and their baby daughter. As an award-winning journalist she regularly frequents some of the best (and some of the worst) hotels all over the world.

Anonymous is currently the manager of a five-star central London hotel. For the past fifteen years he has worked in almost all of the capital's other luxury hotels.

Also by Imogen Edwards-Jones

MY CANAPÉ HELL
SHAGPILE
THE WENDY HOUSE
THE TAMING OF EAGLES
TUSCANY FOR BEGINNERS
THE STORK CLUB
AIR BABYLON
FASHION BABYLON
BEACH BABYLON

HOTEL
Babylon

IMOGEN EDWARDS-JONES
& Anonymous

CORGI BOOKS

HOTEL BABYLON
A CORGI BOOK : 9780552151467

Originally published in Great Britain by Bantam Press,
a division of Transworld Publishers

PRINTING HISTORY
Bantam Press edition published 2004
Corgi edition published 2005

17 19 20 18

Set in 11.5/16pt Sabon by
Falcon Oast Graphic Art Ltd.

Corgi Books are published by Transworld Publishers,
61–63 Uxbridge Road, London W5 5SA,
a division of The Random House Group Ltd.

Addresses for Random House Group Ltd companies outside the UK
can be found at: www.randomhouse.co.uk
The Random House Group Ltd Reg. No. 954009.

The Random House Group Limited supports The Forest Stewardship
Council® (FSC®), the leading international forest-certification organisation.
Our books carrying the FSC label are printed on FSC®-certified paper.
FSC is the only forest-certification scheme supported by the leading
environmental organisations, including Greenpeace. Our
paper procurement policy can be found at
www.randomhouse.co.uk/environment

MIX
Paper from
responsible sources
FSC® C016897

Printed and bound in Great Britain by Clays Ltd, St Ives plc

For the 'A' Team –
Eugenie Furniss and Stephanie Cabot

With grateful thanks to the handsome Doug Young and all at Transworld for their marvellous publishing, plus the charming Anonymous for his patience, humour and rather delicious home-made biscuits.

Prologue

All of the following is true. Only the names have been changed to protect the guilty. All the anecdotes, the stories, the characters, the situations, the highs, the lows, the scams, the drugs, the misery, the love, the death and the insanity are exactly as was told to me by Anonymous – someone who has spent his whole career working in hotels at the heart of the capital's luxury hotel industry. However, for legal reasons, the stories now take place in a fictitious hotel known as Hotel Babylon. Narrated by Anonymous, more than a decade is compressed into twenty-four hours. Everything else is as it should be. The rich spend money, the hotel makes money and the chambermaids still fight the bellboys over a two-pound coin. It's just another twenty-four hours in an expensive London hotel.

7AM – 8AM

It was a big night last night and, Jesus Christ, do I feel shit. I've got what sounds like roadworks going off in my head and a tongue like a shagpile carpet. I hadn't really intended to get pissed, but it was Michelle's leaving do so I couldn't really help myself. That's the thing about working in the luxury hotel business: you're surrounded by so much hedonism and debauchery that at the end of a long hard day at the coalface of the service industry you just want to get hammered.

We all ended up doing shots at Samantha's on Oxford Street. It's a hangout for hotel staff who want to drink long and late into the night. It's a well-known place, if you work in any of the big hotels in the capital. All you need to do is show your hotel ID card, and you're in. There were loads of us there last night to see

Michelle on her way. Well, Michelle's a popular girl. She's been on reception with me for a couple of years, and she's leaving this place to go on to Claridge's. Or is it the Dorchester? She's told me many times, but I'm afraid I still can't quite remember.

Anyway, it was a good night. Plenty of gossip. James, head of purchasing, who is prone to filling old bottles of 1982 Château Rothschild with plonk to impress girls he takes home, disappeared with one of the waitresses. One of the maids was violently sick everywhere. But the best thing I heard was that one of the girls in house-keeping caught Michelle giving the manager, Adrian, a blowjob. Amazing. I tell you, if you knew Adrian you'd probably be even more shocked. He is one of those posh boys who came to us through the Savoy training scheme; all stripy shirts, cufflinks and citrus-smelling aftershave. The sort of bloke you would never expect to drop his trousers in a men's toilet on Oxford Street.

But then again, I have been working in hotels long enough now not to judge people on appearances. It's always the straights in suits who have cases full of rubber and porn mags; it's always the weird-looking blokes who just drink mineral water and go to bed early; and it's always the married women who want to sleep with the staff. But there is one thing they all have in common. There's one thing that absolutely everyone does when they come to a hotel: they steal. TV sets, teaspoons, ashtrays, bathrobes, drinks from the ludicrously named 'honour bar', KitKats, crisps, carpets, furniture, works of art. You get men who are shelling out £3,500 a night (not including breakfast) who will piss in a miniature bottle if it means saving them from coughing up for a Teacher's whisky from the mini bar.

Anyway, what is particularly appealing about Michelle's behaviour last night is that she's got to do her exit interview with Adrian later on today. The exit interview is normally one of those little sit-down chats where the manager, or personnel manager, goes through your strong and your weak points, telling you where you can improve, where you are good and where your particular talents lie. Oh, to be a fly on the wall in that meeting! Roll on eleven o'clock. At least that is something to look forward to today.

It's a bit quiet in reception this morning as I walk in. My mate Ben, who is doing nights this week, is nowhere to be seen. I know I'm a couple of minutes late. It's 7.05 a.m. by the time I have hung up my coat in the staff cloakroom and walked back up the stairs. But he shouldn't have clocked off already. He is supposed to wait until I get here, to debrief me on what's been going on overnight, and then get himself off home.

'Oi, Derek,' I say to the doorman, who is looking a little the worse for a whole night sitting in his leather-padded chair. 'Any idea where that lazy git of a receptionist is?'

'What, Ben?' asks Derek.

'Yeah, Ben,' I nod.

'Have you tried in the back office?' he suggests.

'Of course.'

There is a small office behind reception where reservations make up the bills, receive faxes and deal with the ever-changing, ever-annoying occupancy plan on the computer. It is a claustrophobic place you try not to spend much time in during the day as it smells of instant coffee, stale biscuits and bad breath. At night, however, its long, flat desk doubles as a bed. Ben has been told off for kipping in the office before. His is the first face guests see when they come into the hotel. And this is a luxury hotel where rooms go from anything from £200 to £2,000 a night. The face they are supposed to see should exude luxury; it shouldn't be some crinkled, slept-in piece of shit with stapler marks on its cheek. I walk in and, sure enough, he is there. Flat on his back, his mouth wide open, catching flies.

'Oi, Ben! You bastard! Wake up!' I shout.

Jesus, does the man jump.

'What? Shit!' he says, leaping to attention like someone's shoved a cattle prod up his backside. 'Sorry? Oh, God, it's you,' he mumbles, running his hands through his lank brown hair, looking relieved that he has not been properly busted. 'I only dozed off for about five minutes. I thought I'd catch a few before the red-eye guests start coming in from Heathrow.'

'Yeah, right.'

'Honestly, man, I haven't been here long,' he protests, brushing down his rather shiny suit. 'Anyway, what was Michelle's thing like?'

I tell him about Michelle and Adrian and he starts to laugh. He thinks it's the funniest thing he's heard all week. 'D'you think he'll talk her through her technique? Give her marks out of ten?' He says that it's almost worth staying up to see her come in at eleven for her exit meeting, and asks me to phone him later with all the details.

He tells me he had a quiet night. Nothing too heavy that he couldn't handle. There were a couple of drunks left in the bar who were a bit difficult to shift, and some girl who walked through at three a.m. swinging a plastic carrier bag full of vomit like it was the latest fashion accessory. But other than that, he says, I'll have to ask Derek where he thinks the hookers might be when it comes to checking out, or chucking out, later. He says he wasn't really paying attention. But we both know that he was either in the bar serving himself a few vodka shots to keep him going or he was flat on his back in the office. I smile. It is annoying being on split shifts with Ben, as he always does the bare minimum and seems to get away with it. Actually, it is more than annoying – it really pisses me off. Today more than most, I suppose, because I am so hung over.

'Anything else I need to know?' I ask Ben as I play with the complimentary mints on the counter and click my free hotel pen.

'Not really,' says Ben. 'Except I gather there's some Yank coming in today. A Texan.' He grins. 'Chink, chink, chink.'

'Oh, right,' I say, perking up a bit.

'Oh yes.' Ben smiles, rubbing his hands together. 'Everyone loves a Texan.'

'I'll see you later,' I say to him, giving him a small shove on his way.

'Yeah,' he replies, pulling up the collar on his coat.

'Seven p.m. tonight.'

'Yeah, right.' He sniffs. 'Give me a call when Michelle gets in.' He winks. 'I'm going to miss her.'

'I thought you'd lost your heart to Jackie.'

'Sure, mate,' he says, shooting me with his right index finger. 'See you later.'

'Yeah, right,' I say, sounding a little surprised.

You see, Ben's been having this affair with Jackie, a pretty Australian head housekeeper, for at least three months. I've covered for him a few times on reception, which is how I know. They have the same routine every time. She usually rings down and says something like,

'Room 212 needs inspecting.' He then runs up the stairs like a dog on heat, they stick a 'Do Not Disturb' sign on the door, do it for about half an hour, and then she sends in a maid to clean up the room. It's been going on for a while now so I thought it might be love, or at least something along those lines. But apparently not.

'See you later,' I add, shooting him right back as he walks out of the revolving door.

There is no time to dwell on things because as soon as Ben disappears the phone rings.

'Hello, reception,' I say as breezily as seven beers will let me.

'Hello,' comes this American voice. 'This is room 514.'

'Good morning, sir.'

'I ordered a steak for breakfast this morning about half an hour ago and it still hasn't arrived.'

'I'm terribly sorry, sir. Have you spoken to room service?'

'Room service, shmoom service,' he says. 'I keep calling, no-one picks up, and then I get transferred to you.'

'Right, sir, that happens after three or four rings.'

'Well, I'd like you to get down there and sort it out for me.'

'I can't really do that, sir,' I say.

'Can't or won't?' he asks, beginning to raise his voice. 'I have a very important meeting in an hour. If I

17

don't have my steak before I go to the meeting I'll blame you and the hotel and I'll invoice you for all the inconvenience you've caused me.'

'Right, sir.'

'Don't right sir me,' he says, becoming really quite irritated. 'Do something about it!'

'I'll do it right away, sir,' I say.

'Good!' he shouts, and hangs up the phone.

'Room service?' asks Derek from his leather chair.

'Yep. An American who ordered steak.'

'Not again,' says Derek. 'Why do they do that? What's wrong with a bit of bacon and egg in the morning? Do you want me to go?'

'Don't worry, mate,' I say, thinking I might get myself a swift cup of coffee while I'm down in the kitchen. 'I'll go.'

'I'll hold the fort then,' he says. 'Till you get back.'

Derek's a decent sort of a bloke. He's been a doorman and night porter for over twenty years and he's worked here for the last five. He inherited this job from his uncle. This place is a bit more upmarket than the four-star heap he used to work in just around the corner. He always says that he'll pass this post on to one of his three sons. He can earn over a grand a week in tips, so it's the sort of job people like to keep in the family. But things are changing. The days of passing concierge and doorman jobs on from father to son are almost gone. The trendy modern hotels such as the Sanderson and the Metropolitan want male model material poncing around outside, while the other establishment places tend to be owned by big corporate chains for whom tradition doesn't actually cut much ice any more.

'Do you want me to pick you up a coffee?' I ask as I turn to go downstairs.

'No, don't worry, mate.' He sniffs. 'I'm off in less than an hour. Then I won't be able to sleep.'

God, sleep, I think as I walk down the stairs towards the kitchens and the staff canteen – that's what we all bloody need. No-one sleeps properly in this business. It's not even 7.20 and the early shift in the kitchen have been at it for at least a couple of hours. The breakfast chef came in at about five a.m. He's been par-cooking bangers ever since. Not only has he been making up the staff breakfasts since about 5.30, he's been feeding the guests since seven.

The basement stinks of bleach and bacon. The air is so hot and thick in the corridors that it is hard to breathe. I walk into the kitchen and it's fogged with the fat of a hundred frying eggs. There's one bloke standing in front of the huge piece of hot, flat stainless steel, flipping. His face is grey. It shines with grease. His eyes are glazed as he stares ahead; his gaze is fixed on the eggs in front of him. He looks young, in his early twenties. I don't recognize him at all. He must be new. The turnover is quite high down here among the young guys. Who wants to work a fifteen-hour split shift in this hell? However, by the time you've worked your way up through the ranks to a sous chef position, it seems like no-one wants to leave. The good chefs get over a hundred grand a year; if you've got your name over the front door you can triple or quadruple that.

The bloke doesn't hear me when I shout. Perhaps it's the noise of the food; either that or he is so dog tired his brain's switched off.

'Oi!' I shout again. This time he moves. 'The Yank in 514 wants to know what has happened to his steak.'

The chef doesn't say anything. His face barely reacts. Instead, he points with a couple of swift jabbing movements of his palette knife at a hunk of meat sizzling right at the back of the hot plate.

'How long?' I ask, and he flicks me the Vs, which I presume to mean two minutes. 'Good.' I nod. 'Hurry it up.'

He doesn't react. He just turns to the stack of trays laid up behind him with cutlery, napkins, salt, pepper and toast and starts sliding the fried eggs onto the plates. Occasionally he substitutes them for a spoonful of scrambled eggs from the large vat next to him. He then adds a couple of slithers of bacon from under the hot yellow lights to his left. It all looks pretty disgusting, yet somehow, after it has made its long, chilling journey along various corridors in the hotel and ends up in someone's bedroom, it doesn't seem so bad. And they don't come cheap either: you'll pay anything from £12.50 to £25 for a full English in one of the capital's luxury hotels, and we, of course, love it because they cost under 50p a plate to make.

I walk out of the kitchen and the phone in the next-door room starts to ring.

'Hello, room service,' answers another young man dressed in white.

I slope off down the corridor towards the staff canteen for a quick coffee. All this food has made me want a cigarette. The staff canteen is always cold and damp, and it smells of cheap cigarettes no matter what food they have on offer. Although, bizarrely, I have to admit that the food they actually serve is not bad at all. Bearing in mind that they have about £1.20 per person, per day, to feed us all on and that most of the staff eat at least two main meals in the hotel every day, they don't seem too disgusting. We quite often get the left-overs from any banqueting that has gone on the night before. We have the old salads and some of the leftover pastries from tea. But we also get some good hotpots and stews, the odd chilli con carne, and there's always the curries they make for the Bangladeshi cleaners who hose the place down at night. There are a couple over in the far corner at the end of their night shift as I come in. Bent over their food, like someone might steal it, they don't even talk to each other.

I get myself a cup of black coffee and sit down opposite a bloke in a brown maintenance coat who I presume to be a Pole. I don't mean to be racist, but there are certain things you can take for granted in a hotel. The first is that the majority of maintenance guys are Polish. The second is that night cleaners are mostly from Bangladesh, and the third is that chambermaids are never English.

I remember once, at a hotel where I used to work, we had this linen porter who actually was English. We all thought it was a little odd. But we went with the flow. He was in his fifties. He could have been on his uppers or something, you never know. Anyway, one day he broke down, burst into tears in front of all of us in the canteen, saying he couldn't keep it a secret any more: he had to confess that he'd been in prison for murdering his wife with an axe. He left the next day, and I have never worked with a fellow Brit linen porter or chambermaid since.

The coffee and the cigarette perform their delicious alchemy: my heart starts racing and my brain feels a little more awake. I check my watch. Shit! It's 7.45. Where the hell did all the time go? I run up the stairs two at a time and steam into reception. My other half for the day, Liz, greets me with a steely stare.

'Where the fuck have you been?' she says, trying to look stern.

'Downstairs sorting out some room service order,' I reply. 'Anyway, you were late.'

'Five minutes,' she insists.

'Whatever,' I say.

There is no point arguing with Liz. I've got to work with her all day and it is easier to say nothing, as she's one of those people who can hold a grudge and give you the silent treatment all morning if she wants to. In her mid-twenties with blonde hair and great tits, she is one of those trolley dolly girls middle-aged men really fall for. She always has a tan but never seems to go on holiday; her stiff eyelashes curl back on themselves and her fingernails are made of the strongest nylon. She, Ben, Michelle and I are on a four days on, one day off rota that includes a week of nights. But now Michelle has gone and we're a receptionist down. We're awaiting a replacement, hopefully arriving tomorrow.

'Any problems?' I ask.

'Only one of the waitresses, Marie, has called in sick,' says Liz.

'Marie?' I laugh. 'I bet she's sick. She copped off with James from purchasing at Michelle's party. What did she say was wrong?'

'Food poisoning.'

'Food poisoning? I didn't know you could get that from gin and tonic.'

'Yeah, well.' Liz shrugs. 'Judging by what Derek told me just now about what went on last night, I'm sure she won't be the only one phoning in sick.'

'No.' I smile.

'Do you think Michelle will make it in?' Liz asks.

'I hope so,' I reply. 'I could do with a laugh.'

The telephone goes.

'Hello, reception?' says Liz in her sibilant, heavy voice. 'Mmm. Mmm. Right,' she says. 'I'm afraid we don't actually have the morning-after pill in our first-aid box, madam,' she declares, 'but if you hang on a couple of minutes our concierge, Tony, is arriving at eight a.m. and he will know the closest place where it is available. OK?' she asks. 'Um, yes,' she adds. 'I'll call you as soon as he arrives.' She puts down the telephone.

'Glad you got that call,' I say. 'It makes up for the pregnancy testing kit I had to get last week.'

8AM – 9AM

Tony walks through the revolving doors dead on eight a.m. His coat is plush, his suit is sharp and his shoes are highly polished. His shirt is a crisp Daz white and his black tie is from Prada. His dark hair is smooth and parted down the side, and he is sporting one of those contagious grins that make you want to be his friend. Actually, there are many things about Tony, besides his smile, that make you want to be his friend.

For starters, there is almost nothing that is going on in London that Tony doesn't know about. He is a walking, talking *Time Out* magazine. He knows where to go, where to eat, where to dance. He knows the doorman and bouncer on every club worth going to. He knows which Hollywood celebrity is playing which theatre and where they drink. He can get you a table at the Ivy, Nobu,

Hakkasan, Sheekey's, Petrus, the Wolseley or Gordon Ramsay's at a moment's notice. He can get you tickets for sold-out shows. He can get you deals on expensive cars. He can get you girls, drugs and rent boys. He can get you a villa in the South of France. He knows about this most beautiful place a concierge mate of his once rented at great expense for Courtney Love. It's heaven on earth apparently, not that Courtney would know: she paid the money but never bothered to turn up. But Tony can sort you anything – weekends in the country, bus trips around London. He can jump the queue at Madame Tussaud's. He can tell you where to get your watch repaired, your shotgun cleaned, where you can find the finest sari material in town. He knows where to late-night shop. He knows where to get a small gift for your wife. He knows just the new shoes you are looking for. He wears his concierge golden keys motif on his lapel with pride, and well he might, because they are the exclusive keys to open any door in town.

'All right, Tony,' I say as he comes in.

'All right, mate,' he says back. Tony's in a good mood. But then Tony's nearly always in a good mood. You'd be pretty happy if you took home a couple of grand a week in tips and backhanders and almost none of it ever saw the taxman. 'I hear last night was a good one,' he adds.

'Yeah,' I reply. 'How did you know about that already?'

Tony smiles, says nothing and taps the side of his nose. Meanwhile, Derek's up stretching and off out of here. Tony's arrival, along with the doorman Steve, means the end of Derek's shift. And as Tony sits down behind his desk, going through his post, checking through the Cotswold tour pamphlets he has a 10 per cent stake in, Steve is already opening the door to a flustered-looking bloke who looks like he's straight off a plane.

'Good morning, sir,' says Steve. 'Shall I take your bags?'

'Yes, yes,' says the flustered-looking bloke, dropping everything at his feet. He walks through the door and on towards reception.

'Good morning, sir,' I say, as Liz picks up another ringing telephone.

'Andrew Oliver,' says Mr Oliver, in one of those rootless transatlantic accents that mean he could come from almost anywhere. 'I have an early check-in. My secretary organized it. Paid the extra in advance.'

'Right you are, sir,' I say. 'I'll just go and check.'

There is nothing a hotel likes more than an early check-in or a pre-registered (pre-reg) guest. It's one of those 'happy days' moments when we get to double-book the room. It is a simple process. You get one bloke who pays for his night in the hotel and then you accept another early booking, making the punter pay for the night before to ensure early occupancy. So you are in effect charging for the same night twice. All we have to do in the hotel is make sure the first bloke is out before the second bloke arrives. Otherwise the shit hits the fan.

'Right, Mr Oliver,' I say, picking up his Canadian passport. 'We have you booked in to room 514.'

'514,' he repeats with a long, relieved sigh that smells of airline food.

'Yes, 514.'

I smile, but every single steak-eating American alarm bell in my body is starting to ring. Reception, we have a problem. Room 514 is not empty. In fact, room 514 doesn't look like it will be vacated in the next half hour and then it has to be cleaned and re-stocked and all the while I'm going to have Mr Oliver breathing coq au vin down my neck.

'Right, 514,' I say in such a way that he already knows there's trouble.

'What?' he asks. 'There can't be a problem. I've already paid. I've got a fax here to prove it.' He puts his heavy briefcase on the side and clicks it open.

'No, sir,' I say quickly, 'it has nothing to do with your booking. We have your booking here.' I gesture with my free hotel pen. 'It's just that we had a bit of a problem last night. The man who was staying in your room yesterday suffered from, um . . .'

'Food poisoning,' says Liz. 'Terrible, terrible food poisoning. Dreadful. He hasn't been able to leave his room for twenty-four hours. Oysters, I think he said.'

'Oysters?' asks Mr Oliver.

'Yes, oysters,' repeats Liz, almost beginning to believe her own story. 'No-one's been able to move him at all. Doctor's orders.'

'Anyway, sir,' I smile, 'the hotel is full, so I'm afraid we don't have a room available for you at all at the moment. But if you give us half an hour I'm sure we can sort something out for you.'

'Half an hour,' repeats Mr Oliver weakly.

'Yes, sir,' I say. 'I tell you what,' I add, like the thought has just occurred to me, 'why don't you have a complimentary breakfast in the dining room – eggs and bacon, coffee, that sort of thing – and we'll come and get you as soon as we have a room available.'

Mr Oliver is clearly too tired to kick up a fuss. All he wants is a warm bed, a cup of coffee and CNN on the telly. But instead he shuffles off in the direction of the dining room while I take a quick imprint of his gold corporate American Express card.

'Well, that went OK,' says Liz, with a flick of her blonde hair.

'Yeah, better than Ben at the beginning of the week,' I say.

A few days ago Ben made the terrible mistake of coming out with a rather bad lie when confronted by an irate American, straight off the red-eye from New York.

Instead of coming up with the usual food poisoning story to explain the lack of pre-reg rooms, he said that there had been a flood and maintenance were clearing it up. The American didn't believe him. He demanded to see the room. Ben said that it wasn't possible due to its terrible condition. The man called Ben a liar right close up to his face. Ben said that if the man really insisted he would take him to the room. The American did insist. And Ben took him to a room at the end of the second corridor where we were fortunately having some building work done. But the American still didn't believe him and asked to see the manager. It was a sorry story that ended up costing the hotel a complimentary stay and a bottle of champagne. Adrian was not impressed.

The phones are beginning to go mad now. This is the time of day when guests start calling up asking you to make up their bills and members of staff really start calling in sick. Today's a Friday, so I'm expecting it to be quite bad. It's always Mondays, Fridays and week-ends that are the sick days. The problem has got so bad now that if you call in sick these days you don't get paid. If you can provide some sort of doctor's note, then you will get SSP (statutory sick pay); if not, then tough. Why should the hotel pay for your hangover? Talking of which, mine is feeling pretty bad at the moment. I'd kill for a glass of water and some Nurofen.

The telephone goes again.

'Good morning,' I say.

'Hello, it's Jacinta,' comes a female voice.

I know immediately it's one of the maids calling in sick. It's all so lame. I know she is lying. She knows that I know she is lying yet we all go through the same pathetic charade. At least her excuse is slightly different from the usual 'food poisoning' pretence I have to pretend to sympathize with. She claims she has something wrong with her 'plumbing'. I'm not sure whether she means her drains or her womb, so I say something along the lines of 'bad luck, I hope it improves' before hanging up the phone.

Anyway, she's a bit late to be calling up and crying off work as most of the maids and the housekeeping staff should be here before eight a.m. This is, after all, the busiest time of their day when they should be cleaning and tidying the rooms as quickly as possible. The quicker the turnaround, the quicker they can get through their quota of rooms and go home. The last thing any good hotel needs is a dirty room sitting idle and costing cash. They all have a list of how the room is supposed to be left: two bath towels on the rail (tucked inside), face cloths rolled and placed by the basin, towel rail on low, desk lamp on, glass beakers behind the taps, radio off and air conditioning on. Moreover, any chambermaid worth her salt wants to get into the rooms as early as possible – almost as soon as the guest is thinking about leaving – because some guests leave tips in the room and the last thing they want is either Jez or Dave, the two bellboys, to get in there before them. Last week I was walking past a room on the third floor and found a twentysomething Portuguese maid and twenty-two-year-old Dave fighting over a two-pound coin. Some old hotel hands, who fly and stay all over the world, will leave their tips in bellboy-proof areas, like under the pillows; others who are less versed in their stealing ways leave them on the desk in the middle of the room. Then it's up to the maid to shift herself to get what she deserves.

And take it from me, they really do deserve whatever little extras they get. The stuff they come across you would not believe – dirty underwear, used condoms, sperm-crisp porn mags, lines of coke, old syringes, well-used sex toys. People behave so sadly in hotel rooms the results can be quite shocking. I remember the story of a pop group who had taken so much diarrhoea-inducing cocaine that they ended up wiping their arses on the curtains because they'd run out of toilet paper.

Working as a chambermaid has to be one of the shittiest jobs in the hotel. And when I say shittiest, that's exactly what I mean. A couple of months ago this posh middle-aged woman laid an enormous turd in the middle of her bed. It was the weirdest thing. The woman was staying with her daughter and they were sharing a room – and, I think, even a bed. The daughter went out early for some reason and the mother left at about nine in the morning. She had an amusing chat with me as she walked out the door, telling me about the art exhibition she was on her way to see. Meanwhile she'd left this great big shit in her room and told no-one about it. The poor chambermaid nearly passed out when she discovered it. She couldn't work out why the room stank so much while she was cleaning it, until she pulled back the bed sheets and discovered why. The whole thing was so shocking that Jackie in housekeeping eventually had to clear it up because the maid simply couldn't face it. What was even more weird was that the woman came back again in the evening and made no mention of it at all. They left the next day and – can you believe this? – they didn't leave a tip.

At least they do get tipped sometimes. The chefs downstairs, who work in what I think have to be some of the worst conditions in the hotel, don't even get that. When I say worst, I really do know what I'm talking about, because I had the misfortune to be one once. I couldn't hack it. The bullying, bastard behaviour that goes on down there, you wouldn't believe. The chefs are shits, and boy do they enjoy dishing it out.

I remember my first day like it was yesterday. Unless

you're on breakfasts, you come in around this time. All the chefs do, as they've got to get their *mise en place* ready, which basically means chopping and preparing all the food prior to service. You're on a split shift, which means that we do eight a.m. to three p.m., then we have three to five p.m. off, which is time usually spent in the pub or down the bookie's, and then we come back in again until eleven p.m. It's a bastard because it is so hot and sweaty down there it's like some sort of medieval torture chamber. And the things they do to you. On my first day they made me stand on a hot stove and explain at the top of my voice why I should be allowed to work in their sodding kitchen. I burnt a hole through the soles of my shoes before they let me get down. I had blisters on my feet for a week. As the new boy I was also made to gut fish and turn potatoes.

Turning potatoes is one of those monkey jobs that can send a man mad. It involves topping and tailing a new potato and then taking the skin off the sides in such a way that you end up with a small barrel. When I started out I could only do about two a minute; by the end I could work my way through one bucket in about an hour, which roughly works out at about five a minute. I turned potatoes all day every day for three months. I ended up doing them in my sleep. I dreamt of those stupid little barrel shapes. It was a nightmare. But at least I got out. There's some South American bloke at the Savoy whose only job is to turn potatoes. He's been doing it for years. I think they managed to get him a chair quite recently, which must have made his year.

There was one thing I did learn about turning potatoes: although speed is obviously of the essence, it doesn't do to finish the job too quickly. I did make the mistake once of going up to some sous chef bastard or a chef de partie who was on potage, making soups and stuff, and saying that I'd finished and had nothing to do. 'What? Nothing?' he yelled. 'You said you've got nothing to do?' I nodded. 'Well, come with me then,' he said, and he took me into the back of the kitchen where there was a row of three industrial freezers. They're huge things that could freeze a grown man. He opened one of the freezers, pulled out about six bags of frozen peas the size of pillowcases, ripped every one of them open and poured all the peas back into the freezer. 'Right,' he said. 'I want you to get in there and pick every single one of those peas out of the freezer and put them back in the bags. And don't you ever tell me again that you have nothing to do in the kitchen.' I had to bend over and pick every single one of those peas out with my bare hands. It took me three hours and my fingers were blue with cold by the time I had finished. So, as you can probably tell, I am not overly fond of the kitchens.

I'm not overly fond of Liz at the moment either. The way she keeps clicking her nylon nails together this morning is beginning to get on my nerves. Maybe it's my hangover that's making me a bit more touchy today. Normally she doesn't annoy me that much. The phone goes again. Liz ignores it. She is far too busy resting her breasts on the counter, flirting with some fat bloke, asking him how much he enjoyed his stay. I decide to answer.

'Hello, reception,' I say.

'Hello, this is room 160,' comes a female voice. 'I spoke to someone earlier. About a certain matter.'

'Right,' I say.

'It is a little sensitive,' she says.

'OK,' I say. 'Maybe I can help?'

'Well . . .' She clears her throat. 'I rang up to ask if someone could get me the morning-after pill nearly an hour ago and the girl in reception said that she would get back to me and, um, she hasn't.'

'Oh,' I say. 'I'm terribly sorry, madam. If you'll just hold for a moment I'll see if I can sort something out.'

I walk over to Tony, who is sitting at his desk just to the right of the door counting up how many theatre and opera tickets he has sold so far this week, working out just how much his 10 per cent cut is. He likes this little earner, as he can get up to £400 a month flogging *Cats*, *Les Misérables* and *The Mousetrap* tickets to punters.

'Er, Tony,' I say.

'How can I help you, mate?' he says, looking up from his calculations.

'Morning-after pill?' I ask.

'Oh, right.' He sniffs. 'The chemist at the end of the road,' he says. 'He does give it us if we ask but they do prefer it if the lady goes in herself as they tend to have to ask all sorts of questions.'

'Right,' I say. 'I get the impression she would prefer it if we went and got it.'

'OK then,' says Tony, standing up, 'I'll send Dave.' Tony clicks his fingers at Dave, who is standing by the luggage trolley, buffing the brass. Dave, who is young and keen, immediately stands to attention, drops what he is doing and comes over to Tony. 'He could do with the exercise. He's been sitting on his backside all morning, haven't you, Dave?'

'Yes, Mr Williams,' says Dave.

'Do you know the room number?' asks Tony.

'160,' I say.

'160,' he says, his face breaking into a smile. 'Isn't that the woman who walked through here last night swinging a plastic bag of vomit?'

'Oh, I don't know,' I say.

'I think it is,' he says. 'I bet she's feeling pretty rough this morning.'

'Yeah.' I nod. 'That makes two of us.'

'Yeah, right. Roll on eleven o'clock,' says Tony, rubbing his hands together. 'I can't wait to see the look on Michelle's face.'

9AM – 10AM

Dave walks through the revolving doors on his way out into the sunshine just as Adrian, the manager, spins in round the other side.

'Morning, sir,' says Tony, stacking together a pile of open-top bus tour pamphlets.

'Where's he off to?' asks Adrian, indicating over his shoulder with his left thumb.

'Morning-after pill, sir,' smiles Tony. 'For room 160.'

'Oh, right,' says Adrian.

'Yeah.' Tony is still grinning. 'Apparently it has been one of those nights.'

'Really?' Adrian smiles too, missing none of Tony's tricks. 'I wouldn't know myself, I've only just arrived. All right?' he says to me.

'All right, sir,' I confirm right back.

'Hangover?' he asks.

'No, not at all,' I lie.

'Good,' he says. 'That's what I like to hear. Some professionalism in reception. Good morning, Liz,' he continues, as he walks towards his office.

'Morning, Mr Thompson,' she replies, nodding and giving him her brightest, breeziest service industry smile.

Well, Adrian is a good-looking man. Tall, with brown hair and green eyes, he has risen fast up the ranks of the hotel corporate ladder, which is unusual for a posh bloke who has got a bit of a lad's reputation. I mean, getting blowjobs off the staff is not something a man in his position is supposed to be doing. He is running a business that has a turnover of some £35m a year. Like the captain of a ship, he should be leading from the front, commanding from a position of wisdom and respect. But Adrian's probably a bit too popular for his own good. The staff like him. He goes to their leaving parties and misbehaves. He also always organizes a good Christmas piss-up where he has been known to try to drink the chefs under the table.

He and Tony are good friends, mainly because Tony gets Adrian things – tables in restaurants, tickets to concerts, little deals here, trips there; last year he sent him a limo to collect him from the airport when he came back from holiday. Tony often helps Adrian out of tight spots. He organized Adrian's brother's stag do, making sure they got in everywhere around town, and arranged a few discounts along the way; in return, Tony more or less gets a free rein to do what he wants. He gets to keep his theatre ticket commissions; he gets to ensure that we use only one mini cab firm; he also gets to flog his trips to Dorset and the Cotswolds, and his Stratford upon Avon cheap day returns.

Not that Adrian is the cleanest of cleans. I heard that he was once fired from one of those groovy boutique hotels in France, in one of those upmarket ski resorts. The story goes that when he was doing nights on reception he used to invite all his mates into the hotel after hours and open up the bar serving free drinks until dawn. Unfortunately, one night when Adrian got particularly plastered he decided to lie down behind one of the sofas and have a kip. In smaller hotels the bloke doing nights on reception doesn't usually have anyone else working with him – unlike here, where there is always someone else, like the night porter, on duty. Anyway, while Adrian was apparently fast asleep behind the sofa, two thieves walked into reception, helped themselves to the passkeys and began systematically robbing the rooms. Adrian woke up to sounds of guests shouting '*Voleur!* Thief!' as they ran down the stairs after their belongings. Adrian's reaction was to leave the hotel before the manager arrived and spend the day skiing, returning the next evening to pick up his paycheque and belongings. The French didn't bother to put it on his record. I think because he was young and a student and had been working there for free, they decided to overlook it. But then, that sort of economy with the truth happens a lot in hotels.

There was a restaurant manager who worked here for a while who was eventually fired for stealing. It was only when Adrian actually bothered to ring up the place where he'd last worked that he found out he'd been fired for the same thing before. But in the last hotel they had come to some sort of arrangement. He had been a good restaurant manager. He had kept the place running smoothly, brought in some celebrity clients, making such a fuss over everyone who came in that he made the hotel a destination the glamorous wanted to be seen in. So they decided to overlook the three cases of wine he stole and the way he'd pocketed over £500 in pooled tips. They cut a deal with him, promising him that if he left of his own accord they wouldn't mention his light-fingered indiscretions on his employment record. So he moved over here, and he was fine for the first six months or so, bringing in the punters, running the place smoothly. Then people started to notice things in the monthly audit. It was only a matter of time before he was caught.

We've got a stock-take going on later today, or so I

have been told. There's a Bombay Sapphire thief in our midst and they want to find out if anything else has gone. Someone has trousered something like seven small bottles of Bombay Sapphire in the last twenty-four hours alone. It's an odd drink to be nicking. It's normally the vodka that goes walkabout as you can't smell it on people's breath. Either way, it has been going on for a couple of weeks now and it is really beginning to piss Adrian off. He is in half a mind to start going through all the chambermaids' handbags when they leave at six p.m. That lazy git Mustafa, who sits downstairs in his security booth all day watching daytime TV, never seems to catch anyone. Anyway, Adrian thinks that if we have an outside auditor come in and go through all the stock it might put the wind up the thief and make him/her think twice about doing it again.

The telephone rings and Liz picks it up. Her moist, glossy lips make an annoying popping sound as she speaks. I really should keep busy because otherwise I know today she is going to drive me mad. It's the guy in room 302 who wants to check out. I remember him from the day before yesterday. He is one of those sleazy-type guys with dandruff on his collar and egg on his tie. To be honest, he just looks like he needs a good wash. Anyway, Liz has to go to the 'little girl's room' (how annoying an expression is that?) and she wants me to take over the call. So I type in his room number on the computer in the small office behind the desk and press print. Where's that monosyllabic reservations assistant Ewan when you need him? The machine goes crazy, churning out reams of paper with different 0906 sex-chat numbers on it. Normally these calls cost something like 50p a minute, but in the hotel it is £10 for sixty seconds and room 302 has been hitting the porn lines late into the night. I tear off the sheet and stare. He has been dialling various porn numbers almost solidly between 2.13 a.m. and 4.02 a.m. and he now owes us a grand total of £850.

It does sound expensive, but he is by no means the worst. A couple of weeks ago there was this bloke on his own who ran up a £3,000 phone bill over the two days in his room. It was extraordinary. We did call (when we could get through) a couple of times and tell him that he was running up rather a large bill but he didn't seem to care. His sister had paid for his room in advance and we did have her credit-card swipe behind the desk, so we weren't too nervous. However, when he came to check out he said he could not pay the bill. Eventually, after much wrangling, we called his sister who turned up and hit the roof. Bizarrely, her anger was directed at us for letting it get so out of control. When I finally informed her that we had spoken to her brother on at least two occasions she became suitably contrite and paid up. Or at least I think she did. Adrian came down out of his office to sort it out. I think I heard the woman make mention of sending a cheque.

So, although room 302's is not the largest 0906 porn chat-line bill I have seen, I know it is going to be large enough to cause problems, especially as the man was booked in by his office and he is clearly on some business trip. It is quite hard to explain an £850 porn bill to one's boss.

I walk back out into reception with my metre-long bill.

'Oh dear,' says Liz, raising her overly plucked eyebrows. 'Don't tell me we've got a talker.'

'It looks like he's been a bit chatty, that's for sure.'

'Porn?' she asks.

'What else?' I say, beginning to fold up the printout.

'Oh OK, I don't know,' she replies huffily, with an annoying little shimmy of her offended shoulders. 'He could have been on the phone to his wife.'

'Yeah, right. No-one talks to their wife that much. Anyway,' I say, looking up at the sound of the opening lift, 'keep quiet, here he comes.'

Dandruff man approaches the front desk looking like he has hardly slept a minute last night, which judging from the length of his porn bill has to be the case.

'Good morning, sir,' I say. 'I trust you had a pleasant stay.'

'Very good,' says the man, his suit shining in the morning sun. 'Slept like a log.'

'Good, sir.' I smile, handing over the bill half in and out of the envelope. 'Would you like to check your bill, sir?'

'Yeah.' He sniffs as the long length of paper unfurls in front of him. 'Eight hundred and fifty quid?' he says suddenly. 'Eight hundred and fifty quid? You say I've spent eight hundred and fifty quid on the phone?'

'Yes, sir,' I say.

'That's outrageous,' he says. 'Eight hundred and fifty quid on the phone? You can't charge that.'

'I'm afraid that is our standard rate for a premium-rate telephone line, sir.'

'Premium rate? Those aren't premium rate!' he says.

'I'm afraid they are, sir,' I say.

'No they're not!' he says.

'I am afraid they are, sir.'

'Will you stop being afraid!' he shouts, his cheeks bright scarlet with anger.

'Please don't raise your voice, sir,' I say.

'I did not raise my voice!' he says, raising his voice.

'Fine, sir,' I say. 'Your room is two hundred and fifty pounds a night for two nights, you have spent thirty-two pounds in the mini bar . . .'

'On two whiskies!' he says, slapping the top of reception with his hand.

'Two whiskies, some chocolate, a bag of crisps and some mineral water.'

'Oh, Jesus Christ, crisps and some mineral water,' he adds sarcastically. 'That really is going to break the bloody bank.'

'And you have spent eight hundred and fifty pounds on the telephone.'

'This place is daylight robbery,' he says, shaking his head and releasing some flakes onto the counter. 'I'm sorry, I'm not paying eight hundred and fifty quid on a phone bill. You should have warned me it would be this expensive, and anyway, they aren't premium-rate lines.'

'0906 Hot Honeys is a premium-rate line,' I insist. 'It tells you that as soon as you dial up.'

'How do you know?'

'Because we have had many customers use it before.'

'Can we come to some sort of arrangement?' he asks.

'I am very happy to make up separate receipts, if you want, sir?' I suggest.

'Right,' he says.

'We could also waive about fifty pounds off the bill,' I add. I have done this plenty of times before. It usually makes them so grateful that they pay up the rest immediately. It saves an awful lot of fighting for the sake of £50.

'Really?' he asks, sounding surprised and ingratiated at the same time. 'That would be ever so nice of you.'

'No problem, sir,' I say.

'Can I put the room on the credit card,' he says, licking his thumb, 'and I'll pay the phone bill in cash.' He pulls out a wad of £50 notes and starts peeling them off one by one, placing them on the counter. 'There we go.' He smiles. 'Eight hundred quid.'

'Thank you very much, sir,' I say. 'I'll just run your card through. Would you like any help with your bags?'

'Oh, no thanks,' he says, looking down at his small black holdall. 'I think I can manage this.'

I walk into the back office with his green corporate American Express card and swipe it through the machine. While I stand waiting for the connection, I ignore the miraculously returned Ewan, who is making up a bill for Liz, and stare through the window at the meat van as it pulls up outside the kitchen back entrance below. A man in a white coat and white paper trilby hat starts unloading legs of lamb, sides of beef and pork.

I remember from when I worked in the kitchen that between nine and ten a.m. was when all the deliveries arrived. And, God, did you have to be careful. When it comes to deliveries, you really have to have your wits about you. The scams are endless. And the problem is, because the products used in the luxury hotel business are so goddamn expensive, no-one knows quite who is doing whom. The suppliers do the hotel, the staff do the hotel, and the hotel tries to do everyone.

One of the most lucrative scams I have heard about went on at the Lanesborough. The bloke who was in charge of deliveries had something going with the meat supplier. He would order five kilos of Parma ham, for example, when Chef had only ordered one kilo. The hotel would pay for the five, the delivery man would only take one and the other four were sent back to the meat supplier who sold them on, halving the profit with the delivery man at the Lanesborough. The scam ran for about six months until they were discovered, and the man in charge of deliveries, as far as I can remember, ended up doing time.

But they're all at it, as you can imagine. Chefs get backhanders from suppliers all the time. Otherwise, why would they choose one Jersey Royal supplier over another? They're all clamouring to get their produce into our kitchens. Think of the number of potatoes we turn a year. At Christmas you should see the things that come through here just to keep the man sweet. Turkeys, sides of beef, whole salmons, trays of Dover sole, bags of prawns, slabs of foie gras, baskets of truffles – I bet Chef never sets foot in the shops between Christmas and New Year. He sits there, fat as a goose, feasting on all his free festive fare.

The suppliers do get their own back sometimes. They can be quite crafty when it comes to bookkeeping. It is the big orders you have to be careful about, especially the vegetables. When you have got an order as long as your arm with endives, beans, broccoli, raspberries, blueberries and cauliflowers, who is going to notice the tray of apples that never arrived? But once you've signed for an order, you can't complain. You don't have a leg to stand on. And they're always hassling you into making a mistake. The van always arrives late. You have Chef screaming for his carrots, you have the supplier screaming that he's late and needs to get on with his deliveries, and in the meantime you have to count through every box of oranges that is on the list, because if you make a mistake you're the one who ends up having to pay for it. Either with verbal abuse from Chef or a cut off your wages.

You see, at the end of the day Chef likes to balance his books. He is usually on some sort of bonus scheme. I suppose it's a way the management can keep the kitchen under control. If Chef can bring in his kitchen on, or even under, budget, he gets an extra £1,000 a month or 2 to 3 per cent of his bottom line. So it's worth his while giving you an earful. Not that he is the sort of man who really needs an excuse.

You have to check all the goods over thoroughly as well. It's best to go through them all with a fine comb as they're always trying to palm you off with dodgy stuff – rotten strawberries, bad cabbages, dead lobsters,

Dovers that are past their sell-by date. Top hotels require top ingredients, in perfect shape. If you are charging up to £45 for a main course, it's all got to be good. And usually it is. All the meat that comes in the back here has had a better life than most of the staff who work in this place. Chef appears to know who its parents were, where it lived, what it ate, how much opportunity for play it had, and whether it had a good bunch of mates! I swear he gives more of a shit about the sides of beef that come in here than about the Bangladeshis who clean his floor.

The green corporate American Express card is finally accepted, I tear off the slip and walk back out into reception. Liz is checking out an affluent-looking couple who appear slightly the worse for wear.

'Have you had anything from the mini bar?' she asks, her nails clicking again.

'One,' replies the young man.

'One what?' asks Liz.

'One mini bar.' He smiles.

'What one mini bar?' asks Liz again, looking confused.

'Yes,' says the young man. 'One whole mini bar, right down to the Malibu.'

'Ooh, please don't mention the word Malibu,' says the woman, holding her head. 'I can do without being reminded of that.'

As Liz tries to work out the cost of a whole mini, I hand over the credit-card slip.

'There you are, sir,' I say.

'Cheers.' He sniffs, depositing some more dandruff flakes on reception.

'I do hope to see you again soon,' I say, as he bends down to pick up his bag.

'Yeah, right,' he says, as he walks across the marble floor. 'I don't think so.'

I put a pen in my mouth to stop myself from giving him the finger as he exits through the revolving door.

10<small>AM</small> – 11<small>AM</small>

Liz receives the manager's telephone call asking us in for the morning meeting. Normally one of us is required to attend while the other keeps an eye on the front desk. There are still plenty of check-outs to do and someone has to ensure there are no prostitutes left in any of the bedrooms.

Prostitutes are the bane of our lives in the luxury hotel business. Our place is a veritable Mecca for them. You can see why. We have a place that is packed with rich clients they are only too keen to relieve of all their cash. And we also have a place that is packed with rich clients who are only too willing to be fleeced. Louche, well oiled and on their own, buoyed up by business expense accounts, there is nothing they like more than a bit of 'how's yer father' while their wife, or

52

girlfriend, is on the other side of the world. The statistics are amazing: something like nine out of ten men who stay on their own in a hotel end up asking for 'company'. We, on the other hand, as a reputable establishment, can't be seen to be condoning prostitution, or even promoting it in any way. But to say that it doesn't go on, to pretend that hordes of whores don't swing through our doors on a nightly basis, and to say that sometimes Tony doesn't have a hand in it or get a backhander out of it, would be a lie of epic proportions.

In fact, the place is overrun with them, and now's about the time of day when we really have to keep an eye out. Tony knows a fair few of them, and if he's done his job correctly he'll know more or less which guest came in accompanied and which guest ordered up a bit of extra room service in the middle of the night. And it is now up to us to make sure that the girls leave. Otherwise the problem is, once the bloke has gone off to his meeting in the City or wherever he is supposed to be, they start thinking they're in bloody *Pretty Woman* and order up things like room service, or hairdressing, or a whole load of shit from the concierge service. It is a nightmare, and then, of course, the guest starts complaining that he didn't order a smoked salmon breakfast at 10.30. So now's the time to really keep an eye on room service and the telephone lines, and to keep tabs on who has checked out and who shouldn't, or couldn't, possibly be using the service in their room.

Liz and I have a quick conversation trying to work out who is going to man the desk and look out for prostitutes, and who is going to the manager's meeting. I have to admit I'm slightly desperate to go to the meeting. The idea of sitting down to a milky coffee and a couple of stale institutional biscuits on a plate has real appeal. I think of pleading to her better nature but then quickly realize that Liz doesn't have one. So I pull rank.

'I have a feeling we have a couple of important guests arriving today, and as the oldest face on the front desk I do feel I should go,' I say, crunching on the pen in my mouth.

'Fine,' she says, looking a little annoyed.

'So you'll keep an eye on anything that looks a bit suspicious in the rooms, then?'

'Yes.' She exhales, like it is the most boring question she's ever heard.

'OK then.' I smile. 'See you in a while.'

'Have fun,' she says sarcastically.

Now I really want to punch her lights out. 'You too,' I say, smiling instead.

I walk towards the glass double swing doors that lead into the main lounge area. It is 10.10 and already there are a couple of skinny women with stiff blonde hairdos wearing gold and beige who are smoking, drinking coffee and having a meeting of some sort. The lounge area is a mixture of old and new. The walls are covered in mirrors with fabulous old gold lamps that give the place a decadent French feel, yet the furnishings are quite modern: fat sofas, leather chairs, low gold-leaf tables. It is an odd mixture, yet it works enough for us to have a constant troop of fashion models coming in to have their photos taken here.

Past the corridor that leads towards the bar and in the far corner of the lounge area next to some enormous golden statues holding flaming lamp torches is the door to the manager's office. Actually, he has a suite of offices. He has a sort of outer office where his secretary, Angie, works, and where all the important faxes for the hotel are delivered; then to the left he has this inner office, which is all wooden panels and leather, with an enormous desk along one side of the room where he sits, backlit by the window; and just off to the right of Angie's desk is another much larger office with a conference table in the middle surrounded by high-backed chairs. The wood and leather office is used when he is charming brides to shell out £25,000 on their weddings, and for when he wants to bollock staff. The large conference room is used every day for the morning meeting. And the morning meeting is attended by everyone.

Well, almost everyone. Jackie, the blonde-haired head of housekeeping who is having an affair with Ben, represents the cleaners and chambermaids. James, the sandy-haired dork who is head of purchasing, is there too, alongside the food and beverages manager, the banqueting and events manager, the maintenance manager, the head of security (the personnel manager is off on honeymoon), the restaurant manager and the head chef, who does all the talking when it comes to the food. Tony also turns up, as do Gino the head barman and Lynette the reservations manager, and there is always the front of house manager or someone from reception to keep Adrian up to date.

The meeting usually starts the same way. Angie, who exudes all the faded grandeur of one of the golden statues in the lounge, comes in with her hard, pale yellow hair, pink lips and lavender-scented cardigan. She is carrying a tray that sports a large silver pot of coffee and another similar pot of tea, a jug of milk, a pot of sugar and a plate of assorted biscuits. There is usually some sort of initial holding back on the biscuit front during which everyone carefully picks a dry Rich Tea or some other bland brand; it is only on the plate's second journey round the table that anyone attempts to go for a Bourbon. But we are always careful that there are two chocolate digestives left for when Adrian comes in late, which he always does, every morning, hot off the telephone from someone important.

'Morning, morning, morning,' he says, walking briskly to the head of the table, smoothing down his pink and blue striped silk tie as he goes. He's a one for ties, Adrian. He has a large collection, mostly given to him by guests. The guys from the Gulf states who pack the place during August and drop tens of thousands in a month tend to give him three or four Hermès ties at a time. But today's jaunty number is looking a bit on the cheap side. Perhaps Dave forgot to collect all the others from the dry cleaner's. 'Right,' he says, sitting down. 'Anything in the duty manager's log book that I need to be aware of? Any horrors? Any nightmares?'

The manager's meeting is normally quite a serious affair. In the smaller hotels they can be quite amusing. I remember in the small place I worked in before, we all used to use it as an opportunity to chat and have a laugh, to have a bit of a bonding session. Someone would certainly have mentioned to Adrian something about last night's little indiscretion and we might have had a joke at his expense. But when the hotel is as big as this one and there is £35m of custom to deal with, plus all the glitches and the problems that are going on, we only ever have kick-back when Adrian is in the mood. And today it seems he is quite talkative. I think perhaps it is because of what he did last night. He is trying to pretend that he is part of the group; he is, forgive the pun, sucking up to us a bit.

I tell him about the woman walking through the lobby with the bag of vomit, and he laughs. I also tell him about the man who shouted and screamed about his porn bill, and the little problem with the pre-reg Canadian. Adrian congratulates me on my £50 discount, saying it sounded like the best way of calming the man down, and he notes the new room number of the over-tired Canadian and declares that we should send up a bottle of champagne. He takes a look at last night's duty manager's book and asks Chef to explain the problem the American businessman had with his early-morning steak. Chef's at a loss, blames it on someone junior and promises to give them the bollocking of their lives.

'That's all very well,' says Adrian, 'but because you didn't do your job properly, getting the steak out in time, the Canadian couldn't check in at all. We are all mutually dependent. We are a team, and we must function as a team.'

Chef mutters something into his whites.

'I know it's difficult, Chef,' placates Adrian, 'but that's why you get paid three times more than anyone else in your kitchen. Anyway,' he continues, 'Lynette, what have you got for us?'

Tall, thin and mousy with double-glazed vision like a

wombat, Lynette takes her reservations position very seriously indeed. It's her job to go through the list of VIP guests arriving today and decide who gets a half or a full bottle of complimentary champagne, who gets a wallet with the hotel's name in it, and who gets a teddy bear, a candle or some other 'loyalty treat'. Ten stays gets champagne and five stays a teddy bear, or something like that. She stacks her pages on the table and for some reason feels that she should stand up. This clearly amuses Adrian, as he breaks into a smile.

'Well,' says Lynette, 'we have a few things. Firstly, the difficult Mrs Dickson is back.'

'Right,' says Adrian. 'I thought we were going to have her blacklisted.'

'Yes, well,' says Lynette. 'That is quite difficult to do, seeing as her husband has shares in the company. No amount of telling her that we are full is going to put her off. She feels she owns the place, and, by right, I suppose at least her husband does, a bit. Anyway, she is bringing her Yorkshire terrier this time, so someone will have to be around to walk it.'

'It's like having Geri Halliwell to stay,' interrupts Adrian with a large laugh. He is definitely trying to pretend that he is one of us today. We all smile. We've all heard his Geri Halliwell story before. How while at the Halcyon, where she stayed after her house was burgled, there always had to be someone on hand to

59

walk her wretched little dog, Harry. Adrian tells us again how much everyone hated that goddamn dog, then goes on to say how she ordered some running machine to be put in her room for around eight grand and how she only ever seemed to hang her clothes on it. She apparently lived on club sandwiches and room service. She didn't eat in the restaurant and would send people out for food.

Everyone laughs.

'Yes, well,' says Lynette again, after allowing us a suitable pause for group amusement. 'So I have put her in the only room she hasn't complained about so far.'

'That reminds me,' says Adrian, clicking his fingers. 'Do you remember the story about Richard Gere, who asked the Hyde Park Hotel to change its carpets? He said he couldn't bear the spotted stuff they had in all their rooms, so they refurbed one at vast expense and he never came to stay there again!'

'Yeah!' Tony laughs. 'Didn't they also put in an extra large shower for Pavarotti because he had trouble getting into the bath?'

Adrian laughs. 'Honestly, the things we do.'

He then launches into his favourite Michael Jackson story: forty-eight bottles of Evian poured into his bath at the Lanesborough, one after the other, apparently. The water hardly came halfway up the sides, and even then it was cold. To this day Adrian has no idea what he did with it. Perhaps he just got in and then added the hot from the tap. Adrian shakes his head. 'No idea.'

'Yes, well,' interjects Lynette. 'We also have Mr Masterson arriving today.'

'Mr Masterson?' asks Adrian.

'The Texan oil baron.'

'Oh yes, right, him.' Adrian nods.

Boy, Adrian must be feeling dreadful. His brain can't be working at all. Everyone else around the table knows exactly who Mr Masterson is, and we are all sitting up accordingly. A fat, florid, ebullient Texan, he acts like the guy who invented tipping. He never stops handing out £10 notes. When he's staying in the hotel, you'd be amazed how few people go off sick.

'He has sent through a request for some Trinidad Diplomatics to be placed in the hotel humidor,' says Lynette.

'Some what?' asks James, his posh blond hair flopping over to one side.

'Trinidad Diplomatics. They go for five hundred pounds a cigar at the Lanesborough,' declares Lynette, rather smugly, like a girl who has done her homework, which she clearly has.

'Well, I've never heard of them,' says James.

'What?' declares Gino, watching the profits from his bar disappear before his very eyes.

'Keep your hair on, mate,' says James, leaning

forward. 'My cigar dealer is turning up in about half an hour; I'm sure he'll know where to get his hands on a couple of boxes.'

'A couple of boxes!' repeats Gino, like someone who has been sick on his shoes.

'Look, man,' says James. 'There's no point in asking Hunters and Frankau at this short notice. I'll have to see.'

'I have no desire to know whom you are dealing with,' says Adrian, with a wave of his hand, 'just so long as the hotel is properly stocked.'

'My caviar bloke is arriving today as well.' James smiles.

'Good,' says Chef.

'Where's he from this time?' asks Adrian.

'Some trawler in the Caspian, via Iran and then Frankfurt, I think,' says James. 'Anyway, it's half the price.'

'And I hope that the saving will be passed on to the hotel?' asks Adrian.

'Of course,' says James, in a manner that implies some of the so-called savings may well go elsewhere. 'I also have a rare cognac and brandy sale today.'

'Great, of course it is today.' Gino grins, clapping his hands with delight. 'You have my list already?'

'Yup,' says James, patting his top pocket. 'I have already spoken to Sotheby's and we have reserved that

1802 JBE Massougues cognac your Japanese friends like so much.'

'Excellent,' says Gino, looking forward to selling that on at £500 a shot.

'And I'm hoping that bastard Salvatore at the Lanesborough won't get his hands on the bottles of 1800 Bignon brandy I've heard are still up for grabs. You know, that one you like selling for seven hundred quid a shot,' says James, biting the end off his Bourbon biscuit.

James must have one of the best jobs in the hotel. Not only does he spend all his time flicking through fancy catalogues looking for fine wine sales and whisky, cognac and brandy auctions, spending somebody else's money, he also gets to go on all these amazing trips abroad. He gets invited to stay in the champagne châteaux in Reims in France, as a guest of Veuve Clicquot or Moët et Chandon. There, he gets pumped full of champagne and foie gras. In fact, they drown him in hospitality to thank him for his orders and in the hope that he will order more. He gets to go and see the juniper harvest in Tuscany as a guest of the gin company. And then someone will fly him to the South of France to look at some new soft cheese. Much like Chef at Christmas, when James comes in to work it is essential that he brings his car. He gets so many free gifts, hampers, cases of wine and sides of salmon, there is no way he could get all his bribes home on public transport.

He and Chef also have plenty of deals going on between them. For example, James might suggest a new brand of olive oil, and when Chef orders thirty-five bottles of the stuff, both he and Chef get a couple of litres free. The same goes for more luxury items such as smoked salmon and more obscure products such as game. The kitchen takes twenty-four brace of grouse, Chef and James divide up the ensuing perks between them. I heard that his girlfriend threw up last year on all the free chocolates he got given for Christmas.

'I'm afraid I have to go,' announces Chef, getting up from his seat. 'I have the cheese man arriving in about ten minutes at the back door.'

'Right, fine, go,' says Adrian.

'Thank you,' says Chef as he runs out of the door. 'If you have any Celine Dion requests like taramasalata and pitta bread in every room, just give me a call.'

All I can think of is the cheese man as Chef runs out of the door. My stomach is rumbling despite the three biscuits I have just eaten. The cheese man used to be one of my favourite things when I worked in the kitchen. He turns up every other day in his small van and parks out the back of the hotel. Then Chef, or sometimes one of the sous chefs, goes out and sits in the van to taste slivers of delicious cheese from all over the world. He chooses anything from whole Stiltons and strong Cheddars for the cheese board to fetas for the salads. The choice is vast, and the smell once you get inside the van is overpowering. Sometimes you get little squares placed on crackers to taste; sometimes he hands over slices that are almost transparently thin and melt on your tongue, building their flavour up at the back of your nose. What I wouldn't give to spend twenty minutes now in the cheese van and gorge myself on treats.

And he's not the only one queuing up for Chef's approval right now. The man who sells mushrooms is there with his basket of morels and carefully wrapped truffles. Perhaps even the fishmonger with his trays of hake. There used to be a man who brought in sea urchins from France. They'd come on the early flight into Heathrow, clear customs and make it to the hotel by about now. But I don't know if there is much call for that sort of thing any more. Sea urchins were quite a late eighties thing, don't you think?

Lynette runs through her list of guests, reiterating that we have to be extra nice to Mr Masterson and the shareholder's wife with the dog. She also announces that there is some drinks do on in the Banqueting Hall tonight, and that we should keep an eye out for drunken waifs and strays and anyone who looks like they haven't been invited.

'Right,' says Adrian with a clap of his hands. 'That all looks about OK. Anyone have anything they want to add? Housekeeping?'

'No, fine,' says Jackie. 'Only just to remind everyone that there is an outside stock-check coming in today.'

'Yes, that is correct,' says Adrian. 'They have been specifically told to do the bar.'

'Shit,' says Gino, his head slowly falling into his hands.

'Sorry about that, mate,' smiles Adrian. 'Anyone else? Good. I'd better get on; I've an exit meeting to perform. I'll see you all later.'

'Right,' I say, gathering up my pieces of paper as quickly as I can. I don't want to hang around for a chat. I'm going to have to leg it back to reception if I'm not going to miss Michelle's walk of shame.

11 AM – 12 PM

I arrive in reception at a jog. Liz has never seen me so keen to get back to my post after a management meeting. Normally I'm loitering around having a cigarette downstairs and sneaking in a quick cup of coffee before coming back out front. There are some days when I might even go for an early lunch with the rest of the kitchen staff and some of the Polish blokes in maintenance. I sit there, silently shovelling in bowls of pasta like the rest of them. But today there's a reason to make it back to the front desk by eleven a.m.: Michelle.

My face is quite pink by the time I reach the desk and I'm sure I'm sweating out last night's alcohol.

'Has she come through yet?' I gasp.

'Who?' asks Liz, stapling bits of paper together.

'Michelle, of course!' I say.

67

'Oh, her,' sneers Liz. She and Michelle have never been the best of mates. Cut from the same cloth; it's just unfortunate for Liz that Michelle's cloth is just that bit younger, perkier and possibly of higher quality. 'She hasn't shown her face yet.'

'Oh good.' I grin. 'I'd hate to miss it.'

'Miss what?' asks Liz.

'Her walk of shame!' I laugh.

'Oh right,' says Liz, sounding surprisingly uninterested in her rival's downfall. Then again, it's probably all the attention Michelle is getting that is pissing her off. 'I can't say that I am terribly interested.'

'Oh,' I say, looking round. 'Where's Tony gone?'

'He's gone to help Jez and Dave get rid of a woman on the third floor,' says Liz.

'Right. I missed that.'

'Yeah,' smiles Liz. 'While you are thinking about Michelle the rest of us are getting on with our jobs.'

She goes on to tell me that Jaguar was in last night and that she has had problems trying to get her out of Mr Mayes's room after he went to work. She says the whole thing came as a bit of a surprise. And I have to agree with her, because Ben should have told us that Mr Mayes checked in last night. He must have done it quite late. But Mr Mayes's can almost check in when he likes. He is a hotel regular. He's way beyond the complimentary wallet stage. He lives in Manchester and he comes down to stay in the hotel about three times a month. He works in the entertainment industry, and spunks it like crazy when he stays here. He always orders a couple of bottles of Cristal champagne on room service and he always takes a couple of grams of coke. He's not very discreet about it either: it's all we can do to stop him from chopping it out in the honour bar. And he always has a hooker with him. He has four favourites who for some reason best known to himself he's named after cars: Mercedes, Jaguar, BMW and Roller. We all turn a blind eye to his activities because he drops so much cash in the place, but sometimes the girls can be difficult. And today sounds like one of those days.

'She's ordered breakfast and I had to tell her she couldn't have any unless she was prepared to pay cash,' says Liz. 'And then she just shouted at me down the phone. She was effing and blinding and she kept on saying that if we didn't let her have breakfast on the house she and the other girls would take their business elsewhere. She said something like Mr Mayes spends about five grand a month in this hotel and if we wanted his custom we would have to accommodate her.'

'That sounds messy,' I say.

'It was,' she says. 'So as soon as Tony came out of the meeting I sent him up to sort it out.'

'Good idea,' I say, now slightly bored of the story. Tony is always getting sent up to sort out the hookers. That's part of his job.

Then, just as we are talking, Tony comes out of the lift with Jaguar in tow. She is an amazingly attractive woman. Long legs, long dark hair and great breasts – she could be a model if she weren't a prostitute. She swans out of the front door in her high black boots, giving Tony a little friendly wave as she goes.

'Jesus Christ, Tony,' I say as she walks out of the door and up the street, 'what did you say to Jaguar?'

'Nothing too bad.' He grins. 'Something along the lines that Mrs Mayes was due in the hotel any minute and if she wanted to keep her rather lucrative agreement with Mr Mayes going she should scarper before the whole thing went pear-shaped.'

'Good thinking,' I say.

'The old ones are always the best,' says Tony. 'They work every . . .'

His voice peters off into nothing. I don't bother to reply because we are both staring at the main door where Michelle's getting out of a cab, ten minutes late for her exit interview. She is wearing a pair of knee-length boots, flesh-coloured tights and a very short mini skirt. It's a combination not dissimilar to the recently departed Jaguar. She looks a lot more attractive out of the dark suit and light shirt she usually wears on reception. Steve the doorman's mouth hangs open as she swans through the revolving doors, her head held high. Even Dave stops polishing his brass.

'Morning everyone,' says Michelle, her Australian accent still audible after three years over here.

'Morning Michelle,' says Tony. 'Good leaving party?'

'Excellent, thank you,' she replies without breaking her stride.

'Looking forward to talking to the head? Or should I just say giving head?' He laughs.

'Ha, ha, ha,' says Michelle sarcastically, heading for the glass swing doors. 'At least I'm getting out of this place.'

'Oooh,' says Tony, pretending to sound impressed. 'Onwards and upwards to the Savoy? I hear the manager's very accommodating.'

'Piss off,' says Michelle, standing between the two doors and giving Tony the finger.

'Enjoy your exit,' smiles Tony. 'You've given us all great pleasure.'

'Yeah, right,' says Michelle, rather weakly.

'Some of us more than most,' Tony adds.

Jez and Dave snort with laughter. Only Liz doesn't seem that interested. She is busying herself by pleasantly directing a couple of Home Counties women in corduroy skirts and fun jumpers, clutching plastic shopping bags, towards the lounge for their mid-morning coffee. Lady day trippers love this place. We are not far from Sloane Street and within an easy cab ride from all those destination shops they seem to enjoy so much like General Trading and Peter Jones. During sale season we have at least twenty or thirty women drinking coffee and snacking on homemade shortbreads at any one time. Their conversation always seems to be dominated by bargain bed linen and the price of home furnishing material. But the hotel loves them. They cost us almost nothing. A pot of coffee and some biscuits can be cobbled together for less than 10p per person, and we charge them £10 plus service for coffee for two. Coffee-morning women are one of those excellent little earners that really should not be sniffed at. They don't make much mess, they don't hang around very long and they require minimal maintenance. We couldn't be happier.

The bar staff also seem to be in a good mood as they walk through the door. They are laughing, and talking in Italian. I don't know why, but bar staff are nearly always Italian. Three of them work in our main bar: Alfredo, Francesco and the ever-loyal Gianfranco, who follows head barman Gino wherever he goes. They are all friendly, good-looking blokes, but they don't really mix that much with the rest of us. I think it has something to do with the hours they keep: they come in just after eleven a.m. and they don't leave until the last man standing in the bar decides it's time to go to bed. Their long hours are more than made up for in tips, and the later they stay, usually the more drunk the punter, and therefore the fatter the tip. There is nothing they like more than a gang of guys from the Gulf states cracking open a few bottles of 1919 Dalwhinnie whisky and really going for it, sucking on their Monte Cristo No. 2s. There was one legendary session I heard about last August during which this group of Saudis dropped £18,000 in one evening in the bar; they added a £1,000 tip that was divided among the bar staff. We didn't hear the end of it for weeks.

Anyway, Tony's obviously determined to wipe the smiles off their faces this morning because when they are halfway across reception he shouts, 'Hey, you lot!'

'What?' asks Gianfranco, turning around.

'Looking forward to your stock-take today?'

At the mere mention of the word 'stock-take' all their shoulders slump.

'Don't tell me you've forgotten?' laughs Tony.

'Don't tell me we weren't told,' replies Gianfranco.

'Oh dear,' smiles Tony. 'Enjoy yourselves, boys.'

No sooner do the barmen disappear through the glass doors to change into their black ties and set up in the bar beyond than the outside auditor arrives. At least I presume it is him. He is wearing a calf-length overcoat and is carrying a briefcase and a clipboard.

'Good morning, I'm Mr Kent,' he says as he puts his clipboard down on the counter. 'I am from Hotel Auditing and I have an appointment with the manager, Mr Thompson.'

'Right, sir,' I say, reaching for the telephone, marvelling at his imaginatively named company. 'I'll just call through and tell them that you are here.'

The announcement of Mr Kent's arrival is enough to send a frisson of fear through the whole hotel. Word gets round very quickly that some outside bod has come to check up on everyone. And there is nothing hotel employees hate more than a stock-take, particularly in the booze department.

The problem with alcohol is that most of us think that one of the perks of working in a hotel is that you can serve yourself a quick sip, or a shot to help you through your working day. Gino and I are always having a few glasses here and a few glasses there, especially during a difficult night. He often comes through with a small glass of brandy or vodka and slips it on reception for me. It is totally illegal, but normally everyone turns a blind eye to this sort of behaviour. Unfortunately, the whole point of outside auditors is that they pick up on these things. They sell themselves to hotel managers as the sharpest eyes in the business, and the money you pay for an outside audit is supposedly more than made up for by the things they spot and the cash you consequently save.

In the old days, petty pilfering used to be a whole lot easier. You'd slip off with a half-drunk bottle of vodka now and then and you'd walk off with a Bailey's around Christmas time, to save you buying one on the way home to give to your mum. It was always the gins, the vodkas and the Bailey's that went for some reason; the whiskies and the wines weren't ever really touched. Mainly because they are all kept in this special cellar that stores wine at a perfect temperature; the bottles are turned regularly by the cellar man and you need two sets of keys to get in there. Although, if you really do put your mind to it, all things are possible. But nowadays, since we converted to the computer system, it is a whole lot more difficult to help oneself to anything.

There are a few tricks of the trade that still work. The old one of filling up empty vodka and gin bottles with water and placing them behind the bar does work just so long as no-one spots what you are doing. Another trick requires you to really be in with the bar staff. It involves short-serving the customers. When they ask for a double, you serve a single, charge for a double and hope they don't notice. If they are drunk enough they usually don't. You then keep a tab on how many shots you served short on, and by the end of the night you can usually leave with a couple of bottles of vodka that the whole bar has sort of chipped in for. Genius. The last place I worked, I used to leave with a free bottle of vodka a month.

The auditor does also pick up on bottles of water and mixers that the bar staff have genuinely forgotten to charge for. And, of course, ullage – the slips and spills, the late-night sloppy pourings that after a while go to make up a whole bottle of gin. This is the sort of stuff we actually have to pay for. The management keeps behind 10 per cent of what the punters pay in tips and service charges to pay for breakages, theft and shortfalls in the till. But when a bottle of Hildon water is 40p at cost, sold on to you for upwards of £3.50, then the cost price shortfall isn't usually that bad. However, if you happen to have a Bombay Sapphire thief in the hotel then the month's ullage and theft bill can be quite large.

As Mr Kent is despatched to annoy Gino in his bar, another rather seedy-looking bloke arrives talking on his mobile phone. He has long dark curly hair to the shoulders and a suit that shines in certain lights. He is carrying a heavy-looking holdall bag. But before he has a chance to introduce himself, James flounces across the hall – hand out, smooth shake at the ready – and ushers him off into his back office.

'Who do you think that was?' I ask Liz. 'Cigars or caviar?'

'Cigars,' says Liz.

'How do you know?'

'I recognize him from before. He comes every couple of months, with a very heavy bag, and leaves with nothing but a smile on his face. Anyway,' she adds, 'the caviar guys always look eastern European and smell of salted fish. That bloke looked Latin to me.'

'Oh,' I say with a small shrug. 'I think I might go for lunch.'

Liz agrees. She is on a diet and doesn't really want to go. She shows me the Slim Fast bar she has underneath the leather diary and tells me not to be too long.

Downstairs, it is busy in the staff canteen. Devoid of air and natural light, the rows of tables and chairs shine under the neon strip light and the place smells of onions, sweat and high-tar cigarettes. I pick up a plate and walk along what I suppose could be called the salad bar. There are some sliced tomatoes and basil that look like they were out flaunting themselves at a banquet the night before. There are bowls of rather jaded-looking lettuce and a large bowl of tinned sweet-corn with some red peppers. I curl up my nose. Even the large bowl of pasta and tinned tuna looks like it has seen better days. I walk over to the hot section where all the food was put together at some stage yesterday after-noon and reheated for our delight and delectation. Kept under large, hot catering lamps, it is advisable to peel off the skin before serving. Two young sous chefs are dollop-ing out the chilli. I get myself two spoons' worth and pick up a hunk of white bread. Sometimes I do try to eat healthily but today is just not one of those days.

Looking up and down the rows of seating, I see that the chair next to Alfredo, Francesco and Gianfranco is taken. To tell you the truth I am slightly relieved; I would only have to listen to them moaning about their stock-take all lunchtime. I decide to go off and sit with the chambermaids and a mini bar attendant.

'Hi,' I say as I sit down near three of them. They stop talking Spanish, or is it Portuguese? I always knew I should have worked harder at school. None of them says anything. They are all quite a lot older than me. In their forties or early fifties. Most of them, I should imagine, have children, hoping that they'll do better than their parents. Well, it wouldn't be hard. Earning £4.50 an hour and fighting with bellboys over tips is not the sort of job most people aspire to. And that's in a reputable place like here, and only if they're legal.

'Good morning?' I ask, by way of trying to make conversation.

'Not really,' replies the woman sitting in the middle. 'I have had to clean two used condoms and someone left an old tampon in the bath.'

'I'm very sorry,' I say, shovelling some chilli into my mouth. 'That doesn't sound very nice.'

'I think I have broken a riding crop,' says the woman on her left, putting her hand over her mouth.

'What?' I say, looking up.

'I was vacuuming in front of the cupboard when the door fell open and this stuff came out,' she says. 'Fluffy handcuff things, this rubber suit, and a whip which I shut in the door by mistake and I think I have broken it. Jackie says I have to wait until she has spoken to the owner before I know if I have to pay.'

'Right,' I say, not really knowing how to respond.

'And I discover three KitKats which have been stuffed with cardboard and put back in the mini bar,' says the mini bar attendant.

'I hate it when that happens,' says the one in the middle. 'The effort that goes into making a whole KitKat.' She sighs, her eyes rolling in her head. 'You'd think that it was easier to pay.'

'And,' says the maid to the right, 'they found Anna Maria asleep on one of the beds this morning.'

'No!' says the woman in the middle, sitting back in shock.

'Oh yes. Television on, door closed, the whole thing. Fast asleep on a bed that she had just made.'

They all shake their heads disapprovingly. These women work hard, and for some reason best known to themselves they seem to take pride in what they do. Quite why they would take pride in putting a chocolate on someone's pillow or placing a face cloth at the correct forty-five-degree angle from the basin is any-one's guess. But apparently they do.

I take a bite of my bread and thank my lucky stars that I don't have to deal with skid-marked sheets for a living. At least I have the possibility of moving on and up in my job, to duty manager and possibly to manager. Would you believe me if I said that working in hotels is all I ever wanted to do from the age of six? I know – weird, isn't it? But it's true. It was a childhood dream of mine, to work my way up and maybe have a hotel of my own one day. But these women sitting opposite me can't even dream. It's terrible. They are destined to clean up after other people for ever. Chambermaids don't get promoted. They just get fired. Even the head housekeeping job is usually given to some girl on a management traineeship. Chambermaids start cleaning up toothpaste and they end cleaning up toothpaste. They get their £4.50 an hour, their two to three meals a day and the occasional fiver from some passing American. It makes me depressed just sitting here. I wipe my plate down with my last bit of bread and contemplate going downstairs for a cigarette.

I walk into the staff smoking room and immediately realize the error of my ways. I haven't noticed how late it is. It's 11.55 and the place is full of sous chefs, commis chefs and kitchen porters having their final fag before the lunchtime hell begins. The pale green walls sweat with smoke; I almost can't see across the other side. I can't sit in here for a cheeky one because every guest who arrives in the hotel will smell it on my suit. I'm too lazy to go outside, so I wander slowly upstairs, back to Liz's delightful company.

12PM – 1PM

Back on reception, and Liz is having a few problems with late check-outs. It is around this time of day that you suddenly discover a couple of guests haven't actually vacated their rooms. Sometimes it is one of the chambermaids who rings up to tell the desk that she can't get into a room because it has a 'Do Not Disturb' sign on the door. Or sometimes you notice on the computer that a couple of rooms that should have turned green on the screen and be VI (vacant and inspected) are in fact still red or OD (occupied and dirty). Check-out time here is actually 11.30 and we tend to run quite a tight ship. If someone actually asks to stay on for longer then we will allow them until two p.m. before we start charging them; otherwise they can expect a telephone call asking them if they want to be charged a half-day rate for continuous occupation of the room or if indeed they plan to stay an extra day. We aren't being rude. It's just the maids have so many rooms to get ready before the new guests start arriving we need that time to turn things around.

'I am sorry to disturb you, sir,' Liz is saying when I arrive. 'But check-out is eleven thirty and it is now midday. Will you be vacating the room shortly?' I can tell the man is angry because Liz winces slightly as he shouts in her ear. 'I am terribly sorry to hear that, sir,' she says. 'Perhaps if you came down to reception we could look into the matter.' He says something back and obviously hangs up.

'OK?' I say.

'Fine.' She sighs. 'He says he's had a hundred pounds stolen from his room and that he is holding us responsible.'

'Oh, right,' I nod. 'I bet it's another one of those guys who were so pissed last night they forgot they spent it.'

'Probably,' says Liz. She turns and smiles at me.

'What?' I ask.

'Will you do me a favour?' she asks.

'OK,' I say.

'The thing is, there's another room that hasn't checked out and so far he is not responding to calls. I have rung the room half a dozen times and there is no reply. Could you just go up and see what is going on?'

82

'Do you think we have a stiff on our hands?' I ask.

'Don't be silly,' dismisses Liz. 'It's just a little odd, that's all.'

I take the lift up to the third floor. I am far too tired to take the stairs. When I arrive, the corridor is buzzing with action. There are two Polish maintenance guys right outside the lift trying to mend a rucked-up carpet; further along there's a monosyllabic cleaner who is hoovering the thing. Looking at it, the carpet really does need replacing. In fact, I think it lets the hotel down. Red with a gold strip along the edge, it is bald, shiny and threadbare in places. What we really need is a rock star band to behave badly and we'd all be happy.

There is nothing like a celebrity behaving appallingly to help finance a makeover. I know of one hotel that had its whole dining room refitted, carpets, wallpaper and everything, after a band started a food fight. The manager had a conversation with their manager about how much 'damage' the band had done, and then sent them a clearing-up invoice that financed a makeover of *Changing Rooms* proportions. It was the hotel that cleaned up in that incident. Then again, the hotel always cleans up. I remember smiling when I heard that Oasis had trashed the Atrium of the Landmark Hotel. They'd apparently jumped on tables, thrown some drink around and played the piano, or some such terrible crime. I can imagine the delight on the manager's face as he dreams of having the whole place re-done thanks to Liam and Noel.

I nod to the maintenance guys who are talking to each other in Polish and don't seem to notice me. It is like working for the United Nations sometimes in this place. Sit in the staff canteen and almost no-one speaks English. Actually, half the time they don't even understand what you're trying to say. If you use vocabulary they don't need to know in their line of work, it's beyond them. Just by the bloke hoovering, I find the room. There is no 'Do Not Disturb' sign on the door, so I knock loudly. There is no reply. I knock again. I use my plastic Ving passkey card to let myself in. The place is a mess. The chambermaid is waiting for him to check out before she can do anything, yet the guest is nowhere to be seen. I check the bathroom. Nothing. The best thing I can do is telephone Lynette in reservations to see if we need the room back today, otherwise I am inclined to leave it, wait for the guest to return and sting him with the extra day.

I call Lynette from the room and she starts to have kittens on the telephone. The hotel is overbooked by 20 per cent at the time of speaking and she is desperate to get the room back. Lynette always overbooks the hotel if she can, because since the advent of the mobile phone people are always cancelling rooms at the last minute or changing their bookings. Business moves so fast these days that no-one can guarantee they will be where they say they are going to be at any one time. So she overbooks, and hotel capacity can change as much as thirty times in one day. Lynette is so good at juggling, she should be in the circus. But at the moment she is being a pain in the arse. She is kicking up a bit of a stink, telling me that the man must leave his room, he hasn't booked for an extra night and she has a couple from Lancashire on a wedding anniversary weekend arriving this afternoon.

I stand and think for a bit. What am I supposed to do? I call Adrian's office but Angie tells me he is still exiting Michelle. My only option is to pack up his stuff myself. So I do. I take his suitcase out of the cupboard and pack up all his clothes. I fill his wash-bag with his toiletries and shove them all into his bag. I pack up his books, his newspapers and his car magazines. He has a magazine called *Stuff*, which I have a quick flick through. Then I drag the whole lot downstairs.

Liz is horrified when I tell her what I have done. She places the palms of her hands on both cheeks like that Munch painting and repeats over and over, 'You can't do that, you can't do that!'

'Fuck it,' I say with a shrug. 'I have, so that's it. We need the room.'

Fortunately Liz is distracted by the arrival of the other late-check-out man who is accusing the hotel of theft. For a guest in an expensive five-star hotel, he doesn't look very pleasant. His hair needs brushing, his suit needs cleaning and his face is still greasy with sleep.

'Afternoon, sir,' says Liz, politely but on purpose.

'Morning,' he replies. 'Now,' he starts straight away, 'I'd like to report a hundred pounds missing from my bedroom immediately. Where's the manager?'

'I'm sorry to hear that, sir,' says Liz. 'Are you sure you haven't mislaid it? It is unlikely to have been stolen in the hotel. We simply don't have a theft problem here, sir,' she lies. That's one of our techniques. Always deny that any of the staff could have nicked anything. It is the best policy. Officially his stuff is in his room at his own risk; we won't take responsibility for anything in the room. Valuables should be left in reception or placed in the safe provided. 'Was it in the safe?' she asks. I always ask that one myself. But it does tend to wind them up a bit.

'No, of course it wasn't in the safe!' he says. His voice is beginning to sound pissed off. 'If I knew there were thieves in the hotel I might have put it in there.'

'There are no thieves in the hotel,' she says.

'Then how come I'm a hundred quid down?' he asks, leaning on the counter.

'What did you do last night, sir?' asks Liz.

'I went out to dinner. I went gambling. I came back.'

'Are you sure you didn't use it gambling?' she suggests.

'No. I mean, yes, I'm sure,' he says.

'Well, if that's the case then I suggest we call the police,' she says, picking up the phone.

'D'you know?' says the man suddenly. 'I'm too busy for all of this. Just give me my bill and I'll go.'

That always happens. I don't know whether this guy is trying it on to get some money out of the hotel – which, for the record, we would never give – or if he did genuinely lose it gambling and forgot, or even if one of our light-fingered staff lifted it. Either way, mention the police, as we are obliged to do, and everyone from the chancer to the alcoholic amnesiac always gives in. Eventually he pays up and pisses off. Housekeeping breathes a sigh of relief. That's one less room they have to worry about.

I check my watch; it's 12.40. Michelle is taking a long time with her exit. Either that or perhaps the auditor got in there before her while she was sitting outside waiting.

Traffic through reception is beginning to get a little heavy. The lunchtime drinkers are starting to arrive, coming through to have a swift one at the bar before going on into the restaurant.

The people who lunch in an expensive hotel such as this, famous for its modern and traditional cuisines, can usually be split into various groups. Firstly there are the expense-account lunchers, businessmen who work in and around the area and meet up with an important client here for a long, languid beef on the bone, coffee and liqueurs lunch. Secondly there are the glamorous lunching ladies who regularly meet for fizz and leaves. They tend not to eat or drink too much but they can often stay quite late into the afternoon, only leaving to collect their children from school. And thirdly there are the occasion lunchers, people who are in town to see a show, or who are taking Granny out on her eightieth, or young men introducing their fiancée to their parents. They tend to be larger groups of five or six and they take a long time to order and stay late into the afternoon.

But it is really only the businessmen who go to the bar for a drink first. Gino can tell almost as soon as they stand at the bar and order their first drink who is going to spend some money and who is not worth being ever so pleasant to. I remember he told me once that the men who come in and order a double spirit straight off mean business; the ones who stand and think about what they should be ordering are not worth chatting up, as they probably won't be hanging around for stickies and chocolates later on.

I smile at a couple of likely-looking lardy lunchers as they come through dressed in their smart pinstripe suits, hand-made shirts and red braces. I wish them good morning and I'm concentrating so hard on them that I almost miss Michelle coming through the glass doors.

'Miss Lane,' I say after her as she tries to sneak past.

'Oh, hello,' she says, stopping in her tracks.

'You weren't going to leave without saying goodbye, were you?' I ask, sounding as offended as I can. I like Michelle. We've worked for eight months together on the desk. She is much better company than Liz. She likes a gossip and a drink, and I like that in a girl.

'No.'

She smiles, glancing round at Tony's desk, waiting for some cheeky comment. But Tony's busy. He's got a client at his desk, some young bloke I have seen a couple of times before, a businessman with an office around the corner. He sends quite a few of his Russian clients to the hotel, and he pays Tony £500 a month in cash to make sure both he and his guests are well looked after. Tony has a few deals like that going on. But he likes to keep them quiet. If Adrian found out about his moonlighting he probably wouldn't be too pleased. Outside deals are a bit of a grey area. There is no telling how the management would react.

Michelle comes over and stands behind the huge floral arrangement we have on the counter, hoping that Tony won't see her. Liz is busy on the telephone, snapping off small sections of her health bar biscuit as she speaks.

'So how was it?' I ask Michelle.

'A lot better than I thought,' she replies. 'But he went through everything. All the guest comments that have ever been made about me. All that sort of stuff.'

'Really? That's what took you so long. It sounds very thorough.'

'It was.' She nods. 'Maybe he was making up for the personnel girl being on honeymoon.'

'Did he say anything about last night?' I ask.

'Nothing,' she replies. 'Thank God. I was so embarrassed when I walked in. I mean, less than seven hours ago he was standing with his pants down in a men's urinal in a club.' She giggles. 'I just couldn't get the image out of my mind. But he was totally professional. Amazing, really, how people can switch that sort of thing off and on.'

'Yeah,' I agree. 'But he's like that, isn't he, Adrian? Best friend when he wants to be, boss when he doesn't.'

'I suppose so.' Michelle shrugs. 'Anyway, I suppose I'd better go. You've got work to do.'

'All right?' asks Liz as she puts the phone down.

'Yes, thanks,' says Michelle. 'You?'

'Very busy,' smiles Liz.

'I can see,' says Michelle.

'When do you start?' asks Liz.

'In a week,' says Michelle. 'I'm going on holiday before.'

'Good,' says Liz. 'That's nice.'

'Spain,' says Michelle.

'Good,' says Liz. The telephone rings. 'See you around,' Liz mouths as she picks up.

'I'd better go,' says Michelle again.

'I'll walk you to the door,' I say.

Michelle walks past Tony's desk and he says nothing. Deep in his meeting with the businessman, Tony wouldn't dream of being unprofessional enough to make a sharp comment, although from the flicker of his eyes as she goes past you can tell he is gagging to.

Steve opens the door for us as we walk out into the street.

'Bye, Michelle,' he says, offering her a white-gloved hand. 'Good luck.'

We walk a little further along the pavement, then I kiss Michelle on the cheek and tell her to keep in touch. She lies and says she will. I do the same. But we both know that the only way I will see her again is if I move to the Savoy. That's the thing about working in hotels, you almost have no time to socialize. Most of the time I'm too knackered to do anything, so I sit at home alone and watch the telly. I wave to her as she walks up the street. I'm really going to miss her. It's going to be lonely in reception without her.

I nod towards Steve, who is opening a taxi door, hoping to relieve its occupant of a quid. Steve is good at relieving people of pound coins. Every time he opens a door, every time he hails a cab, every time he carries someone's bag, he gets one. They all sit there in his pocket, jangling. By the end of the week he can have anything from £600 to £1,000 in small golden coins. It's no wonder that plenty of people would quite fancy Steve's job. Even if it does entail standing outside in all weathers, wearing a thick, uniformed coat and being polite to people.

I decide to walk around the corner to the back of the hotel for a quick cigarette. The noise coming from the kitchen around the corner is off the scale. Chef, it seems, is having a hissy fit because his chicken livers haven't arrived. I can hear him swearing and shouting 'livers, livers, livers' from the street. There is steam rising from the open kitchen windows and I can see them all running around in there.

This hour before lunch is always madness. I remember it well. It is often more to do with anticipated tension than anything else. Chef is getting ready to call the orders in. It looks like an easy job, but it's not. In fact, it has to be the hardest role in the kitchen. He has to stand there and take control of, and command the respect of, some 150 people. It is like conducting a symphony: everyone has to be on time and with the beat of the kitchen, and if anyone misses their cue the whole thing falls apart. It is so difficult and so stressful, especially when people fuck up, which they do all the time. There is a real art to it, and God does Chef scream when you get it wrong. Then there are the sous chefs to contend with. Competent in all areas of the kitchen, they buzz around like blue-arsed flies. The chefs de partie, who are heads of sections, in charge of the grill or the vegetables, are always quite anxious as they have a lot to manage. Then there are the first commis chefs who have been in the kitchen for about two years and they're doing all right for themselves on £14K for a forty-hour week where they end up working eighty, but they are still likely to make mistakes. Then there are the second commis chefs, who are about eighteen or nineteen. They're trainees, like I used to be, who know nothing and are there to be shat on. And then, finally, there are the porters. It is a vast team, working with vast quantities of food. It is hectic. There's a hell of a lot of work to be done. The pressure is high, you are working against the clock, there is no slacking around. So I suppose you can understand why it is always a little hysterical just before the lunchtime rush begins.

I stub out my cigarette to a cheer of delight from the kitchen as a delivery of chicken livers finally makes it through the door. I walk around the front of the hotel and see Tony just finishing with his businessman. He seems happy. He has a wide grin on his face and a large brown envelope of cash in his inside coat pocket. Liz beckons me over quickly, her nylon nails working overtime.

'There you are,' she says. 'I've been paging you. I'm desperate for a toilet break and the phone keeps on ringing.'

'Oh, I'm sorry,' I say, taking the small red pager out of my pocket. 'I've forgotten to turn it on.'

'Really,' she says, rolling her eyes.

'Leave it with me,' I say, getting back behind the desk. 'You take as long as you like,' I add, thinking I might just give Ben a quick call while she's gone to give him a Michelle blowjob update. But the phone goes again before I have the chance. It's Jackie.

'Hi,' she says. 'I was just wondering if you could send Ben up to check out a room for me. Number 407 really needs inspecting.'

'What, really needs inspecting?' I ask.

'Yes,' she says.

'Well, I'm afraid Ben won't be here until later. He's on nights this week.'

'Oh, of course he is,' she says.

'But I could come up in a minute and help you out,' I suggest.

'Don't worry,' she replies. 'I'll do it myself.' She hangs up.

I start to laugh. 'She's outrageous,' I say.

'What?' says Tony, whose bat-like hearing is always tuned in for gossip.

'That Jackie,' I say.

'She wasn't ringing up for a shag again, was she?' smirks Tony.

'How do you know?' I ask. 'I thought it was supposed to be a secret.'

'Well, firstly, you should know by now, there are no secrets in hotels; secondly, if there are any secrets, it's my job to know them; and thirdly, she's done it before. Ben isn't the first handsome bloke on reception who's been through Jackie's laundry basket.'

'No!' I say, my mouth hanging open. I'm so naive.

''Fraid so,' says Tony with a click of his teeth, firing off a quick shot with his right index finger. 'I think you'll find she's very accommodating.'

1PM – 2PM

With rumours of the obliging nature of Jackie's laundry
basket ringing in my ears, I decided against calling Ben
to update him on Michelle's exit. It is a bit offputting to
know that Jackie's been there and done that before. Not
that Ben's in love with her, mind you. It just makes him
out to be a bit of a fool and their whole relationship a
bit phoney. I don't know whether I should tell him or
not. Would he mind if he found out that he wasn't the
first to inspect rooms with Jackie? Would he care? I
don't know. Is it my duty to tell him anyway? I don't
know. We are friends. He showed me the ropes when I
first came here a year and a half ago. Ben's been on
reception for two years now and he seems happy to stay
here. While I, you know, really want to make the grade.
Make my dad proud of me. Maybe, I think as I gaze

into space and ignore the ringing telephone, maybe I'll tell Ben later when he comes in. It depends what sort of mood he is in.

Liz comes back from her extended toilet break. I don't know what she's been doing but she smells very strongly of perfume. Why do women do that? Cover themselves in perfume? She was just beginning to smell OK after her morning dousing and now she's reapplied. She's drowned herself in the stinking stuff. You can tell the guests don't like it: they recoil slightly when she leans over to show off her tits.

The lunchtime rush is now well and truly on. Herds of men in suits keep filing through reception, the expectation of a fat lunch writ large all over their faces. I know Gino is rattling that cocktail shaker of his, like some serving suggestion for any punter who comes into that bar. There is something about the sound of ice on silver that gets people going of a lunch hour. He'll be shifting those Bloody Marys like his mother's life depended on it.

Tony's at his desk with some young man who has just come in to flog him bicycle tours, if I can eavesdrop accurately. He is looking a bit lean and keen, something I know Tony finds very unattractive. It's usually around this time that Tony receives his salesmen; for the next hour or so people with briefcases and pamphlets will come in and out of the hotel trying to persuade Tony to take them on board. Tony will ask what his cut will be, and depending on the attractiveness of the offer he hears you will either be accepted into his little leather folder of delights or you will very politely be asked to go on your way. Needless to say, the bloke with the bicycle is charmingly turned down.

'We have more of a taxi-based clientele,' says Tony, standing up to shake his hand. 'But good luck, mate, it sounds like an interesting idea.'

Tony is never rude to anyone; he says you never know if you'll need them at a later date. So everyone who meets him thinks they're his new best mate. It's a talent Tony has in spades. The skinny guy walks through the door and Tony picks up his *Time Out* magazine. A concierge's bible, it tells him exactly what's on where and keeps him abreast of little details like opening times and curtain up. He also has his copy of the *Golden Keys Journal* sitting on the desk. Packed with global concierge gossip, it tells him which concierge is doing well and who's moving where in Singapore.

Lynette comes rushing round the corner and into the back office behind reception. She has pages and pages of paper in her hand and looks hassled.

'How's juggling occupancy going?' I ask.

'We're minus ten at the moment,' she says, her magnified eyes blinking.

'What, ten rooms overbooked?' I say.

'I know, I know,' she says. 'But the situation could change at any minute, as you know. I was minus twenty-five two hours ago. Just before we went into the manager's meeting.'

'Right,' I say.

'Who have you checked in? Anyone?' she asks, flicking through all her papers.

'We've had the red-eye guys in so far plus the Canadian.'

'Oh my God, will you check that someone sent him up a complimentary bottle of champagne to compensate for the mess-up this morning?' she asks.

'Yes, of course,' I say.

'Anyone else?' she asks, her pen poised.

'Not yet, Lynette. It's only lunchtime.'

'Lunchtime?' she repeats, sounding confused.

'Yes.'

'Oh, I thought it was about three p.m.'

'No.'

'Phew. I must remember to get some satin sheets put in 505.'

'I'll call up if you want?' I suggest.

'Would you?'

'It's fine.'

'They're for the Texan,' she says.

'What time is he arriving?' I ask.

'Some time this afternoon,' she says, before rushing off back to the manager's office.

I call Jackie to make sure that the Texan has the correct sheets in his penthouse bed. Room 505 costs £2,000 a night (not including breakfast) and I am sure we will be charging him at least £100 extra for his satin sheets. You know how much we like special requests in the hotel industry. I remember at the last place I worked Madonna turned up and complained about the exercise bike we had in the gym, so we ordered her a special piece of equipment and charged three times the price to her room. Well, she'd been quite difficult already, complaining about the colour of the curtains in her room; we had to move her from suite to suite five or six times. But then Madonna doesn't have a monopoly on difficult. I remember a story about Cher's people calling the St Martin's Lane Hotel and saying that she wanted all her food to be organic and from Harrods. So the hotel went happy food mad, shelling out a fortune for her. She also asked for a couple of exercise bikes to be put in her room, so they went and emptied the gym, taking everything up to her room. Cher then apparently arrived, said something like this place is a fish bowl, and walked straight out of the hotel. God knows what they did with all the food.

But when it comes to requests, the weirdest thing we had to get was, of course, for Michael Jackson at the

Lanesborough. He asked for all this stuff from the States, so we had to get someone to send over chocolate bars, jellybeans and a drink called Gatorade. I suppose with Michael all these things are par for the course. Jackson is the only star I know who brings his own chef with him, only to have him serve up children's food like chicken nuggets, burgers and fish fingers. Jackson also had his suite turned into an amusement arcade, full of computer games like Space Invaders. We also put another television in the room so he could have rolling cartoons on all day long. Now I think about it, he must be the most over-requesting star I have ever come across. But then he was also the most generous towards his fans.

There were always hundreds of them hanging around outside the hotel, chanting his name in the vain hope of luring him to the window. The room service guys and I used to take the piss sometimes. We would rattle a curtain, put on one of our white service gloves, and then, as the screams grew louder and louder, we would give the crowd a little white-gloved wave. They'd go mad. And we would collapse behind the curtain laughing. Once we tempted them so much. We waved and waved and we could hear the crowd shouting, 'It's him! He's here! He's coming out to see us!' Then one of the boys pushed me out onto the balcony. Five hundred flashbulbs went wild. I have never heard such a collective sigh of disappointment when they realized it was just me.

Anyway, there was always a hardcore group of fans who set up a proper camp next to the security fencing, with their tents and their sleeping bags, and on cold nights Michael would send out a hundred cups of hot chocolate for them, which I thought was rather kind. No-one else ever did that. They, of course, would then go mad all over again.

Jackie is a bit irritated by my call. I don't know whether it's because Ben is on nights and she can't get her usual daily service, or that she is genuinely annoyed that I have been told to check up on her. Of course she has organized the sheets. She is totally aware that the Texan is arriving today, and the room has been arranged accordingly. I hang up on her, rather wishing I hadn't bothered to call.

Meanwhile, Liz is jotting down a message on a piece of paper.

'Yes, sir, of course, sir, absolutely, sir,' she says. 'I'll send someone right away.' She hangs up. 'You wouldn't take this to a Mr Maison in the dining room, would you?' she asks, smiling a wide, lip-lined smile.

'Right,' I say, resigned to the deal. 'Do you have any idea what he looks like?'

'Blue shirt, red tie, bald head,' she says.

'That'll really narrow it down,' I say, picking up the note.

I walk into the restaurant. Golden chandeliers, high-backed chairs, linen-covered tables, bustling service and bubbling conversation; the place is traditional, packed and smells delicious. Red wine, truffle oil, roast beef, sizzling grilled fish – their aromas fill the air and my mouth immediately starts to water. There is something about a good hotel dining room that just exudes decadence. All I need now is the waft of a fat cigar and the scent of leather to remind me of the good old days at the Savoy Grill.

That place was amazing. Before its Marcus Wareing makeover, it smelt of old money and establishment. It was old school at its best. Racks of lamb, beef on the bone and twenty-four different ways to prepare a potato, from pommes sables to pommes soufflé. When I worked there, it really was the days of the big spenders. Roger Moore used to love it in there. There was an occasion when he and two other guys came in for lunch. They didn't hold back in the slightest, and by the end of a six-hour session they ended up with a bill of £4,500 between the three of them. They paid in cash, putting a big wedge on the table. So I picked up the money and then came back twenty minutes later to find another big wedge sitting there. They were all slightly the worse for wear, so I walked up, thinking that they might have been slightly forgetful.

'Gentlemen,' I said, 'you have actually paid the bill.'

And one of the guys turned round and said, 'No, you idiot, that's the tip.'

I remember picking up the £200 wad and all the way back to the side of the room trying (and failing) to work out how to avoid the *tronc* system. This is one of those egalitarian systems where all tips are pooled and split between the waiting staff. At the Savoy Grill you could earn quite a lot of money. I'd get up to £400 a month in cash, but the headwaiters and the manager were taking about £2,500 to £3,000 home per month. Service was never included on the bill and everyone always tipped in cash. The only way around the *tronc* was to cover the cash in a napkin as you were clearing the table and pocket it. But woe betide you if you got caught.

It was a very interesting place to work. Margaret Thatcher was in there all the time. She was a great whisky drinker. She was always on the double whiskies, and she would always have the same table, number 4. If you were anyone in the Savoy Grill you would have a banquette table down the side – tables 4, 5, 6, 7 and 8. They were at the far end of the oak-panelled room. It is almost like an old gentlemen's drinking club. The tables were enormous but you would only ever really have two people at each one. But because of the high alcove walls, it was very intimate and no-one could hear your conversation. So many deals and affairs went on there, it was amazing.

I think because it was so discreet, the Queen Mother was a regular, and she loved it. When I was working in the kitchen, we would all take the piss, joking that she needed a stepladder to get to the table, she was so small. But she was actually great. Her full security entourage would sit on one table, and she would hobble in and sit at another. She would always dine late and only ever ate with friends, never with any other members of the Royal Family. She would always order off the menu. She really liked simple food. She was mad for fish and chips. She drank sweet Veuve Clicquot (which they made specially for her) or champagne cocktails, which is a shot of brandy, a sugar lump and some angostura bitters. She would have a maraschino cherry put on top. She'd follow her drink with an order of fish and chips. After lunch she would have green chartreuse followed by a yellow chartreuse. It was hilarious. It was always all systems go in the kitchen, the chefs slicing the potatoes so that every single chip was the same size and cut to perfection. So she would have fish, chips and fresh garden peas, not the mushy variety. I swear she treated the Savoy Grill like an upmarket caff.

Princess Diana also loved the Savoy Grill, and Claridge's. I remember once I went into the kitchen at the Savoy to collect the half a dozen oysters she'd ordered. One of the chefs who was opening them all up said to me, 'I'm going to snog Princess Di,' and as he said it he licked his hand and wiped it across the oysters, before we served them to her. I didn't really know what to say or whether to serve them or not. But I did. The Diana Effect was amazing. People always seemed to go a little crazy around her. I will never forget meeting her. All she had to do was look at you with those amazing blue eyes and you were smitten.

The Queen used to be more of a Claridge's person. In fact, she liked it so much that it used to be known as the Royal Family's second home. She used to attend these enormous banquets there with 1,500 people. They were so vast that the banquets would be spread over various rooms. There'd be a reception first, with champagne and cocktails; then dinner would be announced and everyone would sit down. However, every time the Queen went past, everyone would have to stand up and bow or curtsey. And she would walk past about four or five times an evening. As waiters, we would have to stop what we were doing immediately, get in a line and bow while she went past. Unfortunately, we'd corpse. I suppose it was like laughing in church. We knew we were not allowed to, but we just couldn't help ourselves.

The oddest thing I remember about the Queen is that all she drank was Campari and orange, which has to be one of the worst drinks going. Prince Philip, on the other hand, drinks lager, or bitter. When I was working there he was a fan of Ruddles Ale, and a cocktail called a Silver Bullet, which is Wolfschmidt Kummel, gin and lemon juice. It comes in a round tumbler on ice, and it's lethal.

It was the oddities about the royals and the celebrities I waited on that I always used to find entertaining. Kathleen Turner was a great petits fours plunderer. Every time she ordered her post-prandial coffee at the Savoy Grill she would wrap the petits fours in a napkin, put them in her handbag and then claim she never got any. I caught her doing it once and she called me over.

'You've seen me putting these in my handbag, haven't you?' she said.

'Yes, madam, I have,' I replied.

'You're not going to tell anyone, are you?'

'No, madam, I'm not.'

And I then went and got her another whole big tray of them and put them on her table. She ended up giving me a £50 tip which I most definitely didn't put into the *tronc*.

Not all famous people are that delightful. In fact, Noel Gallagher has to be one of the rudest people I have ever met. I remember being at the Lanesborough once around Christmas and he had certainly been indulging in some festive spirit. He and a group of people had been sitting there since lunchtime, and it was about nine p.m. There were people queuing for the table. The restaurant manageress declined to serve them any more drinks, saying she needed the table back for the evening and suggesting that they retire to the bar. Gallagher refused to go, saying that it was his table and he wasn't moving for anyone. She said fine and that she would give them another half an hour. When she returned and asked again if they would move through to the bar, he just got up and said, 'Do you know what? Fuck off!' He then threw a glass of wine in her face and left.

But it's not just celebrities who behave badly; sometimes hotel staff can do the oddest things when they come into contact with the rich and famous. I remember once I was escorting Mariah Carey into her hotel room when I noticed a maintenance guy, with his trousers down, sitting on her loo. I stood there slack-jawed. I couldn't bloody believe it. Fortunately, Mariah was looking the other way. It was only when I got him out of there that I learnt he was a fan and had simply wanted his buttocks to be close to hers.

I glance quickly around the restaurant and note that there doesn't seem to be anyone famous in here today. I walk up to Andre, the restaurant manager, and ask if there is anyone in here who fits the description of Mr Maison.

'Blue shirt, red tie, bald head,' I say.

Andre is in a panic. He has three tables waiting on main courses and a waiter who seems determined to get his coffee made for his table for two before serving the mains, which is pissing the kitchen off no end. He is also so high on caffeine he is sweating and can hardly concentrate. It makes me laugh. I can't believe the waiters in here are still up to their old tricks.

When I first arrived here, it used to be a standing joke to give Andre too much coffee. He has a heart problem so isn't really allowed to drink it, but he allows himself a couple of strong espressos in the morning. However, after eleven a.m. it is decaff only. But to be frank for a second, Andre is a bit of a shit. He is the sort of restaurant manager who removes a fork after you've laid up the whole dining room, then demands that you check your tables again to see if you notice anything, bollocking you severely if you don't. So the waiters used to deliberately over-caffeine him. When he'd ask for his decaffeinated coffee just before service started, they'd give him a triple espresso in the hope of sending him into the stratosphere. Today, judging by the dank sweat on his white forehead, is clearly one of those stratosphere days. I always think, he'll drop down dead one day and then there'll be a few waiters who might have to ask themselves a few tricky questions.

I spot Mr Maison over on the other side of the room,

lunching with two other bald men in ties. As I approach, I notice they are drinking a red Château Palmer, Margaux 1989, at £450 a bottle. They seem to be celebrating something. I hand over the note and Mr Maison makes great play of fishing his wallet out of his high-waisted trousers. I stand and smile and wait, thinking it would be nice to see a brown note come out of the pocket, but a blue would be fine. Instead, he fishes out 50p from the depths of his trousers and pats it into my hand. I'm half inclined just to let it fall onto the floor. But I'm broke, and these things all add up over time.

I have to admit that I am a little despondent by the time I get back to reception. The knowledge of the Texan's arrival today is the only thing keeping me going.

2PM – 3PM

It's relatively quiet on reception at the moment. Liz is tapping her nylon nails on the desk. She is loudly sucking on a mint while looking through the passports of some French couple who have just checked in. She smiles as she works out exactly how old the woman is.

'Can you believe she is forty-four?' she asks, looking up, her cheeks firmly sucked in as she gets to grips with her mint.

'Well, I can't say that I saw her properly. They were heading for the lifts when I came out of the restaurant,' I say, finding all the slurping coming from Liz's mouth almost as annoying as the drumming of her nails.

The French couple's bags are still sitting by the front desk in the shiny brass luggage trolley. Neither Jez nor Dave is very keen to take them up to the third floor.

For, just as the Americans are famed for their generosity, so the French are fêted for their general tightness when it comes to tipping.

However, they are not unique in the long-pockets-short-arms department. The Italians are also rubbish, as indeed are the Spanish and the Greeks. The Japanese are generous, and the Russians seem to be so delighted suddenly to have so much money that they can't help splashing or sharing it around. But the most welcome hotel guest has to be the Arab – even more profligate than the American. The guys from the Gulf spend money like water and drink rare whisky like water. I remember a girl in the hotel I worked in who was once given two first-class return tickets to India because she had been so helpful to this Saudi. The concierge was a little furious as he thought he was entitled to a bit more than the £500 watch he'd been given. But that is one of the problems when the real big spenders come into the hotel: we all start to get a little greedy. You can almost smell the service seeping back into our industry this afternoon as we are all on tenterhooks waiting for the Texan to arrive.

I look at my watch and smile. I know that all hell is still breaking loose in the kitchen downstairs, with orders for main courses still coming in and the pastry chef finally proving his tantric worth.

I used to have a mate who was a pastry chef. They

are very odd blokes indeed. I think they're nearly always stoned. At least, my friend was. They work in a totally different environment to the rest of the kitchen. Their room is cool to prevent any of the ingredients from melting, and calm because of the detail and precision of the work. If the head chef is a culinary artist, the pastry chef is an engraver. Nothing a pastry chef does is loud or flamboyant. The ones I have met are always quiet, introverted, perfectionist types who can spend hours making a rose out of icing. They can also make baskets out of sugar, and pipe cream into holes you never knew existed. They are largely ignored by the rest of the kitchen, but really come into their own during afternoon tea. Their handiwork is there to be admired on the sweet trolley or dessert menu. Having said that, in a more traditional dining room like the one we still have here, it is usually the more old-fashioned or nursery type of pudding that goes down well, like apple pie, bread and butter pudding or rich chocolate pot. Although we do have various fruits in Grand Marnier or berries in some sabayon for our more progressive clients.

Liz's tapping nails are really annoying me, so I decide to go into the back office to check the emails. Ewan is often too busy dealing with faxes and telephone calls to check the email five or six times a day, just in case something important comes in. Anyway, I don't mind doing it. It gives me a break from the desk, although the stale smell of the back room can sometimes put me off. Ewan's on the telephone talking someone through their weekend mini break in his dull monotone voice. I nod; he nods back. I dial up the server. Five emails arrive on the screen. The first two are reservations requests so I forward them to Lynette and Ewan's personal in-boxes; the third is junk mail from Ryanair telling us about some more flights they have for free; the fourth is some wine company advertising some new South African stuff; and the fifth, entitled 'Help Needed!', is a little odd.

It is from a woman who appears to be questioning a £10.70 mini bar bill we have sent her. But the more closely I read the email, the more I realize that she is not actually questioning the bill, but asking us to change its date. 'I was not supposed to be staying at the hotel at the time of the bill,' she writes. 'And my husband has unfortunately opened and read your letter. Now, as you can imagine, I am in big trouble and I need to find a solution.' She then goes on to give two email addresses – one her husband can read, one he cannot – while begging us to change the date of the bill and thereby her time of stay in the hotel. 'My marriage depends on your response,' she writes. 'I shall now send you an "official" request from my other email about the bill, so that when you reply my husband can see the response. I am counting on your readiness to help.'

God, I think as I print off the email, all this hassle over an unpaid orange juice and a bottle of water. Poor woman. The idea that your marriage might collapse because you didn't own up to those two beverages as you were checking out seems very harsh to me. I walk out of the office and share the news with Liz. She reads the email three times over, her eyes round, her mouth half open as she enjoys the drama of it all. She pretends that she remembers the couple in question and starts describing them intimately. I ignore her.

'What do you think we should do?' I ask.

'Email her back on husband-mail and say we got it wrong, of course,' says Liz, like I am some dumb moron.

'Do you think so?' I say. I am tempted to do as Liz says, but sense there is something fundamentally not quite right about it. And having already made one faux pas already today – packing up a guest's room without his permission – I think I should probably go and ask Adrian. 'I think I might go and ask the manager.'

'If you really think you can't make a decision on your own,' replies Liz with a dismissive wave of her hand.

'I think it's for the best,' I say.

'Right,' she says, leafing through some papers on the desk. 'Whatever.'

I take the printout and walk through the glass swing doors. She's only jealous, I think, that I picked up the email.

I am ushered into the office by Angie and find Adrian at his desk surrounded by fruit baskets, bottles of champagne, leather wallets, a teddy bear and 'Compliments of the Manager' cards. His Mont Blanc pen is poised as he is signing welcome slips for important guests.

'I'm sorry to bother you, Mr Thompson,' I say, standing by the door.

'Come in, come in.' He beckons me, his gold cufflink glinting in the sun. 'What seems to be the problem?'

I hand him the email and explain what has happened. He puts down his pen and reads it through, a mild grin of amusement on his face. He looks up.

'Poor cow,' he says. 'That must be one of the worst ways to be caught out, over a mini bar bill.' He laughs. 'How tragic is that?'

'So shall I write and say that we got it wrong on her husband's email, then?'

'I'm afraid not,' says Adrian.

'Oh?'

'Well, that would technically be fraud,' says Adrian. 'And if this case should ever come to court and our bill was used as evidence, we would have to lie in court or be caught lying in court. Either way, it is not a good look for the hotel.'

'Oh,' I say. 'It's just that I do feel a bit sorry for the woman. She sounds so desperate.'

'I know.' He shrugs. 'But really, for the sake of the hotel, I'm afraid we just can't get involved.'

'Right,' I say. 'So what should we do, then?'

'Well, nothing,' he says. 'Write something along the lines of "I'm afraid I can't help you with this matter" and leave it at that. If she writes again, bring it to me and I will have to write back to her.'

'Oh,' I say, picking up the printout. 'Is that really all we can do?'

'Yup,' says Adrian, picking up his pen again. ''Fraid so.'

As I turn around to leave his office, there's a knock on the door and Tony walks straight in.

'Tony?' says Adrian.

'Sir,' he says. 'I think there is some bloke casing the joint.'

'Right,' says Adrian, sitting up in his chair. 'What makes you say that?'

'Well, it's either him, a guest, or a new bloke in maintenance I haven't met yet. Either way he came into the hotel, took the lift to the third floor and disappeared.'

'Disappeared?' asks Adrian.

'Yeah, well,' says Tony, suddenly sounding rather sheepish. 'I was talking to a client on the telephone and it was Liz who noticed him. She says his red baseball cap was pulled a bit low over his face and suggested that I send Dave up to investigate. By the time Dave got up there the man had gone.'

'Oh,' says Adrian, getting up from behind his desk. 'Have you informed Mustafa in security?'

'Yes, first thing I did. He's checking his CCTV screens right now.'

'Good, because I don't need any paintings going walkabout. The police have already been in and warned me about a gang who are doing the area at the moment.'

Adrian goes on to explain that the picture thieves have already done the Cadogan Gardens and Blakes Hotels this week. Apparently, they brazenly walked into the hotel, took the pictures off the walls in full view of everyone working there, and walked out with them. Everyone in the hotel thought they were simply a couple of blokes from maintenance doing their jobs. Blakes has been hit a couple of times before, he says. Last time a gang walked in and started taking out tables, chairs, glassware and cutlery, and because they were doing it in such an overt and obvious manner no-one stopped them.

'Do you remember that bloke who stole all those TVs?' says Tony. 'From that place My Hotel?'

He then tells me this story about a thief who booked himself into two rooms in a new hotel, My Hotel, in

Chelsea. All the rooms in the hotel have these state-of-the-art flat-screen computers on which you can receive emails and watch TV. They are amazing and worth about five grand each. Anyway, the thief asks the concierge to send someone up to Harrods to buy him two computer bags, which of course he duly does. Then the thief calmly puts the two TVs into the computer bags and walks straight out of the hotel with them. The hotel tried to track him down but found that he had booked the two rooms on a stolen credit card.

'You've got to be so careful,' says Adrian. 'Do you remember those five laptops that went from a conference room in the Lanesborough?'

'Yeah.' Tony nods. 'Hadn't they all gone for lunch? Left the events room unlocked, and when they came back the place had been filleted?'

'That's right,' says Adrian. 'Terrible business.'

It's not like the hotel doesn't expect a certain amount of thieving. Ashtrays, teaspoons, bathrobes – they are all factored in to the price of the hotel room. But when it comes to things like fridges, loo seats (two wooden and Victorian ones from the Savoy), carpets and paintings off bedroom walls we start to get annoyed. The 10 per cent we add on to room rates for theft won't cover the gilt chair that is taken down the fire escape and shoved into a van at the bottom.

'It's not so much the price of replacing the paintings,'

admits Adrian, 'it's the bore of having to choose and find the replacements.'

As Adrian instructs both Tony and me to keep our eyes peeled around the hotel, there is another knock on his door. Sally comes in. Dressed in a dark suit with smooth, straight, blonde hair and two dark blusher triangles on her cheeks, Sally is the glamorous face of the hotel, in charge of PR and sales. She liaises with journalists, hands out free hotel stays and goes to tricky conferences about image and better communication, but her main job is what is known in the business as 'show rounds'. She spearheads the hotel's pitching on the lucrative wedding, conference and cocktail party circuit. It's her job to take prospective brides around the hotel, gently plying them with champagne as she persuades them to drop something like £40K in the hotel in one night. You can see why the hotel is only too happy to lay out a few canapés for the happy couple to taste or open a few bottles of champagne in their honour. But it is a stiffly competitive market and it is normally about one in ten of the brides Sally shows round who ever chooses to cut her cake in the ballroom.

Afternoons are Sally's busiest time because she can only really operate when the hotel is quiet. Part of her job is also to show various journalists or potential conference clients around the rooms available in the hotel, and for that she needs green-lit, VI, clean, un-occupied rooms – something which is only readily available in the short window between two and three in the afternoon.

She stands in Adrian's office with a broad grin on her face, looking from me to Tony and then back to the manager.

'You're not still pleased with yourself for saving tonight's cocktail party from near disaster, are you?' asks Adrian, taking the lid off his Mont Blanc pen again.

'No,' says Sally.

'What, then?" asks Adrian. 'You aren't wanting more plaudits just for doing your job again, are you?'

'Well, a bit.' She smiles. 'I have just secured us a large wedding for five hundred and fifty guests on a Sunday night!'

'On dodo night?' asks Tony.

'Who gets married on a Sunday night?' I ask.

'They're a very nice Jewish couple from north London,' says Sally.

'Extremely nice.' Adrian smiles. 'Well done, Sally.'

'I can't believe it,' she says. 'It was touch and go between us and the Mandarin Oriental. I had to under-cut them by a couple of thousand, but we can always make it up in corkage.'

Part of the appeal of these large events is the corkage.

The hotel can charge upwards of £10 simply to open a bottle of wine or champagne you have supplied yourself. It's amazing. Not only does it sting you for opening the alcohol, it stings you again when you come to pay. It has been known for places to say that you drank forty bottles when in fact you consumed only thirty-two. I remember a wedding we did recently where they drank sixty-five bottles of champagne and Adrian charged them for eighty-five. They also drank 120 bottles of water and we charged them for 200. Well, who is going to bother to count? If you're rich enough to drop £40K on a wedding, you really aren't the sort of person who is going to go down into the depths of the hotel and start counting up the empties at two a.m. And the amount of pilfering that goes on has to be seen to be believed. I remember a mate of mine once did a thirty-hour shift at this wedding and managed to help himself to eight bottles of Dom Perignon. He wrapped them one at a time in his tea towel and took them to his locker downstairs, telling everyone that he was going on a toilet break. The hotel also loves a big room hire. It charges from £300 an hour for a room that would normally be sitting idle. Banqueting, award ceremonies, conferences and weddings are win-win situations for any hotel.

Tony and I congratulate Sally as we leave Adrian's office and walk back to reception. I show Tony my email. It is important to include him in the gossip and try to keep him on side. I resolve to try a bit harder at making Tony my best friend.

Back in reception, Tony and I stop dead as we come through the glass swing doors. Neither of us really knows where to look. Tony snorts slightly as he tries to get himself together; I dig my fingernails into the palms of my hands as I walk towards the desk.

'Good afternoon, ladies,' I say.

Two heavily bandaged heads turn very slowly in my direction. They are both wearing dark glasses and have clearly just come out of hospital after having their faces lifted.

'Hello,' mumbles one of them, and immediately regrets it, wincing in pain.

'Mmm,' mutters the other as she fumbles through her wallet trying to find her credit card.

'Is it four days that you will be staying with us?' asks Liz, checking through her pile of paper.

'Mmm,' agrees the taller bandaged woman.

'Right,' says Liz, talking to them both as if nothing was out of the ordinary at all. 'We have put you in adjoining rooms so that you can keep each other company.'

'Hum hm,' mutters the taller woman again.

'I'll get Jez to take up your bags for you. Remember, no bending down for either of you.' Liz smiles. 'I hope you feel better tomorrow.'

The two women walk very slowly towards the lift. Each and every step appears to cause them pain. We are used to plastic surgery patients in the hotel. They always check in during the early afternoon, after their doctor has given them the all-clear on his lunchtime round. But it is still a bit of a shock to the system when they arrive. You don't really know where to look. How are you supposed not to notice when someone has lips like a pantomime duck? What are you supposed to say when a pair of Zeppelin breasts walk into reception half an hour before their owner? The whole thing is a bit mad. What makes me laugh is they somehow think that a pair of shades makes them look a whole lot better.

English women tend to come in pairs. Two friends undergoing the knife together, like it's an alternative to a fun lunch or something. Foreign women are nearly always nipped and tucked on their own, but they arrive with an entourage that can sometimes include several small children. They all stay three or four days locked up in their rooms, ordering soup on room service, and then leave to have their dressings taken off somewhere on Harley Street, before checking out of the hotel as if nothing had happened. Most of the time they receive no telephone calls or visitors. They leave as incognito as they arrived, ready to present their new face, lips, backsides and breasts to their amazed and sceptical friends.

'Oh, that looks painful,' says Liz as the elevator doors slide shut.

'Like some fucking freak show,' says Tony as he sits back down at his desk. 'One of them looked like she should have done her backside at the same time. No point in having a face that looks like you're in a permanent state of alarm if your arse is down by your ankles.'

'Ssh,' says Liz, 'they might hear you.'

'What, through all that lagging?' I say, laughing as I pick up the phone.

$3_{PM} - 4_{PM}$

Liz and I stand at reception talking about what parts of our bodies we would like to have enlarged, reduced, lifted, tucked and separated. She starts to point out faults in her appearance I have simply never considered worrying about before. She says that her calves are too fat and she would like some sort of extra shape in her upper arms. These are two body parts I was utterly unaware of until now. She would also like the bags removed from under her eyes. I suggest that the bags come with the job. But, unfortunately, now that she has pointed them out, I tend to agree: she could do with having her lower lids tightened up somewhat. For a young, overtly attractive girl, she doesn't half look shagged out. She answers the telephone, and as she smiles and talks someone through switching on the television in their room, her bags are all I can think about.

Suddenly, James comes flouncing through the glass swing doors. His Hugh Grant hair flops everywhere as he approaches reception.

'Hi,' he says.

'Hello,' I reply.

'Have you seen my caviar man anywhere?' he asks, sounding unusually concerned.

'No, not so far.'

'Shit,' he says, his fringe falling forward as he lowers his head. 'I've got Chef breathing down my neck. Our friend the Texan has ordered a bucketload of the stuff to be on ice in his room when he arrives.'

'Oh,' I say.

'Yeah.' James nods and rolls his eyes. 'I, my friend, am in the shit.'

'What does he look like?' I ask.

'Who?'

'Your caviar dealer.'

'Oh,' says James. 'I've no idea, but he'll be surly and Slavic and possibly a bit grubby-looking. They nearly always are. He's called something like Sergei, or Sasha. I don't know, I haven't dealt with him before. A mate in the restaurant trade tipped me off about him last week.'

'Right,' I say.

'Will you keep an eye out for him?' asks James.

'Sure,' I say.

'I would hang around here myself, but I've managed to track down some Puligny Montrachet 1980 for a really good price and I don't want those shits at the Dorchester getting their hands on it.'

'Right.'

'They're also promising some stuff from 1942.'

'Good.' I nod. Second World War wine is gold dust these days.

'Yes, it is,' says James, swishing back through the glass doors. 'It *is* bloody good.'

'I'll call you if I see anyone,' I say.

'Cheers,' says James. 'You're a mate.'

As I stand there pondering what it must really be like to be one of James's mates, I notice a whole load of kitchen staff file past the front of the hotel. Some are still dressed in their chef's whites with pale blue or check trousers, others are in their jeans, jumpers and thin coats; all of them are hunching their shoulders in the cold, accompanied by wisps of cigarette smoke.

The kitchen staff are on their split-shift break. The lucky things. God, what I wouldn't give for a hair of the dog pint right now, or a vodka shot to keep me going. Those guys have now got two hours they can call their own, and I can guarantee that most of them are going to the pub.

Well, there's almost no point in going home, is there? When I first started working in the kitchen and had no mates, I did pop home a couple of times before I realized my mistake. I slept all the way there on the Tube, dribbling onto my own shoulder with exhaustion, and when I finally did get home I made myself a sandwich, watched some kids' TV and took the Tube back, sleeping all the way again. I soon understood there were probably better uses of my time.

So mostly I'd go to the pub. It was a good way for me to bond with the group and let off steam. I'd sit there with the rest of the commis chefs and waiters bitching about what went wrong at lunch and about who landed us in the shit due to their incompetence at the grill, or something like that. It was a laugh. Six or seven languages on the go at the same time, but somehow we all managed to chat. I used to knock back about two or three pints and half a packet of cigarettes during my break. We'd normally come back a little pissed after our time out, but no-one ever seemed to notice or mind. We'd all shove back the mints on the way back to disguise any alcohol on our breath. But if anyone had made a fuss, I think they'd have had a mutiny on their hands. You can't expect 150 blokes to work their arses off sixteen hours a day without some sort of respite. Anyway, after half an hour in the boiling hellhole that is the kitchen, we'd sweated ourselves sober.

There were a few who didn't drink at all. They were the ones in the really shitty jobs who normally didn't speak much English and who were sending half their wages home to some other country. Either they were too broke to drink or they were too knackered. Some of them had other jobs, cleaning somewhere else, and used these two hours to pass out in the staff room, catching up on some shuteye.

The stoners didn't have much to drink either. They'd rather have a few spliffs than pints any day, and they'd sit in the corner of the pub eating crisps, zoning out and going round the corner for tokes. It always used to amaze me how they made it through the next shift. Dope makes you tired and want to go to bed. I was usually knackered enough before the dinner service without a joint adding to my problems. I always suspected that they supplemented their drugs a bit later on, adding coke or speed to the mix. Some of them would finish the shift at eleven p.m. really quite hyper and high, keen to go on drinking somewhere else, while the rest of us could barely manage to put one foot in front of the other to make it home.

Liz has got her hands on the afternoon post. She is dividing it up into sections, sorting out Tony's weekend jaunt brochures from James's fine wine catalogues. There's an awful lot of the stuff. It seems odd, when most of the bookings are done over the telephone these days, that we still get so much rubbish through the post. Liz takes the pile into the back office. A naturally nosy person, she likes going through the post before letting Ewan anywhere near it.

'Fantastic!' announces Tony, slamming down his telephone, evidently satisfied. 'That'll be an excellent piss-up if ever I've heard of one.'

'What?' I say, leaning on the counter. With Liz in the back room it is a good time to let standards slip for a second.

'That was the PR for Chutney Mary – you know, that curry place in Chelsea.'

'Yes. Never been there myself, but I've heard it's a good place.'

'Well,' smiles Tony, 'they've organized a concierge piss-up next week and they've asked me to come along. There are thirty of us. All concierges. But they say I can bring a couple of mates along.'

I can see both Jez and Dave stiffen with anticipation. Normally when Tony gets invited to these things, which happens about twice a month, it is a toss-up between the two of them who goes. It is supposed to be part of their training process, their way of finding out which places are good to eat at, which are on their way out, what is worth the trek across town. The last thing you want to do, as a concierge, is recommend somewhere that is mediocre, especially when the client is dropping £2,000 a night in your hotel.

'Sounds good,' I say.

'Yeah,' he agrees. 'It's always good to share notes with some of my mates from other hotels. You get the best stories. It's always nice to hear what's going on in the other places.'

'I'm sure,' I say.

'Want to come with me?' he asks.

I stand up, slightly shocked. Jez and Dave slacken with rejection. 'What, me?' I ask.

'Yeah, you,' he says. 'It might do you good to have a laugh. It's all free,' he adds, as some sort of incentive.

'When is it?' I ask, like I'm a busy person with an agenda, a diary, a social life, a life or indeed a girlfriend. None of which I've got. I used to have a girlfriend but she dumped me months ago because I kept on having to do nights, and I haven't got around to getting another one for exactly the same reason.

'Next Thursday,' he says.

'Sounds great,' I say, getting out my empty diary. 'I'll jot it down.'

As I'm noting down my date with my new best friend, I suddenly notice a suspicious-looking character wandering around the lobby with a large holdall bag, wearing a red baseball cap pulled low down on his face. Suspicious to say the least. He doesn't have enough purpose in his stride to be a maintenance man, although sometimes you can be forgiven for pulling them over, the way they stroll about their business. I catch Tony's eye. Quick as a terrier,

I can see he's on to him: his body is stiff, his eyes are bright and he's following his every move. The description certainly fits the man who was hanging around earlier. Are those rolled-up paintings in his bag? The only thing that worries me is he's not making the fastest exit I have ever seen. Even so, he does look dodgy. But you have to be careful when approaching people in the hotel. They can easily be guests, and it is more than your job's worth to ask them to open their bags. They can be rock stars, or celebrities in a 'street' disguise. Winona Ryder used to confuse us all the time; she'd dress up like a man in order to put off the paparazzi when leaving the hotel. Such people have to be approached with caution. However, Tony seems to be throwing that to the wind as he walks up to the man.

'Excuse me,' he says. The man turns round. 'Could you open the bag, please?' The man looks shocked. He puts his hand over the bag and shakes his head. 'Could you please open the bag, sir,' asks Tony again. 'It would be better for you in the long run if you were seen to co-operate, son.' The man is still shaking his head. 'Right,' announces Tony. Aggressively shoving the man with one hand, he grabs the bag with the other.

'Nooooo!' says the man as he collapses in a crumpled heap on the floor.

'I did ask politely,' says Tony, unzipping the bag. 'Oh,' he says as he looks inside.

'What?' I ask, coming out from behind my desk in somewhat tardy support.

'Give James a call, will you,' he says. 'Tell him his caviar man has arrived.'

'Oh,' I say, stopping mid-stride.

'Yes, bit embarrassing,' says Tony, walking towards the wall. 'Sorry, mate,' he adds, offering the man a hand.

The caviar man says nothing. He refuses Tony's offer of help and, brushing himself down, puts his hand out for his bag of caviar.

James is more flustered and flouncy than usual when he rushes out of his back office and into reception.

'You didn't hit him? You didn't hit him?' he says to Tony. 'Please say there was no physical contact. Otherwise he won't come here again.'

Tony denies all knowledge of any contretemps and the caviar man doesn't speak good enough English to contradict him. In a matter of seconds, James has scooped the man up and taken him into his back office for some calming vodka and some gentle Beluga, Sevruga and Oscietra dealing.

The hotel will normally buy all the bloke's got in his holdall. It's not like it will be difficult to get rid of the stuff in a place like this. The guests spoon it back like blackberry jam. Mr Texan oil baron has ordered half a kilo for his room already, if I heard correctly earlier. James, I know now, will be doing a bit of a tasting with his silver spoon. When he's spending thousands of the hotel's pounds, he's got to be careful that he's not buying shit. That's one of the problems when dealing with the black market: you have no recourse if you make a mistake. So the caviar man will be in there for a good half hour while James checks the seals on all the jars, opening the occasional one just to see they haven't been tampered with. Then Chef will be doling out the fish eggs to whomsoever asks for them. We could even get a few takers for tea.

It's ten minutes to four, and the tea crowd should be turning up soon. I've actually noticed a few tourists coming through into the lounge for tea already. They can cause a few problems sometimes. We're an upmarket destination five-star hotel so we have a no trainers, no shorts policy in our lounge, which can make it rather tricky when it comes to tea. The thing is, no-one likes afternoon tea more than the Americans, and they, no matter their size, tend to favour shorts and trainers. So it often ends up being a quid pro quo situation. If there's a large group who look like they might spend a lot of money, we let them in; if it's only a couple who look a little overawed by the place, I usually tell them to go to the café around the corner.

But, as with everything in the hotel business, tea is about making money. And there is nothing a big hotel like ours likes more than afternoon tea. Think of the mark-up. The cost price for a pot of tea, some cakes and dainty sandwiches, plus a couple of strawberries, scones and some cream, is less than a pound. We charge £11.75 per person and £5 extra for another pot of tea. At the last place I worked it was £28 for a full stand of sandwiches and cakes, which I know for a fact cost them £2 to make. We don't even make the mini éclairs or strawberry meringues on the premises any more. Our stoner pastry chef is usually too busy making canapés or mad creations for banqueting to spend hours making dainty cakes these days. We buy them all in. They are delicious, but they're not made here any more. When our pastry chef does have the time he can make the most exquisite, beautiful works of art, but nowadays he's only really required to do that sort of stuff for weddings.

Gino also likes to try to get in on tea. It is a good time of day for him to get rid of some flutes of champagne at £10.50 a glass and less than £2 at cost. Depending on how busy his bar is with post-lunchtime boozers, I have often seen him walk through the lounge carrying a bottle of chilled champagne by way of a serving suggestion.

Apart from the Japanese and American tourists for whom an English tea has constant appeal, the tea crowd has changed a bit over the years. It used to have, much like morning coffee, a Home Counties feel to it – women, all dressed up for town, taking their godchildren/girlfriends/mothers out to tea. These days, however, it has become rather more glamorous. The ladies who lunch now also do tea, although obviously not on the same day. Since Kate Moss and Sadie Frost were seen sporting cups and saucers at Blakes, we have noticed a big difference in our tea takings, and that's mainly in flutes of champagne. Girls' teas are now big business, and no-one is happier than Gino.

But August is the best month in the hotel calendar for afternoon tea. Actually, August is the best month in the hotel calendar for almost everything, as we are obviously crammed with Arabs. And the Arabs love their tea. At the beginning of the month, when they arrive, they will slip the restaurant manager £100 or so to make sure that they have sole use of a particular dining table in the restaurant, and an area in the lounge. And then they go mad.

Money is of no object whatsoever, and there's real oneupmanship. Their time clock is totally different from the other guests' in the hotel. They get up between two and three in the afternoon and come down for breakfast, which is actually afternoon tea. Dressed up to the nines in the most amazing stuff you have ever seen, the women go totally over the top. They meet for tea and try to work out who has got the most expensive jewellery or who is ordering the most. Although we enjoy it all, they can also be rather annoying, because their teas always go on rather a long time. In fact, a bit too long. When you want the dining room back at 5.30

for pre-theatre dinner, they are still hanging around.

What usually happens is that the women will leave at around five p.m., armed with sackloads of cash, and go out hardcore shopping, while the men sit around doing a bit of business. Then they all disappear and come back again at about 9.30 for dinner. They eat an enormous amount, the men hammering back vodkas while pretending to drink water in front of their wives. Then they hit the nightclubs and casinos, and the strip clubs in Soho, coming back at about three a.m. In places like the Lanesborough, which has a special Arabic menu for the month of August, they can then go on to order room service.

However, the last thing you need at this time of day with nearly all your kitchen staff on a break is any sort of rush on. I remember I heard about a smaller hotel in Kensington that was once caught on the hop by London Fashion Week. A quick stilettoed sprint from the Natural History Museum, where most of the shows take place, they were once descended upon by a gaggle of models; Naomi Campbell, Claudia Schiffer and various other skinny beauties all piled in at once. The restaurant was absolutely dead, then all of a sudden, at 3.45, it was heaving with loads of models ordering Fat Chips, Cosmopolitans, Bloody Marys and champagne. They came in, ordered, ordered, ordered, stayed for forty-five minutes, paid their bill and then, bang, they'd gone. The restaurant was totalled – glasses everywhere, bowls everywhere, ashtrays brimming over. Then, bang, all of a sudden they were hit again at about 6.15.

The next day, the hotel got a list of when the shows were on so they knew when the fash pack was coming. They fried prawn won tons, prepared crudités and cooked some chipolata sausages in honey; they made jugs of Bloody Marys and Cosmopolitans; they put bottles of champagne on ice; and they didn't even bother setting the restaurant for dinner. They stripped it all out and left it at that. The models returned and cleaned the place out, except for the crudités, which, bizarrely, no-one touched. In two days they sold ninety-five portions of Fat Chips (£2.75) and 200 glasses of champagne – a remarkable achievement.

I'm leaning against the counter, listening to Tony talk to some restaurant PR on the telephone, when I notice a large black limousine pull up outside the hotel. I can tell the man is important because Steve immediately stands to attention – that man can smell a tip coming half a mile up the road. He walks slowly backwards towards the glass door of the hotel and gives the window a little tap with his white gloves. Tony looks up and immediately stops what he is doing. He puts down his telephone and says loudly to Jez and Dave, who are busy packing up luggage on the trolley, 'Oi, boys, look sharp, our friend the Texan has arrived.'

4PM – 5PM

Mr Masterson's arrival sends a bolt of electricity through the hotel. Anyone who had previously been half asleep or underperforming is now suddenly wide awake and on full beam. It is amazing what the smell of big bucks does to a service industry. Suddenly, nothing is any trouble. Doors that were previously closed are now wide open and everyone is so terribly jolly.

Steve is the first off the blocks. He speedily opens the door of the limousine, greets Mr Masterson by name and has the luggage out of the car and into the hotel before the Texan has managed to button up his camel-coloured cashmere coat. Steve receives a £20 note for his diligence and bows, walking away backwards from Mr Masterson like he was royalty. Which, I suppose, in hotel terms, he is.

Next to give Mr Masterson the full wattage of his bright smile is Tony. Out of his seat, his hand out in meet-and-greet mode, Tony welcomes Mr Masterson back to the hotel and asks him about his flight. It is not strictly his role to do that, it's more Adrian's territory, but he earns £50 for doing so.

In fact, as word spreads through the hotel of Mr Masterson's arrival, everyone comes out of the woodwork. James escorts his caviar man to the door and 'bumps' into Mr Masterson as he is checking in, mentions he's sourced his Trinidad Diplomatic cigars and earns himself £50. Gino pops out from behind his bar, leaving the auditor for one second, to tell Mr Masterson about the arrival of a delicious special whisky he might want to try. Gino gets two £50 notes for his trouble. Even Andre, the caffeine-fuelled restaurant manager, finds a reason to be in reception when he really should be finishing the teas. He reminds Mr Masterson that he has saved him his usual table and gets £50 for his pains. Lastly, Adrian comes out from the back office. Expansive smile and full-on service industry charm at his disposal, he greets the Texan like he is his oldest friend in the whole wide world. They shake hands and slap backs, enquiring after each other's health like they both care. Adrian reserves this sort of welcome for guests who spend more than £10,000 a pop in the hotel. God knows how exuberant he would have been towards David Beckham and his £433,157 bill at the Hotel Santo Mauro in Madrid.

I let Liz check Mr Masterson in. I think being surrounded by so much toadying and obsequious commercialism is enough to put anyone off. I don't know why I'm surprised by everyone's reaction. They have been talking only of this man and his vast wealth for days now. Their running around after him for handouts shouldn't come as a shock. Anyway, Liz surpasses herself. Flicking her hair and thrusting her cleavage forward, she flirts with him like he is some drop-dead handsome movie star instead of a short, bald, florid seventy-year-old man. But he seems to enjoy it and hands over another pink £50 note as he collects his room key. The man has handed out nearly £500 within five minutes of arriving and he hasn't yet made it to the lift.

Jez and Dave fight for the pleasure of taking Mr Masterson's luggage to his room. They have one small Louis Vuitton suitcase each. For a very rich man, Mr Masterson seems to like to travel very light.

'Enjoy your stay,' I say to him on autopilot as he walks past.

'Oh, I didn't see you there,' he says, sounding a little surprised. 'That's very kind of you,' he adds, slipping a £20 note onto the desk.

I am a little mortified. The grand stand I was trying

to make, steering clear of all the other sycophants, hasn't actually gone according to plan. I now look just as bad as the rest of them.

'No, honestly, there is no need,' I say, pushing it back towards him.

'Really, son,' drawls Mr Masterson, already halfway towards the lift. 'Take it. There's plenty more where that came from.'

'Um, thank you, sir,' I say.

'Thanking you,' he replies.

As the lift door closes behind him, an explosion of chatter begins. The lobby sounds like an excited school playground with words like 'Can you believe it!', 'pink notes' and 'amazing' being bandied about all over the place. The energy level of the whole establishment seems to have doubled with the arrival of one person.

'Well, I thought he was charming,' says Liz, flicking her blonde hair and clicking her nylon nails.

'You would,' I say.

'What's that supposed to mean?'

'Nothing,' I say. 'I'm going outside for a cigarette.'

We're not normally allowed to smoke outside the front of the hotel as it is not good for the image of such a pukka establishment. You can imagine that a whole group of waiters wading around in old butts is not the most attractive of things for an arriving guest. But I'm not really in the mood to care. It's odd, because usually

I'd have been all over the Texan like herpes. I'd have had my head so far up his arse I'd be wearing him like a glove puppet, but today all this fawning has given me a headache. Perhaps I'm more upset about Michelle leaving than I care to admit. We were quite good mates, and the idea of endless shifts with Liz is bringing me down. Or perhaps it's the fact that I toasted Michelle's departure a bit too enthusiastically last night that is making me feel so contrary and morose.

I sidle up to Steve, who is stamping his feet. It's already quite cold and dark and he has got another four hours of standing out here, opening doors and being polite.

'All right?' I ask.

'Great.' He nods, his thick nose all red and running with cold. How he stands it out here in all weathers I'll never know.

We've got four doormen who work for the hotel: Graham, Derek, Steve and Dennis. Steve and Dennis are cousins. It's the old keeping-the-job-in-the-family idea at work again. Dennis has been at it for seven years, but Graham and Derek are relatively new additions to the fold. But then, everyone is relatively new in comparison to Steve. Steve's been standing out here for thirty years. Working four days on, four days off, he does a twelve-hour shift from eight a.m. to eight p.m., opening doors and keeping the front of house clean and respectable. He officially earns £11K a year, although with all those pound coins he collects you can times that by five. He has become so much part of the furniture that some of our regulars buy him little presents when they come and stay. His welcoming face is part of the traditional continuity of the hotel. He makes guests feel welcome when they arrive, and sometimes he even uses their name when he opens the door, making them feel grand and important in an instant. Little do they really know that he is a moody bastard who drinks like a fucking fish on his days off. The massive broken veins that branch across his thick nose are less to do with exposure to the elements than with nights at home with a bottle of whisky. But he doesn't seem too bad-tempered today. Perhaps it's the £20 note burning a hole in his pocket that has lightened his mood, or the fact that he has done his four days already this week and in three hours' time he'll be on a four-day break. He even strikes up a conversation.

'You all right?' he sniffs.

'Been better,' I say.

'Going to miss your friend?' he asks, stamping from one foot to the other.

'Who's that?'

'Michelle.'

'Yeah.' I nod. 'More than I'd thought, actually.'

'She was quite sexy.'

'I didn't think you'd noticed.'

'Yeah, well,' he says, a chapped smile breaking across his red face, 'I see more than any of you lot ever give me credit for. You all think that Tony is the eyes and ears of this place. But you're wrong. I see every coming and going from here, and just because my back is turned to reception most of the time doesn't mean I'm ignorant of what is going on.'

'Right,' I say, taking a drag on my cigarette.

'I know about Ben and Jackie in housekeeping as well,' he says.

'Right.'

'I know,' he repeats, tapping the side of his nose with his gloved hand. 'That shocked you.'

'Well, it has a little, as it happens,' I say.

'Yeah,' he says as he turns towards a cab pulling up outside the hotel. He smiles as he walks towards its door. 'Oi,' he adds, turning quickly round to face me. 'Don't stub that bastard out here. Take it with you.'

I pick my butt off the pavement and follow the guest slowly in through the revolving doors. Fortunately, from a smoking receptionist's point of view, the guest is Mrs Robertson. Bless her. A dear old biddy in her late eighties, Mrs Robertson has been living in the hotel since her husband died two and a half years ago. She is sweet, charming, reasonably chatty but, sadly, deaf as a post.

She's so deaf, in fact, that we've had to devise this special method of getting room service into her room. She has a room on the top floor of the hotel with a nice view over London that she likes to gaze out on occasionally, in between watching the horses on the telly. For the first year of her stay, her racing addiction was a nightmare. She used to have her TV on so loud that whenever we brought up her morning tea, or any of her other meals, she would never hear any of the room service guys knocking on her door. We're not allowed to enter rooms unless we have been invited in, so the room service boys would stand outside her room rapping on her door for hours at a time. Reception would at the same time be calling madly on the telephone, but she wouldn't hear a thing. Eventually, Tony came up with an idea. Through a mate of a mate of his, he sourced a remote control for the television that we could keep outside her bedroom door, and any time anyone wanted to get Mrs Robertson's attention we'd turn down her volume through the crack under the door. She, of course, was thrilled with the idea; everyone else was relieved.

'Good afternoon, Mrs Robertson,' I say as I overtake her on the way to reception.

'What?' she says, turning her small, wrinkled face towards me.

I have to say I'm a bit fond of the old dear. I lost my

147

grandmother a couple of years back and Mrs Robertson sort of reminds me of her. I like the way she always wears a proper hat and a pair of gloves when she leaves the hotel. There are not many people around who still do that.

Then again, she's quite popular with most members of staff in the hotel, mainly because she is always polite and not much trouble. I remember one old lady at one of the places I worked who was mean and cantankerous and used to piss all over her chair. We eventually had to put plastic covers on all her seating and add rubber sheeting to her bed. But in the end she had to go. She was treating the place like a nursing home and there was no-one qualified to look after her.

On the whole, there is an ambivalent attitude towards long-termers in the hotel business. You would have thought we would be only too delighted to have guaranteed occupancy of rooms for a great length of time, but it can be a right pain. For a start, it's not all little old ladies wanting their afternoon tea and a biscuit in front of the telly. There are plenty of long-termers who are foreign businessmen who have been placed here by their bank or some other wealthy employer. Stuck in a hotel for two months while trying to find somewhere to live, they become demanding, treating the place like their home; they develop regular affectations, like a raspberry-only breakfast, or start wanting the concierge to organize their lives even when they are in the office, booking flights and taxis all the time. They want their hotel room to be treated like an apartment, which means that the maids get little or no access, yet they complain when the room has not been cleaned.

We also get guests who are having their flats or houses refurbished who check into the hotel for months at a time. They are difficult customers mainly because they're stressed and money is tight, so they tend never to order room service and bring their own alcohol into their room. Long-stayers usually get a monthly invoice, and it is always the house refurbisher who complains about his bill, going through it with a fine-tooth comb. However, there are some who prefer to pay in advance instead of the monthly invoice; we take a lump sum off their card and then inform them when it has run out. Mrs Robertson is the advance credit card type. We usually favour advanced payment for the elderly, for obvious reasons.

There is, however, one type of long-stayer the hotel can't get enough of, and that's the millionaire who, like Mick Jagger at Claridge's, keeps an apartment in the hotel, which he'll visit once or twice a year. He'll pay for use of the room for a whole year in advance, on the understanding that it is kept empty, awaiting his whimsical arrival. Except, of course, it isn't. I remember a terrible story I heard once about Kerry Packer turning up at the Savoy only to find he could not get into his room. He had a suite there that he rented 365 days a year and only used for three or four weeks maximum. Anyway, he turned up unannounced one afternoon to stay in his suite and the hotel had rented it out to someone else. While reception delayed him, saying something along the lines that there had been a leak in the suite and they were just sorting it out, a whole load of people were despatched to take all the other guest's stuff out of the room. Packer apparently sussed what was going on and threatened to take his business elsewhere if he didn't get into his room within the next ten minutes. They managed to pull it off. I have no idea how they explained the upheaval to the other guest. The man would have been in an expensive suite. They must have comped him his whole stay and apologized profusely.

'Good afternoon,' I say again to Mrs Robertson.

'Oh, yes.' She nods, finally, after lip-reading my question. 'I had a lovely lunch with my grandson at Simpson's on the Strand.'

'Good,' I say.

'Jolly good,' she replies.

'Would you like your room key?' I ask.

My voice is bellowing around reception and Tony is looking a little annoyed. This is one of the busiest times of day for him. It's the time when he has to confirm all the tables he has booked at various restaurants around London. If he can't fill his tables tonight, he must let the establishments know so that they can pass the tables on to others further down the food chain. It is also around this time that guests in the hotel start ringing him up asking him to book restaurant tables. So Tony is in one of his terrible catch-22 situations: should he release his table at the Ivy or Sheekey's and risk getting a telephone call in the next ten minutes asking for a restaurant table, or should he hang on and risk pissing off the maître d' who will be less inclined to do him a favour on another occasion? These are the sorts of decisions that make a good concierge, the sort of concierge other hotels want to poach, which is a practice that goes on all the time. There was someone sniffing around here only the other day. Tony, of course, reported it to Adrian, who immediately gave him a pay rise. Good concierges are hard to come by and a luxury hotel always wants to hold on to them.

Mrs Robertson hasn't heard my last question, but I go to get her Ving key card anyway. The flash of Tony's eyes is enough to make me think twice about asking her again.

'What's got his goat?' asks Liz, looking up from a calculator. She is desperately trying to balance the front till. A job I take great pleasure in delegating, given half the chance.

151

'Dunno,' I say, handing over Mrs Robertson's key card.

'Don't tell me they've run out of circle tickets for *The Mousetrap*,' says Liz.

'Yeah.' I laugh. 'Or there's been a rush on at *We Will Rock You*!'

'You two can piss off,' stage-whispers Tony as he puts down the telephone.

'I heard that,' announces Mrs Robertson, standing by the lift.

'How the hell . . . ?' mouths Tony as she turns to get into the lift.

Both Liz and I shrug.

Tony's telephone goes. From the whiteness of his smile, I guess it must be an important client. Liz gets back to balancing the daily float, accounting for all the outgoings, like morning-after pills, that we have had to pay for today. I decide to give housekeeping a quick call just to make sure that all the rooms are ready and back for business before the early-evening check-in rush. While Jackie yawns into my ear, complaining about a broken lamp in room 240, Jenny the flower girl arrives.

Blonde and bubbly with a flamboyant pashmina draped over her shoulder, Jenny turns up at various times during the week to replace all the flowers in the hotel. She does bedrooms on Mondays, common parts on Wednesdays and the main reception, dining and bar areas on Fridays. Flowers may sound like a trifle when it comes to the main event of running a hotel, but they are really quite important. They set the tone of the place and are significant enough for a place like the Bentley Hotel to spend £4,000 on blooms a month; for a medium-size place like here, our monthly florist's bill comes to £3,000. It's a nice little contract if you can get it. You can also triple your money if you get bookings for banquets or weddings.

Jenny's been through her country-bunch phase and seems a bit keen on all those tropical flowers at the moment. All fleshy glamour and no smell, I have to say I'm not that fond of them. But then I only have to work next to the things all week, so who is going to ask for my opinion?

She usually arrives with the arrangements already done, bringing them out of a small mini van she parks outside the front, with specific instructions for Steve to look out for traffic wardens. She then spends the next ten minutes tweaking her flowers *in situ* while talking about her two children to Liz. I swear, I know more about her goddamn family than I do about my own. Her two are in bed with the flu at the moment, and Liz, for some reason, moans in sympathy. I move up the other end of reception to get away from their chat. I've only got another couple of hours to go and I'm beginning to feel the lateness of last night's party.

All I fancy is an early night after sitting on my sofa with some soup.

'Shit!' Tony exclaims very loudly and very unprofessionally.

'Language,' says Jenny, turning around.

'Pardon me,' says Tony with a tight smile. 'But you might be a little pissed off if you'd just cancelled all your tables at the Ivy only to have the most important guest in the hotel call up and ask for a table for six.'

'Oh dear,' says Jenny, tweaking some fleshy red thing with a white stamen that looks like a satellite dish.

'Not Masterson?' I ask.

Tony nods, and puts his head in his hands.

5PM $-$ 6PM

No amount of gorging himself on humble pie is going to help Tony out of his situation. He held on to his tables at the Ivy for as long as he thought was humanly possible, and now he is in the shit. I can hear him whispering down the telephone. His head is low as he talks into his chest. He always does this when he is trying to cut some sort of deal. But from the constant scratching of his forehead I can tell it's not working. He puts the phone down slowly and stares into the middle distance, obviously trying to think.

Liz and Jenny finish talking about Jenny's children and Jenny walks through the glass doors, one orange arrangement in her right hand and a bowl of green leaves in her left, on her way towards the bar. As she walks through the doors, Gino comes bursting out.

'Bloody hell fuck!' he says, walking towards reception, only to collapse onto the desk with dramatic exhaustion. 'Do you know,' he announces, rolling his eyes, 'there are times in one's life when one is allowed to kill someone, and mine is here. Oh my God,' he exhales. 'That little shit of a stock-taker. I swear to fucking God he is counting my bloody olives! One . . . two . . . three . . .' His pinched fingers pluck imaginary olives out of an imaginary bowl.

'What?' squeals Liz, leaning over. 'Literally going through them all?'

'No, stupid!' says Gino, his eyes rolling again. 'But he may as bloody well be!'

'Oh, right,' Liz says quickly, putting her head down, suddenly very interested in a pile of paper in front of her.

'Really,' says Gino, shaking his head. 'We are three bottles of Britvic orange short and a bottle of vodka down, and someone has half fucking inched a Bailey's. Really,' he says again, his hands together, pleading, 'who fucking cares?'

'There is a Bombay Sapphire thief in the hotel,' states Liz, her lined lips pursed.

'We all know that, sweetheart,' says Gino, 'but that's in the maids' bloody department, not with me! I don't sell miniatures, now do I?'

'I was just saying,' says Liz.

'Say away,' says Gino with a flick of his wrist. 'But it has nothing to do with me.'

As Gino leans on the desk bemoaning his auditing fate, Adrian walks brusquely through the glass doors.

'Oi, Gino,' he says with a click of his fingers. Gino stands to attention. 'What are you doing in your morning suit?' asks Adrian. 'It's gone five,' he adds, tapping the face of his expensive gold watch. 'Black tie.'

'I'm on my way,' says Gino, theatrically. 'I'm just recovering from my stock-take.'

'Now!' barks Adrian, refusing to be drawn into his head barman's dramatics. Gino immediately shuffles off. 'Right, Tony,' continues Adrian without breaking his stride. 'What's this I hear about Masterson and the Ivy? I've just got off the phone to him.'

Adrian parks half a buttock on Tony's desk and starts talking in hushed tones. Tony looks up Adrian's nose for a while, then turns his face towards his desk and nods continuously. Neither Liz nor I can hear what they are saying. We both lean forward, straining to hear. But to no avail.

After a couple of minutes, my attention is distracted by the return of the kitchen staff as they file past the front of the hotel after their break. Fortunately, Adrian's back is turned the other way, as even from here I can tell some of them are pissed. It's the way they are walking, laughing and slapping one another on the back as they come round the corner. No-one could ever be that pleased to be going back down into the kitchens, unless they were drunk. One of the sous chefs runs up to the front window and presses himself against it, kissing and smearing the glass. For one dreadful second I think he is going to moon reception, but I see him clocking Adrian's back and he runs swiftly back to join the group.

You can't really blame them for wanting to soften the blow of the next five hours. I always used to think that the evening run was worse than the morning. You change into your fresh set of whites and immediately the hell begins. For not only are people tired and tempers fraying, the stress level always trebles as there is so much more to do. Firstly you've usually got a whole lot of canapés to make as soon as you get back down there. We've got a party for 400 starting at 6.30 this evening, so God knows how many smoked salmon rolls and blinis they're going to have to churn out before the night is out. There's also a whole load of savoury *amuse-bouches* to get ready for the bar. Luxury hotels run bars where crisps, peanuts and the odd green olive quite frankly don't cut the mustard. One of the ways to justify a £15 martini is to have plates of creamed and piped anchovies on savoury biscuits, halved quail's eggs with lumps of caviar, and prawns on small toasts standing by. All these things have to be made even before the sous chefs get round to sorting out their *mise en place* for the dinner shift, chopping their parsley and slicing their vegetables. I give one of the commis chefs a little wave on his way and thank God I am above stairs these days.

Adrian suddenly gets up from Tony's desk and, patting him on the shoulder, says something along the lines that he is glad something is sorted out. Tony looks relieved. Adrian is a little tense-faced as he walks towards reception.

'Everything all right here?' he asks.

'Fine,' says Liz, her voice sounding oddly high.

'Whose luggage is that?' he asks, pointing to the bag I'd packed earlier that is still sitting behind reception.

'A guest's,' I say swiftly, suddenly feeling really quite sick. I'd quite forgotten my early room clearing. I feel my face go pink. I wonder if Adrian will notice.

'Well, put it away in the back office,' he says. 'It's untidy. When are they coming to collect it? You know we don't like to keep checked-out luggage this long.'

'Yes, Mr Thompson,' I say, bending down to pick up the bag, avoiding all eye contact.

'When's he coming, then?' asks Adrian.

'Um, soon,' I say, hopefully.

'Good,' says Adrian, walking back towards the glass doors. 'Stock-taker gone yet?'

'Um, not as far as I know,' I say.

159

'You're on reception. Is that a yes, or a no?' he asks dryly.

'No,' I say, as determinedly as I can.

'Good,' he says. 'Pay attention,' he adds, turning around and pointing two fingers at his own eyes. 'Keep them open.'

'Yes, Mr Thompson,' I say as he turns and walks back through the glass doors.

Everyone exhales as he goes. The tension dissipates. Even Jez and Dave were looking a little uptight with Adrian around – like they're bloody over-burdened with responsibility!

'He's on the war path,' says Liz, ever one to point out the obvious. 'I wonder what got up his nose?'

'I've got no idea,' I say. 'But I can't stand it when he's like that. You all right over there, Tony?'

'Yeah, fine,' he says, picking up the telephone. 'We're sending the Yank to Sheekey's. I pulled a few strings and Adrian's going to call up and tell him it's a far better place, where you get a better class of celebrity.'

'Right.' I nod. 'No Posh and Becks.'

'Yeah,' he nods. 'That was a close call.'

A rather attractive-looking redhead walks into the hotel. She looks hassled and wet. It must have started raining outside. She is carrying a whole load of small bags including a couple of carriers that look like they're doubling up as suitcases.

'Hi, hi,' she says as she arrives at the front desk. 'Vanessa, Vanessa O'Neil.' She smiles, dropping all her bags at her feet.

'Good evening, madam,' I say, typing her name into the computer.

She leans on the desk and smiles. I smile back.

'Two nights,' she says.

'Right,' I say, tapping away.

We both fall silent, and I slowly start to become aware of an odd buzzing sound.

'What's that noise?' asks Liz, coming over.

'No idea,' I say, leaning forward on the counter, moving closer towards the source.

Jez, who is walking towards the front desk with a view to taking Ms O'Neil's luggage up to her room, stops dead in his tracks, stares at the floor and turns bright red. Ms O'Neil seems oblivious to the noise and carries on looking through her handbag for her credit card.

'Room 460,' I say, handing over the key.

'Thank you,' she says, handing over her credit card.

The buzzing noise carries on, and eventually Ms O'Neil starts to look around wondering where it is coming from. Suddenly Jez kneels down and picks something off the floor.

'Madam,' he stutters, great patches of red spreading across his cheeks, 'I think this is yours.' His eyes remain fixed on the floor as he hands over a big, black, buzzing dildo.

'Oh my God!' squeals Ms O'Neil as she takes hold of the thing and frantically starts trying to turn it off. Twisting and turning it in her increasingly hot and sweaty hands, she looks like she is about to cry with embarrassment. Eventually, she just opens her handbag and shoves the still buzzing dildo inside. 'Um,' she says, turning to face me.

'Yes, madam?' I reply.

I am so firmly biting the inside of my cheek I'm convinced I'm about to draw blood. We stare at each other, both pretending not to notice that her handbag is vibrating.

'Do you mind if I go straight to my room and deal with the paperwork a little later?' she asks, with slow determination.

'No, not at all,' I manage to say, somehow, through my nose.

Ms O'Neil gathers all her bags together, refusing Jez's tentative offers of assistance, and runs towards the lift. You can almost hear the sigh of relief emanating from the poor woman as she collapses against the back wall.

The door closes and I start to laugh, mainly because I haven't been allowed to. The embarrassment of it all is overpowering. Jez is so shocked he simply walks slowly around the corner to share his sex-toy experience with Dave. Liz announces that she feels sorry for the woman and adds that there is nothing wrong with a woman-of-today having a vibrator. Tony thinks it's the best thing that has happened in the hotel all day. He rings his mate at Claridge's to tell him the story. He recounts the whole thing with his fist in his mouth, embellishing as he goes. I can hear the chuckles from here.

Not that Ms O'Neil's big black vibrator bears comparison with half the stuff the chambermaids find in some of the bedrooms. In fact, there are usually a few surprises about now as they start doing the rounds, turning down the rooms.

I always think that turndown is one of the most pointless things chambermaids have to do. For starters, most of the guests are in their hotel rooms around this time, having baths, unpacking, chilling out or watching TV, so the last thing they want is to be disturbed by anyone. Least of all someone who is pottering around their room doing a whole load of pointless things they are quite capable of doing themselves. Quite why you need your bed sheets folded back to a ninety-degree angle is anyone's guess. I also love the way in this hotel the radio is turned low on to Jazz FM and the bedside lamps are turned on, just in case anyone can't come up with that serving suggestion all on their own. The breakfast slip is placed on the pillow and the remote control put in the corner of the folded sheet. The bedcover is removed and put in the cupboard. And the final touch is the complimentary bottle of mineral water from the management, any other leather wallet gifts and, of course, the chocolates on the pillow.

Pillow chocolates must be one of the few things luxury hotels shell out on for little or no reward. The truffles we hand out in this place cost £3.50 a box. They are quality stuff, expensively priced, and we hand them out for free, every night.

Although, when I say free, I am using that term loosely. Were you to do a financial breakdown of one of our hotel rooms, working out how much it actually costs to turn it around on a daily basis, you would be amazed at how cheap it actually is. It is just over £10 per room per day. And that price includes cleaning the sheets and fresh towels every day (£2.95), newspapers (65p), heating, lighting, wear and tear and theft (£1.10), the wages for the chambermaid who cleans the room (£1.25) as well as the price of the cleaning products she uses (39p), the Penhaligon guest supplies (£1.60) and, of course, the most expensive outlay of all, the pillow chocolates themselves (£3.50). Knowing this, quite how we can get away with charging £2,000 a suite a night is beyond me.

With Tony still talking sex toys on the telephone, Liz suddenly announces that she is going to staff supper. I suppose, with only a ten-minute break during her shift so far plus a meagre diet bar for lunch, I can't begrudge her her macaroni cheese and bap with the rest of them.

She walks off downstairs while I check in a middle-aged couple from Bolton who have at their feet a full *Sale of the Century* collection of Louis Vuitton bags, ranging from a family-size suitcase right through to a small vanity case. They seem to have packed a lot for a weekend. The woman is all excited. She tells me three times that she is going to see a show. Her husband is less thrilled. He sighs as he fills in the form and hands over his credit card. He seems resigned to the fact that this weekend mini break in the capital is going to set him back at least a grand in hotel expenses alone.

It's just over an hour until I go home. I lean on the desk thinking about Friday-night telly, possibly a take-away with my Texan £20 and a nice early night. I can't wait. Just a few more check-ins to go. I stare out through the windows and notice the small, white dry-cleaning van pull up outside the hotel. My heart sinks. Dry cleaning is a nightmare. Not only are they always late, they always, without fail, lose something. The hotel has tried numerous companies, some local, some well known and in prestigious parts of town, and the result is always the same: complaints and lost clothes. It is a service, the hotel is, I suppose, obliged to provide; some of the large ones actually do it in house. But unless you are staying for a length of time, I would advise that you avoid any hotel dry-cleaning service like a cold sore.

'Afternoon,' says the dry-cleaning bloke as he walks in, dressed in a blue boiler suit and carrying a pile of white cardboard boxes that look like they should house cakes rather than folded shirts. They're clearly all style over content, this lot.

'Evening,' I say, making sure that he knows I know he is late. The dry cleaning should really be here at about four so that housekeeping has a chance to get into guests' bedrooms in good time should they need it that evening.

He comes back and forth a couple more times, bringing in a cellophane-clad red coat and what look like some smart cocktail dresses.

'That's your lot,' he says, handing me over a clipboard to sign. 'It's all there,' he adds as I start ticking each item off.

'I'm sure it is,' I say. 'I've just got to make sure.' I go down the list, and predictably it's not all there. 'We've got a couple of things missing.'

'Not missing,' he says, 'just arriving tomorrow.'

'Right,' I say, sounding dubious.

'It's all kosher,' he says.

'OK,' I say, signing the bottom. 'And try not to be late tomorrow.'

'Right you are,' he says, taking his clipboard and walking back out to his van.

I call housekeeping to tell them that the dry cleaning has arrived. There's no answer. I contemplate paging them, but Dave volunteers to take the dry cleaning around the hotel. He's a bit quick off the mark. Jez is probably still in too much vibrator shock to remember that you can make at least £20 in tips on the dry-cleaning run.

Dave has only been gone about five minutes when the telephone calls start coming in. Someone who sent two shirts in has only got one back; someone else is missing his tie. Who sends ties in to be dry-cleaned in a hotel? The telephone goes again.

'This is room 404,' comes a female voice.

'Good evening, madam,' I say.

'You've lost my two-thousand-pound Valentino dress,' she says.

'Oh, right,' I say. 'I'm sure we haven't lost it, madam.'

'Well, I put it in for dry cleaning and all my stuff has come back except the dress.'

'I'm sorry to hear that,' I say. 'I'll make sure you get it tomorrow.'

'Tomorrow?' she yelps. 'What do you mean, tomorrow? I need it now, right now! I have a party to go to in an hour. It is a very important party and I need the dress. I have nothing else to wear.'

'Oh,' I say. I cover the telephone. 'Tony,' I whisper. He looks over. 'We've got a dry-cleaning problem.' Tony nods and gives me a telephone gesture, meaning to pass the call on to him.

'Don't you "oh" me,' says the woman. 'I need that dress now. I want that dress right now!' She is beginning to sound hysterical.

'Madam,' I say, 'I'm terribly sorry, the dry cleaner's is closed. We have no way of getting your dress back for you tonight. However, I can personally guarantee that you will get your dress back tomorrow afternoon.'

'Afternoon!' she shouts. 'I'm checking out at eight tomorrow morning.'

'Then we shall forward it on to you, at our expense.'

'Damn right at your bloody expense!' she shouts. 'I'll be invoicing you for the room, the dress, the dry cleaning and anything else I fancy.'

'I'm very sorry, madam,' I say.

'Sorry is not good enough,' she says. 'I've got nothing to wear tonight.'

'I know, madam,' I say. 'And I am just about to forward you to the concierge who can get you any dress you want in town. Don't worry, madam, Tony will look after you. I am about to put you into the most capable hands in town.' I can hear her still shouting at me as I press the re-directing button. 'Incoming,' I say to Tony as I press his extension. His telephone rings and he answers it in his most placatory of voices.

Jesus Christ, I think as I hang up the phone, somewhat exhausted by that exchange, can things get any worse?

6PM – 7PM

I stand there listening in on Tony's conversation. He is an amazingly talented bloke. His ability to calm down a situation, bring out the humour and make people relax is incredible. Within two minutes of talking to the cocktail dress woman I can hear him laughing with her, telling a few jokes and sharing a couple of indiscreet stories about other guests who have been left in worse situations by our dreadful dry-cleaning service. So by the end of the conversation, the woman hangs up actually feeling lucky.

'I don't know how you do it,' I say after he puts down the phone.

'Practice,' grins Tony, across the desk. 'Anyway,' he adds, 'I'd better get a shift on. I've got to see if my mate can get some dresses sent over from Harrods within the next half hour.'

'You'd better get on,' I say.

'Yeah,' he says, looking at his watch. 'Not long for you now.'

'Can't wait.' I smile. 'My sofa and TV await.'

The telephone goes. I pick it up.

'Hello?' comes a very familiar voice. 'It's Ben,' says Ben.

'Oh, hello, Ben,' I say, glad to hear his voice. 'Are you on your way in? We've had quite a day here, mate. Oh my God, you just missed a woman with a big black vibrator in her bag, and the Texan is here handing out pink ones like it's going out of fashion.'

Ben says nothing. He doesn't even laugh.

'Ben?' I repeat. 'Are you there?'

I hear a small, weak cough down the other end of the phone. My heart sinks. My shoulders sag. I know what's bloody coming.

'The thing is, mate,' he starts, 'I'm afraid I don't feel too hot.' He coughs again, as if to reiterate his point. 'It's the flu, you know. It's a bad one. There's a lot of it going around at the moment. I've spent all day in bed, mate, trying to fight it off, you know, trying to get into work, and I have to say it has defeated me.' He coughs again. This one is a little more dramatic. Ben's good at coughing, but then he is a thirty-a-day smoker so he does have an advantage. 'I'm sorry, mate,' he says. 'I just don't think I can make it.'

I am so angry I can hardly speak. 'Right,' I manage.

'Mate,' he says, 'I really am sorry. There is nothing I can do.' He coughs again.

'Yeah, right,' I say.

'Honestly, mate,' he says, his voice suddenly all feeble. 'It's terrible. I really hope you don't get it.'

That little comment really is the last straw, and I'm afraid I lose it. 'Why don't you piss off,' I say suddenly.

'What?' he says.

'Piss off,' I repeat. 'You're always bloody doing this.'

'Are you calling me a liar?' he says, sounding suitably outraged. He adds another cough for effect.

'I'm not calling you anything,' I say.

'Because if you are I will report you to Adrian . . . when I'm well enough to come in.'

'Do what you fucking want,' I say. I can hear him trying to answer back as I hang up the phone.

Well, things have now certainly got a whole lot fucking worse. I lean on the desk, my forehead in my hands, working out the ramifications of Ben's sudden attack of the flu. A double shift. A bloody double shift. One of us is going to have to pull a double shift. And I know for a sad, dismal fact that it is going to be me. Shit. Liz has only just come off doing nights, so she'll make some boring song and dance about not doing it tonight. And

I'll end up doing it. So I may as well save myself the dull song and dance and volunteer to go straight through till seven a.m.

Jesus Christ, I hate Ben. As well as all his house-keeping sex and slacking on the job, Ben is a bit of a boozer. More accurately, Ben is an alcoholic. A drink problem is an occupational hazard in this business. Steve, Ben – there are a whole load of them. I'm not sure whether it is the pressure of work and the odd hours that are the contributing factors or if boozers naturally gravitate to a place where the stuff is available twenty-four hours a day. Either way Ben is an annoying little shit. This is the third time he's pulled a sickie in the last month. He normally gets too pissed to come into work and then calls up with some spurious excuse like his mother is ill, his boiler has broken or he's got food poisoning. He's never that imaginative. Although I have to say that tonight he didn't actually sound too pissed. Normally he is slurring all over the place, and you actually don't want him to turn up for work.

I can't tell you how angry I am. I hate doing nights. There's nothing worse. It's not the staying up that bothers me. I've got a packet of Pro Plus caffeine pills in the back office drawer to make sure I don't sleep on the job, plus I'm sure that Gino – stock-take not-withstanding – will slip me a few vodkas later on when things get desperate. It's just that nights are a nightmare. Between two and three in the morning the hotel always goes a bit mad. Actually, what am I saying? It doesn't go mad, it goes totally in-fucking-sane, and I'm not sure if I'm in the mood to handle it tonight. All I want is a sofa and the telly. Instead, I've got Sodom, Gomorrah and Bedlam rolled into one.

I don't know why it happens exactly; all I know is that something strange occurs to guests as soon as they check in to the hotel. For some reason, even if in real life they are perfectly well-mannered, decent people with proper, balanced relationships, as soon as they spin through the revolving hotel doors the normal rules of behaviour no longer seem to apply. Their boundaries are altered. Their rules of engagement change. They forget their responsibilities. And their inner diva or bastard child roars to the surface. They also think they're invisible. They think they can behave like rock stars on a bender then turn up at reception the next day like innocent little children, butter hardly melting in their mouths. What they forget is that we're sober and we see and hear everything.

I can't bloody wait.

'You look a bit pissed off,' says Liz, coming back from her macaroni supper.

'I'm furious,' I say. 'Ben's pulled a sickie.'

'What? Again?' she asks.

'Yup.'

174

'Are you sure he's not genuinely ill?'

'I can't believe you are actually asking me that,' I say. 'You know Ben as well as I do.'

'Sorry,' she says. 'You're right.'

'Yeah, well . . .'

'I can't do a double tonight,' she says quickly. 'I've got a date and it's been planned for over a week. I really can't cancel it.'

'No, don't worry,' I say. 'I'll do it.'

'You will?' she says, sounding shocked.

'Yeah, well, you've got a date and everything. I'm only disappointing my sofa and I'm sure it will cope.'

'Oh, thank you,' she says, leaning forward to kiss me on the cheek. 'You're a life saver.'

'Stop it,' I say, pushing her away. 'Anyway, it's always nice to have some extra money.'

'That's true,' she says, turning back to the desk. 'Cheers anyway.'

Liz is all jolly and excited. Not only does she not have to do the night shift, she is also going out on a date. Looking at her again as she checks in some businessman, she's re-done all her make-up. Her hair is brushed, she's put more of that disgusting perfume on again and she's put a dark maroon line around her mouth. She's definitely ready to go out.

The Harrods deliveryman arrives, much to Tony's delight, with an olive and gold box full of clothes. Jez is sent up to room 404 and Tony earns himself another fat tip.

Reception is beginning to fill up again. There are locals coming in for a post-work drink before winding their way home; there are gaggles of glamorous girls meeting up for a bottle of champagne before going out to dinner; there are friends of guests of the hotel joining them for a drink before dinner; there are businessmen coming in for a networking drink; and there are the cord-clad dullards arriving for their pre-theatre dinner.

Pre-theatre dining is one of the most annoying things a luxury hotel has to do. And it's not even that popular. But for some reason or another we have to do it. We serve a light supper in the dining room that consists of something like a plate of smoked salmon, a quiche and salad, a bowl of soup or an omelette stuffed with something so that their stomachs don't rumble during the second half. It irritates the hell out of the kitchen, coming as it does during one of its busiest periods of the day, just as everyone is running around like blue-arsed flies trying to get things ready for dinner as well as sending out thousands of canapés into banqueting. We try to knock out the theatre food and get them in and out as quickly as possible, pretending that it has something to do with getting them there before curtain up. Which, of course, is nothing to do with it. It's just that we really don't want them cluttering up the dining room before the real diners arrive.

And they are always the most dull-looking people: petulant teenagers being forced to suffer a cultural night out; middle-aged women with their middle-aged female friends; elderly couples. They are also never going to see anything interesting. It's usually *Les Misérables* or something that has been going for decades.

Having said all that, the most annoying thing about pre-theatre dinners is that they come back for pudding after the show. Just when you thought you wouldn't have to see them again, they turn up at about 10.45, exactly when the kitchen is beginning to wind down after an exhausting night, and demand a sticky toffee pudding to send them off to bed. Honestly, I've never really understood why we do it. There are a couple of women *d'un certain âge* walking through right now.

'Good evening, ladies,' I say.

'Good evening,' they both reply.

I smile and wave them on their way, then I ring through to Adrian's office to tell him about Ben's sudden sickness. I can tell that he is not impressed. Adrian used to be quite good mates with Ben but recently he has begun to keep his distance. Adrian's an ambitious bloke; he hasn't got this far this quickly on talent alone. He's picked his friends carefully, he's been nice to the right people and he knows which clients to suck up to. Talking of which, I've just spotted Mrs Dickson and her horrible yapping dog.

Steve's on her case – or should I say cases – right away. He's got two in each hand as he comes through the revolving door. Mrs Dickson manages to take care of her dog. She looks the other way, or is somehow totally immune to its barking and thrusting attempts at nipping other guests' ankles. Dressed head to toe in pink Chanel, she has hard yellow hair, a powdered white face and clumpy false eyelashes like dead spiders, and bears more than a passing resemblance to Barbara Cartland. Liz seamlessly makes an exit to the back room, leaving me to do the honours.

'Good evening, Mrs Dickson,' I say, impressing her with the personal.

'Is it?' she asks. 'It may be for some, but I've had a terrible journey here.'

'Oh really?' I say. 'I'm terribly sorry to hear that.'

'Good,' she says. 'Now, what suite do you have for me this time? I do hope it is better than the one I had last time. I can't remember which one it was. Sergeant!' she shouts down at her dog as it pulls on its lead and valiantly tries to have sex with Jez's leg. Poor Jez is not having much luck this afternoon. 'Get off that man!' Sergeant continues to bark his annoying little lungs out.

'We have put you in suite 560,' I say with a full service industry smile.

'560?' she asks. 'Where is that?'

'Right at the top,' I say, 'with a view over the communal garden square.'

'Communal?' she says. 'I don't think I want to look down on anything communal.'

'It is really very attractive,' I say weakly.

'That's as may be,' she replies, 'but I think I prefer a more exclusive view.'

'Oh,' I say.

'Oh,' she says back.

While I try to convince Mrs Dickson of the merits of her communal garden view, slightly wishing that I had simply said the word 'garden' and been done with it, Mr Masterson wanders back down into reception. His loud voice drowns out the chatter of people coming in for early-evening drinks and Sergeant's shrill little bark. Jez and Dave stand to attention like soldiers on parade. It is an action that obviously pleases him because he gives them both a fiver. But it is Tony he has come to see. He makes even louder than usual noises about his table at Sheekey's tonight. Slapping Tony on the back, he shakes his hand and gives him another note. Annoyingly, Mrs Dickson's helmet hair is in the way so I can't see its colour. All I know is that Tony looks pleased, so it must be a purple or a pink. Mr Masterson then wanders back through to the glass doors in the direction of the bar.

'Good Lord,' says Mrs Dickson, her white nostrils curling like she has just smelt some frightful odour. 'Who on earth is that?'

'Mr Masterson,' I say, totally unprofessionally. 'He is a Texan oil millionaire.'

'Oh,' she says, like the source smell has been confirmed.

'He's a regular,' I say. 'He normally has your suite 560, but as you have it this time he can't.'

'Oh really?' she says. 'Isn't that interesting, Sergeant?' She picks a complimentary mint out of the bowl on the desk and throws it on the floor. Sergeant consumes it in a matter of seconds. 'I think we'll take 560 after all.'

I check Mrs Dickson in and she and Sergeant get into the lift while their luggage remains in the lobby. Dave and Jez practically draw straws to see who is going to take it up to her room. As with the French couple earlier this afternoon, Mrs Dickson does not believe in tipping, or at least certainly not in this hotel. Because a small portion of it belongs to her husband, she thinks all its staff and services come free. Jez loses yet again and is despatched with Mrs Dickson's bags and what looks like Sergeant's dog basket. It really isn't his day.

Liz returns to the front desk, and I decide to pop

through to the bar to inform Gino that it is not my lucky night either, that I am being forced to pull a double. It's not because I want his sympathy, it's because I want his booze. Well, he has slipped me a couple of vodkas in the past. Sometimes I pay for them, but more often than not he gives me a freebie. He only really does it if I've got to go straight through. Although, perhaps, the findings from today's stock-check will change things.

The bar is heaving when I walk in. There's a real buzz about the place. All the tables are full and the ashtrays are getting that way. There is so much noise that it's a wonder anyone can hear the ebullient conversations they all appear to be having. There's a particularly loud group of young men in the far corner of the room drinking Dom Perignon Vintage 1995 that I know retails at £172 a bottle. And there are a couple of glossy-looking girls at the bar, applauding Gino as he gives it the whole Tom Cruise thing with a cocktail shaker. It's at times like this that Gino's real star quality shines through. He is the difference between a bar that is packed and earning its own space in revenue and a moribund place full of miserable old men with flatulence.

As I stand in the corner, I can tell he is working the room. He serves the girls their Cosmopolitan cocktails and tries to flog them his new 'Berrytini' creation – a martini made with blueberries. He then immediately makes sure that the boys on the other side of the room have enough champagne. At £172 a bottle you can see why he is only too happy to help them consume just that bit more. He walks past Mr Masterson and offers to light his £500 cigar, saluting as he walks back to the bar, another order for a £40 shot of twenty-year-old Talisker whisky under his belt.

'Gino,' I say as I approach the bar.

'Hello there, mate,' he says, his eyes shining with commercial delight.

'I just wanted to say that I'm doing a double shift tonight, so any problems in the bar, any hassle, you know where I am.'

'Yeah, OK,' he says, standing back from the till, letting Francesco cash up. 'And any spare something to come your way?'

'Well . . .' I smile.

'When that stock-taker fucker has gone,' he says, nodding towards the back.

'Is he still here?' I ask, surprised at Gino's frankness with the man so close.

'Yeah, he's leaving in ten minutes,' says Gino, shaking a fist in the general direction of the back-room door. 'I wish he'd fucking hurry up,' he adds loudly, cupping his hand around his mouth, directing his insult backstage. 'He is cramping my bloody style.'

'I heard that,' says Mr Kent as he comes through the door with his clipboard.

'So sue me! I have a forty-pound shot of whisky to serve. You want to watch me do it in case I spill twenty-five-pence worth on the side?'

'No thank you,' says Mr Kent. 'That's me finished for the day.'

'Thank God for that!' says Gino dramatically.

'And may I say,' adds Mr Kent, 'you run a very good bar, Mr Lauri.'

'Finally, fuck, he gives me a *complimento*!' says Gino.

'Yes, well,' says Mr Kent.

'I did tell you, you will not find your Bombay Sapphire thief here. Try housekeeping, Mr Kent, housekeeping!'

'Don't worry, Mr Lauri,' says Mr Kent, 'it's their turn next week.'

'Oh,' says Gino.

'Anyway,' says Mr Kent, 'I wish you a good evening.'

'Good evening,' says Gino.

'Yes, well,' I say to Gino, 'see you later.'

'Absolutely, mate. And don't worry about anything.'

'Oh, OK.' I smile. 'Thanks.'

I walk back into reception, suddenly feeling not so bad.

7PM – 8PM

By the time I get back to reception Liz has already got her coat on. She is pottering around between the front desk and the back office, humming with excitement at her impending departure.

'Oh, there you are.' She smiles. It's amazing how going home can improve someone's mood. 'Two cleaners have phoned in sick.'

'What, already?' I ask.

'Yup,' she says, stapling some paper together. 'Oh, I got you these out of the office drawer.' She hands me a packet of Pro Plus pills. 'It doesn't look like there are that many left,' she says. 'Half a packet. D'you think that might do the trick? Or do you want to send Jez out to get some more?'

'No,' I say, taking four out of the packet. 'I'm sure I'll manage.'

'Are you sure you should be taking that many at once?' she asks.

'I don't see how else I'm going to get through tonight.'

'Are you sure?' she asks again, sounding concerned.

'Yeah, well,' I say, knocking them back.

'See you tomorrow.'

'Yeah. And you'll have a new girl, Michelle's replacement.'

'Mm,' she says, not sounding too keen. 'I wonder what she'll be like.'

'Attractive, I've heard,' I say, just to wind her up.

'Oh, good.' She smiles, looking ever so thrilled. 'Have a good evening.'

'Will do.'

'Night,' she says as she walks past Tony.

'Night,' he replies.

Reception is beginning to take on the appearance of a railway terminus. There are people walking into the bar, people coming in for dinner, and guests leaving the hotel for meetings, meals or drinks somewhere else. A couple of gents in cashmere coats with heavy leather briefcases are walking through to the bar, while other groups of what look like fashion people keep turning up fashionably late for the cocktails and canapés do in I suppose what could loosely be termed our ballroom. Well, it's a room big enough for a ball, and we do tend actually to host a couple in there in the run-up to Christmas. But really it's a large room with some moulding on the ceiling, some gold lamps on the wall, a grand piano and a whole load of gilt catering chairs.

For some reason or another, it is popular and often booked, especially in the evenings. We hold about two or three events in there a week. And although it is catered for by the same kitchen as the rest of the hotel, the waiting staff are entirely different. They are made up of casuals. Casuals who are even more casual than the staff who actually work in the hotel, which is say-ing something. They are paid the minimum wage, get no tips, have no regular working pattern and can be called up to work anything from a six-day week to a no-day week at a moment's notice. As a result the turnover is high, and it's the sort of job that only attracts foreign students, Australians on their gap year, illegals and first-generation immigrants with few language skills and little choice. The casuals are not really considered part of the rest of the hotel. They arrive and leave by a different side entrance; they have one small room with a few chairs in which to change; they are not fed; and they have very little contact with the rest of the staff in the hotel. In fact, if I am being honest, I don't think I have ever spoken a single word to a single one of them.

Two thin girls walk up to reception in stratospheric heels and transparent dresses.

'Hi,' says the blonde one, waving a piece of stiff white card. 'Can you tell us where the perfume launch is tonight?'

'Oh,' I say. That's what it is, I think. 'Through the glass doors, turn left, and it's at the end of the corridor.'

'Thanks,' says the darker-haired girl as they giggle off through the doors.

Steve walks into reception, stamping his cold, desensitized feet on the Indian carpet. He rubs his large gloved hands together, removes his top hat and buffs the crown of his sweaty head.

'Well,' he says, exhaling, 'that's me finished for another day.'

'OK, then,' says Tony, looking up from his desk. 'Are you off, then?'

'Yup,' says Steve, wiping his running, defrosting nose on the back of his hand.

'Been a good one?' asks Tony.

'Good,' says Steve, tapping his jangling pocket like someone in an Asda advert. 'And with that Yank top-up, excellent. It's Dennis up next, isn't it?'

'That's right,' says Tony. 'Talking of the fat bastard, here he is.'

'All right? All right? All right?' says Dennis as he

187

walks up to Tony's desk, suited and booted and ready to go.

'Cutting it fine, Dennis, cutting it fine,' declares Tony, tapping his watch.

'Five minutes,' says Dennis. 'The traffic was shit.'

'Yeah, right,' says Tony. 'You only live around the corner.'

'Got me there,' smiles Dennis, gloved hands in the air. 'Caught me out.' He turns around. 'All right there, mate?' he asks me, giving me an expansive wave across the room. 'I thought I was on with Ben?'

'All right there, Dennis,' I say. 'Ben's pulled a sickie so I'm afraid you've got me tonight.'

'You on a double?'

'Yeah.' I nod, putting my hands together and inclining my head to one side, making as if to go to sleep.

'You poor bastard,' he says. 'D'you know, Tony,' he says turning back around, 'that wanker Ben wants sacking. Twice this week I caught him sleeping in the back office. He's a scumbag shit. Don't worry, mate,' says Dennis, turning back towards me, 'I'll look after you. You stick with me.'

'All right,' I say, smiling back.

I like Dennis. He is always a laugh to work with. Although he's Steve's cousin he is actually nothing like him. He's more like Tony. He's handsome, he's got the gift of the gab, and he is nearly always on top form. He also seems to like his job as doorman – he's been here long enough. And judging by the number of times his mobile phone goes off I'm sure Dennis has got a lot of fingers in a lot of other pies.

He stands around for a couple of minutes sharing jokes with Tony and Steve, but then a cab pulls up outside and he's out the door before you can say one-pound tip.

The telephone goes, and it's Lynette asking about check-ins. She sounds hassled and stressed, and then she finally admits that she has overbooked the hotel. Shit. This is the last thing I need on top of my hangover and my double shift. I hate having to turn away people who have booked into the hotel because they normally go through the roof. It is understandable, I know, but it doesn't make it any more pleasant.

'We've got a couple of junior suites available,' she says, 'and that's it.'

'Yup,' I confirm, checking on the computer system.

'So you can upgrade the next few doubles who come in, and after that, that's it,' she says.

'How about using the large two-grand-a-night suite next to the Texan?' I ask.

'No,' she says, swiftly, 'unless they are regular, regular, regular. But I can't see anyone who is.'

'Right,' I say. 'And where are we sending them tonight?'

'The Berkeley,' she says.

We're always doing this, packing people off to the Berkeley. The Lanesborough also sends its guests there, as well as the Four Seasons. The Savoy passes on to Claridge's, the Berkeley or the Connaught. They do like to try to keep it in the group. The Sanderson uses St Martin's Lane and the Metropolitan, and the two of them reciprocate. Only as a final option, when all else fails, will any one of them bump guests to rival hotels.

'Oh,' Lynette adds. 'Just so you know, you need to add these two names to the blacklist.'

'Right,' I say, bringing up the list on the computer.

Lynette goes on to give me the names of two blokes who are currently doing the rounds at the moment. The police have forwarded their names to the various luxury hotels in the capital and they have provided both a physical description and a run-through of their modus operandi. Apparently, they ask to be shown round to get the layout of the place, then come back at a later date, blag a key card off a chambermaid and rob the place. It's the small hotels or the unmodernized ones that are most at risk of this sort of scam. Nearly all the newer places operate the swipe card system; the old-fashioned cut key makes a place easier to break into. They have to be very careful how they display their keys, as often it really is only a matter of getting behind the front desk to gain access.

It is from about this time onwards that we have to be very wary about who is coming in and out of the hotel. It is usually at night that we start to make mistakes, especially if you're dog tired like me. Although I do have to say that these pills are really beginning to kick in now. It's like someone's pinned back my eyelids with toothpicks. My heart is racing. I shouldn't have taken so many at once, but I was feeling so shit and so knackered. I don't really see that I had any choice.

As I lean forward on the front desk, riding the caffeine rush, a vision of warped femininity slowly comes towards me. An overly tall woman in large high shoes with suspiciously thick, uniformly coloured hair and an awful lot of make-up is checking in. I recognize him immediately. He is one of a couple of our transvestite guests who come to stay for the weekend so they can enjoy the freedom of being allowed to dress how they want without any hassle from their wives or partners. This tall brunette is a regular. He is also, somewhat confusingly, a regular with his wife. On the occasions when he comes here in his brown wig, we have to call him madam; when he arrives with his wife, we obviously call him sir.

'Good evening, madam,' I say. I can see Tony smirking slightly out of the corner of my eye, but I ignore him.

'Good evening,' he says, a surprisingly deep voice coming out of his lipsticked mouth. 'Ms Austin.'

'Right, Ms Austin,' I say, 'you're actually in luck. Due to the fact that the hotel is very full tonight, I shall be upgrading your room to a suite.' He looks thrilled. His bright pink mouth smiles. 'At no extra cost at all.'

'Thank you,' he says, like I have done him the nicest favour in the world ever. 'Thank you very much.'

'It's my pleasure,' I say. And it is. It is always lovely to be appreciated for the things we do, particularly as most of the time we only ever really get grief. 'Will you be wanting a table in the restaurant tonight?' I ask. I can't remember if he is a room service transvestite or not.

'That would be wonderful,' he says.

'Leave it to me,' I say. 'Do you need any help with your bags?'

'No, thank you,' he says, picking up his small overnight bag. 'There's no need to trouble anyone.'

I take an imprint of his credit card, hand over the key card to a junior suite and ask Tony to keep an eye on the desk. As Ms Austin takes the lift to the fourth floor, I follow him in the direction of the glass doors and into the dining room to secure him a table.

The dining room is not yet busy. In fact, it is empty but for a couple of tables of Americans who for some reason like to eat dinner at 7.30. The rest of the room is all laid up and ready to go. There's a palpable sense of the calm before the storm. Andre, the

192

restaurant manager, walks in from the direction of the bar.

'Arrrgh,' he says, shaking a small white clenched fist. 'That bloody Gino Lauri. I am so fed up with him.'

'Why?' I ask. I don't really want to know, but I want a table from Andre at short notice, so I figure it is better to hear his story.

'I go in to hand out some menus to some of the diners in his bar and he throws me out of the place,' he says, beads of angry sweat glowing on his top lip.

'Well,' I say, somewhat stumped. 'Um, that's not very nice.'

'Not nice?' says Andre, turning to look at me like I'm some offensive little turd. 'Not nice? It is more than not nice. It is war!'

Gino and Andre are always at loggerheads, particularly at this time of night. The problem is that they both want different things. Andre wants as many people in his restaurant as early as possible, so he can either get them out quickly or so that he has more time to work on them, getting them to spend money on ludicrously expensive wines like the £12,500 magnum of Château D'Yquem he managed to get James to buy him the other day. Meanwhile, Gino wants the guests to stay in his bar as long as possible so that he can try to flog them ludicrously expensive cocktails. The two of them are, quite simply, never going to agree.

And they are also, quite simply, never going to be friends.

'Right,' I say, not wanting to be drawn into Andre's war in any way, shape or form. 'Good luck.' I smile.

'Yes, well,' says Andre with a dramatic shrug. 'What do you want?'

'A table.'

'A table for what – one, two, three, forty?'

'One,' I say.

'One.' He sighs. 'This is not a table-for-one restaurant. This is a destination restaurant and we don't do tables for one.'

'It's a guest in the hotel.'

'Oh, OK.' He sighs again, walks over to his large wooden lectern and leafs through the oversize leather book in which all the reservations are written. 'He can have number four,' he says, 'at nine fifteen. What's the name?'

'Austin,' I say.

'Austin,' he repeats.

'Thank you,' I say. 'See you later.'

Back in reception, Tony is flat out, booking cabs and calling restaurants to say that some guests are late but assuring them they are on their way. There are also a couple of rooms asking for shirts to be pressed and shoes to be polished, and Tony's sending housekeeping to iron the shirts and telling those who require shoe polishing to leave their shoes outside their bedroom doors in the appropriate bags provided. Someone will deal with them before morning.

The telephone goes again. It's another of the night cleaners phoning in sick, and it's another case of tactical food poisoning. I simply write down the name and ring downstairs to tell them they are three cleaners short so far tonight. There is no point in calling the cleaner's bluff. They get paid little enough as it is; if they want to lose a whole day's pay, it's up to them. But you would have thought it was the last thing they needed. Maybe they are genuinely ill. There is always that possibility.

Mr Masterson comes through the glass doors, not so fresh from the bar. Not only does he look like he's had more than just a few shots of Gino's overpriced whisky, he also brings with him a cloud of Trinidad Diplomatic. The whole of reception stands to attention as he arrives. Jez and Dave place expectant smiles on their jaded faces and Tony finishes his telephone call with brusque efficiency.

'Mr Masterson,' says Tony, getting out from behind his desk and tucking his tie into his trousers. 'Your Mercedes is waiting for you outside.'

'Good,' says Mr Masterson, pointing a red finger in Tony's direction. 'Good man.'

'I have instructed it to wait outside the restaurant for

195

you, sir, and bring you straight back here afterwards. But, obviously, if you have any other plans you only have to tell the driver and he will do exactly as you wish.'

'Good,' says Mr Masterson. 'Very good work.' He walks up to Tony, takes two £20 notes out of his wallet, folds them into four and pops them into Tony's top pocket, tapping them down with his finger. Tony smiles, but I know he hates it when people do that to him. It makes him feel cheap.

'Evening, sir,' he says as Mr Masterson makes his way towards the door. 'Have a good night.'

'Thank you, Tony,' says Mr Masterson, touching the top of his head as he goes.

Dennis is at the Mercedes door like a shot. He tips his top hat as Mr Masterson lowers himself onto the cream leather seats, earning a fiver as he does so.

'Who the fuck does that man think I am?' mutters Tony, taking the money from his top pocket. 'A fucking lap dancer?'

Talking of which, I suddenly spot two women walking into reception who make me feel a little suspicious. I don't know whether it is Tony's lap dancing analogy or the fact that both of them are wearing very short skirts and very high heels that makes me think they might be prostitutes.

Now, I know I said that we turn a blind eye to

prostitutes, but only if they have been invited in by clients. If they are overt, by the hour and soliciting in the hotel itself, they have to go. And these two look very much like they are in the last category.

'Excuse me, ladies,' I say, coming out from behind the desk, approaching with confidence. 'Can I help you at all?'

'No thanks,' says the taller of the two in the shorter skirt.

That is not a good sign. 'Are you sure?' I ask.

'Quite sure,' says the other one.

They are both standing in reception, looking left and right like they have never been in here, so they're clearly not guests. And as they haven't asked for the bar they are clearly not meeting guests either.

'Well, I'm terribly sorry, ladies,' I say with a light laugh and what I hope sounds like acres of charm, 'if that's the case, I'm afraid I am going to have to ask you to leave.'

'Leave?' squawks the tall one.

'We've only just got here,' adds the second.

'Well, I'm terribly sorry,' I say, walking towards the taller one with my arm out to guide her towards the front door. 'We don't allow single women in here on their own.'

'What?' says the tall one. 'What are you talking about?'

197

'I'm afraid you won't find any clients in here, dear,' I say, sort of spelling it out for her.

'Clients?' she exclaims. 'What do you think I am? A prostitute?'

'Well . . .' I laugh.

'Gina!' she says. 'Can you believe it? A prostitute? Jesus Christ! Get those invitations out and get your hands off me.'

'We've been invited to the perfume launch,' says Gina, waving the invitations right close up to my face. 'So you can piss off, you pervert. Honestly,' she scoffs.

'Twat,' says the taller girl as they walk through the glass doors in the direction of the ballroom.

8PM – 9PM

Tony is crying with laughter. He can't believe how badly I handled that situation. Perhaps it's because I'm so tired and run down, but I can't really believe that I did it either. It's not really something I am prone to doing, walking up to random women in reception and accusing them of living off immoral earnings. But, in my defence, we do usually get a couple in during the course of an evening, willing to chance their luck in the bar, and it is my job, along with Tony or Dennis, to see that they don't make it in there.

Tony's putting on his coat and laughing at the same time. 'I can't believe you, I can't believe you,' he keeps on saying. 'Nothing like prostitutes, the pair of them. Nothing like it.' Even Jez and Dave are finding my fuck-up to their liking: they are sniggering, not quite so openly, into their coats.

It is the end of the shift for all three of them, and by the sounds of things they are planning a quick trip to the pub. It is Tony's idea, and Tony will pay for all their drinks. It is his way of building up team spirit and a bit of loyalty. He's clever like that.

'Right,' he says, rubbing his hands together, 'are we all ready for a swift one at the Rose and Crown?'

'Yes, please.' Dave and Jez reply in unison, their tired faces momentarily lighting up.

'See you later then, mate,' he says, waving to me. 'Keep those eyes open for prostitutes.' He sniggers. 'You never know where you might find them.'

'Yeah, right,' I say. 'You can all piss off.'

'So can you,' smiles Tony, pulling up the black velvet collar of his grey overcoat. 'Has anyone seen that paddy Patrick anywhere?' he asks, squinting as he looks outside.

'I'm here,' says the diminutive voice of the equally diminutive Patrick.

'You're late,' says Tony, turning round to find Patrick standing in his grey and gold uniform by the brass luggage trolley.

'I'm sorry,' he says.

'You should be,' says Tony, looking him up and down. 'And get yourself to the gents and do something with your hair.'

200

'Right away, sir,' says Patrick.

'Stop calling me sir.'

'Sorry, sir, sorry,' says Patrick, shuffling towards the upstairs toilets reserved for guests only.

'Not there,' sighs Tony, clicking his fingers. 'How many more times? The staff toilets.' He rolls his eyes as Patrick jogs past him, head down, on his way towards the back stairs. 'See you later,' he says to me as all three of them head off to the pub.

Poor Patrick, I think as the boy trots off down the stairs. Tony's only getting on his back because he is new. Patrick's been with us for three weeks, and all that time Tony's mercilessly taken the piss. He says it's for his own good. How else is the sixteen-year-old squirt ever going to learn? Who's going to teach him the ropes? Learn him the rules? But I suspect it's because Tony enjoys flexing his muscles; you know, spreading it around a bit. Another thing is that Patrick was not Tony's first choice of bellboy/night porter: Patrick has the misfortune of being one of Adrian's appointments. As a result, Tony enjoys giving him plenty of grief. Poor sod. I swear the boy has developed a stammer and stress spots in the time he's been here.

Also, between you and me, I'm sure the lad is not really supposed to be on nights. He's been here such a short time and I have no idea how that can qualify him for the tricky job of night porter. He hardly makes me feel secure. The idea that I can leave reception in his capable hands while I pop outside for a fag or a quick slurp of vodka from the bar is some sort of joke. I mean, he's fine when it comes to delivering faxes, collecting breakfast cards and polishing shoes, but give him some aggressive punter or some pissed-up group of men intent on trashing the place and I bet you a tenner you wouldn't see Patrick for dust.

Only the other day I heard this story about an incident at the Covent Garden Hotel. Apparently, two guys came into the hotel during the night, immediately went up in the lift and quickly disappeared. The guys in reception thought it was a little odd, and the night porter became a bit suspicious and said that he would keep an eye on the lift and the stairs just in case. Anyway, one of the thieves got out onto the roof. He climbed into a guest's bedroom through an open window and helped himself to passports, handbags and luggage before he left. They both then came running down the stairs and the night porter tackled one of them, hurling him to the ground. A huge fight then ensued, the porter keeping one of the thieves pinned to the floor until the police arrived. They picked up the other villain a couple of days later.

Now, call me old-fashioned, but I don't really see old nine-and-a-half-stone sixteen-year-old Patrick pinning anyone, or indeed anything, to the floor until the police come. So all I can say, in the grand scheme of all things violent, is thank God for Dennis.

'All right there, mate?' I say as Dennis comes inside.

'Fine and dandy, me,' says Dennis, sitting down at Tony's desk and putting up his feet. 'You?'

'Been better,' I reply.

Dennis's mobile goes off in his top pocket. 'Scuse me, mate,' he says as he pulls it out. He's not really supposed to be on his mobile during work hours, it's supposed to be switched off. But Dennis is always breaking rules. He isn't really supposed to be sitting at Tony's desk either, especially when there's a leather-padded chair provided for him. But who's going to tell him off? Certainly not me, or Patrick.

Patrick comes back into reception, his dark-red curly hair parted down one side and smoothed flat down on his head, like he is going out to Sunday lunch with his mother. I can't help smiling. He looks even younger than when he went down there.

'All right there, Patrick?' I ask.

'Yes, thank you very much,' he says as he walks back to the brass luggage trolley and starts to rub it down.

The telephone rings on reception: it's a woman on the second floor asking us to send someone up to zip her into her dress. She sounds terribly apologetic. I tell her not to worry as we get this kind of request all the time. One of the weirdest I've heard was when Naomi

Campbell was staying at the St Martin's Lane Hotel.

When extremely glamorous celebrities such as Naomi Campbell come and stay, they often get given one member of staff to look after them entirely. In some hotels you get given a butler who will zip you into your dress or, on some more bizarre occasions, powder down your rubber catsuit for you. These people are often highly trained and are at the end of a bleeper. They know how to fold a sari, they know in which order to place military medals, they can tie bow-ties, advise on white tie, coach guests on how to address ambassadors at receptions. They also know odd things like how to get the rarest of stains out of the frailest of fabrics.

Anyway, in Naomi's case, hers wasn't a butler but a member of staff who was on permanent call to cater for her every whim. At around seven p.m. she paged him in a crisis, demanding that he come up to her room immediately. He arrived smartish to find her sitting on her bedroom floor clearly under the influence of something as she rocked back and forth, surrounded by piles of make-up. She then turned and asked him to help find her lipstick. He wasn't quite sure what to do. He went into the bathroom to find lines of white powder racked up and ready. He came back out, picked up a random tube of lipstick and handed it over. It seemed to do the trick. He then made very quick excuses and left.

Somehow I don't think the zip-challenged woman on the second floor is going to be terribly difficult, so I send up Patrick. He needs to be able to cope with guests in all states of undress and in all sorts of difficult and tricky situations, so he may as well be broken in as soon as possible. He seems reluctant, and he is up and back in a flash. He must have spent all of fifteen seconds doing up the woman's dress. Yet, by the time he is back polishing his trolley in reception, the poor lad is so embarrassed that even the tops of his ears are pink.

Before I can tease him, Lynette comes through reception in her coat. She is on her way home after a long day spent juggling rooms, guests, cancellations and re-bookings. She looks tired. Half her eye make-up is slipping down her face, making her look like a panda.

'There you are,' she says, sounding hassled. But then, I don't know of any time when she isn't. 'Still here.'

'Still here,' I confirm. 'Here all night. Ben is apparently terribly ill.'

'Not again,' she says. 'He's always unwell, that boy.' She stands at the front desk, distractedly shuffling through some faxes. 'Now, right, there we are,' she says, pulling out a piece of paper. 'Right, Mr Andrews. And Miss Cox.'

'Yes,' I say.

'Well, the thing is, they have booked two adjoining rooms, if you see what I mean.'

'Right,' I say.

'And we don't have two rooms left, just a junior suite and a senior suite,' she explains. 'So I wonder if you can ask them to share.'

'Share?'

'Yes, well,' she says, looking slightly embarrassed. 'They've been having an affair for six months at least, so I don't think they'll mind.'

'Oh?'

'Well, they are both from the same company in Scotland, they come here often, they always take adjoining rooms – it doesn't take a genius to work it out. Anyway, it always annoys me that they never use the other room when we could easily re-sell it, which I suppose I have inadvertently done this time.'

'Oh, right, of course,' I say, feeling slightly stupid.

'Do you think you can manage that?' she asks.

'I don't see why not,' I say.

'Offer them the suite, then suggest twin beds, and I guarantee you won't have any problems.'

'Do you think it will work?'

'Well, in my years of experience, it has yet to fail. You have them on the back foot with the affair already; I don't think they'll want any trouble.'

'OK,' I say.

'Anyone else you'll have to dump,' she says,

buttoning herself right up to the top of her red coat. 'Sorry. Goodnight.'

'Night,' I say.

'See you in the morning,' she says.

'I hope not,' I say.

'Of course.' She smiles. 'Sleep well when you do finally get home.'

She walks out into the night and Dennis finally gets off his mobile phone.

'Jesus Christ,' he says, putting his phone back into his pocket. 'I've just heard the best story from my mate down at the Number One Aldwych Hotel.'

'Oh yeah?' I say.

Dennis is always ringing up his mates at various hotels all over London. Not only does he like to know exactly what is going on, anywhere at any time, he has the contacts to find out. After seven years in the business he is also a fount of all gossip, some of it quite scurrilous.

He does tell a great one about Cilla Black and he has a couple of Meg Ryan yarns up his sleeve.

Before Dennis and I can get on to anything juicy and interesting, Mr Andrews and Miss Cox arrive. And Lynette is proved right: it takes less than a minute of explaining and grovelling and obsequious behaviour before they accept the offer of the junior suite and decline the use of twin beds. You'd almost think they wanted to sleep with each other right from the start.

With the furtive lovers despatched to their junior suite, I tell Dennis that I am just going to pop downstairs for a cup of coffee and a cigarette to keep me going. He nods and mouths something along the lines of 'OK'. I'm not sure whether he means me or the person he is talking to on his mobile phone. Anyway, I take my chance.

Downstairs smells of roast beef and disinfectant, and there's a faint whiff of truffle oil too. It's hot, dark and relatively deserted. I walk along the corridor towards the staff canteen, serve myself a cup of black coffee and immediately take a sip. It's cold. Not freezing, but cold enough to have an oily film on the surface. I drink it anyway. It's the caffeine, not a warm drink, that I'm after. I move on down the dark corridor to the smoking room. Even in the darkness I can smell it coming a mile off. I sit down on one of the long benches beneath the line of blue nylon cleaning coats and light up. I sit, smoke and listen to Chef shouting next door.

There's been a run on something. I can't quite make out what it is. It must be something warm and hearty. It always happens when it's raining outside, and tonight it's pissing it down. It's amazing how we all order the same food when it comes to certain weather conditions; you can understand why some big food companies employ people to predict future rain or sunshine because we all react like lemmings. I tell you, as soon as the sun comes out, we're all eating salads; a cold snap, or a downpour, and we are all ordering chateaubriand, if we're lucky enough to be able to afford it.

I've seen it all before. We run out of something delicious like roast lamb, Chef goes mad, gets pissed off with the predictability of his clients ordering the same thing, then eventually tells a waiter he has no more lamb; the waiter then comes out and tells the restaurant manager, who eventually tells all the other waiters. In the meantime, three more orders for roast lamb have arrived in the kitchen and some poor sod of a waiter has to go back out and tell the guests that they can't have their order. Nightmare, I think, as I take a long drag on my fag and thank God, again, that I don't work down here any more. Anyway, I think, a hotel of our standard shouldn't ever run out of anything.

I lean against the greasy wall in the smoking room and close my eyes for a second. There is no way I'm going to last the night, I think; even the pills aren't keeping me awake. I take another drag. Suddenly, Patrick bursts through the door.

'There you are!' he says, all pink and sweaty and out of breath. 'I've been paging you.'

'It doesn't work down here,' I say, taking the red pager out of my pocket. 'There's no signal.'

'Oh my God, you've got to come,' he says, mincing

his freckled hands with worry. 'There's this Saudi guy upstairs and he's demanding a room. He says he comes here all the time and he says that he wants a room right now. I don't know what to do. Dennis said to come and get you quick sharp and I've been running around looking for you everywhere.'

Well, that certainly wakes me up. It's like having a rocket shoved up my arse and a big bag of Pro Plus pills forced down my neck like a foie gras goose. I shift it faster than Linford Christie back up those stairs.

210

9PM – 10PM

I come up the stairs, my heart racing, my hands sweating, to find a large Saudi dressed in white robes and red and white checked headdress waiting for me. Amazingly for a Saudi, his entourage is small – just two women, both dressed head to foot in black.

'Ah.' He smiles as I approach. 'The man we have been waiting for.'

'I'm terribly sorry,' I say, my chest heaving, as I arrive behind the desk. 'It's just that we didn't expect you, sir.'

'I know,' he says with a wave of his hand. 'I didn't expect to be here myself. Business is an unpredictable mistress; one is always at her beck and call.'

'Right,' I say, exhaling as I try to get my breath back. 'I'm afraid to say that the hotel is very full tonight, sir.'

'Oh,' he says. 'Is Adrian about?'

'The manager? Yes, of course, sir, um . . . yes, maybe, possibly . . . um, I'm afraid I don't know. I'll call for you.' I say this like it's the best idea I've ever had.

'Good,' he says. His voice is quiet, yet extremely determined. He places his gold-ringed, manicured hands on the desk.

'Right,' I say, nervously. 'I'll call right away.'

'Good,' he says again.

I look up to see Patrick stumbling in through the doors with a heavy collection of expensive luggage under each armpit. Dennis comes through two seconds later carrying a similar amount. They pile them high, one on top of the other, onto the trolley. The Saudi turns around.

'There are three more in the boot,' he says.

'OK, sir,' says Dennis, walking back out into the cold.

There is no answer in Angie's office, so I try Adrian's direct line, which is strictly – as he has reiterated many times before – for emergencies only.

'Hello,' he says, sounding more than annoyed at being disturbed.

'You're still here,' I say, the relief clearly audible in my voice.

'Of course I'm still here,' he says, like he never goes home to his girlfriend before six p.m. 'I'm checking through the stock-take.'

'Oh good,' I say.

'I'm glad you think it is good,' says Adrian. 'Anyway, what do you want?'

'I have a Mr . . . ?'

'Sheikh ——.'

'I have Sheikh —— here, he's just arrived, and he said he would like to see you.'

'Jesus Christ!' says Adrian, coughing down the line. 'Why the fuck didn't you say? Tell him I'm on my way.'

'He's on his way,' I say with a wide service industry smile as I put down the telephone. 'He won't be a second.'

'Good,' says the Sheikh.

Indeed, Adrian is probably less than thirty seconds. I've never seen him make the distance between his office and reception in such a short time.

'Sheikh!' he says as he bounds through the glass doors, his silk tie flying in the wind. 'How lovely to see you again. Really, it is lovely.' His hands are outstretched in a wide and welcoming manner. In fact, standing there, rooted to the spot, exuding ebullience, he looks a bit like Jesus.

The Sheikh is less forthcoming. He walks towards Adrian and offers his right hand. 'Good evening,' he says. 'How very pleasant to see you.'

'Yes, wonderful,' says Adrian, tugging on his hand like a one-armed bandit. 'Excellent, excellent.' He finally releases the Sheikh and comes round behind the front desk. 'Right,' he says, looking down the occupancy chart on the computer, 'what do we have available for one of our old friends?'

Old friends? I almost snort. I've never clapped eyes on the bloke in my life. Although I do know that sheikhs are obviously important people. He could possibly be the bloke who came in last summer, when I was on holiday, and bought Michelle a pair of diamond earrings for being so special, and who also gave Tony a Cartier watch. Lord knows what he must have given Adrian for him to be that far up his sheikhly arse, but it must have been something quite spectacular.

'Did you and your girlfriend enjoy your trip to Monte Carlo?' asks the Sheikh.

'Oh, very much so, very much so,' says Adrian. 'Terribly kind of you. Terribly kind indeed.'

So that was it. No wonder Adrian ran from his office. It's just a shame, then, for all concerned that the Texan has the best suite in the hotel. The Sheikh will have to make do with second best for the first time, I imagine, in quite a while.

'Oh, there we go,' says Adrian, looking up and grinning from ear to ear. 'How lucky, the best suite in the hotel is available tonight. Right at the top.'

'The same as I had before.' The Sheikh is smiling and appears satisfied.

'Ah,' smiles Adrian. 'Right, not quite the same room,' he says. 'It *is* the same, but different. It is the same size, with two bedrooms, a lounge, two bathrooms and another separate seating area, but it is slightly different.'

'Oh?' says the Sheikh. 'But the last time I came to stay I had the best suite in the hotel.'

'Yes,' agrees Adrian, now rather regretting his initial boast. 'We have two best suites.'

'Interesting,' says the Sheikh. 'I had no idea that there could be two bests. One, I thought, had to be better than the other. But then my grasp of English never has been very good.'

'Ha! ha! ha!' Adrian laughs somewhat hysterically as he turns around to fetch the key card. The Sheikh hands over his black American Express card. 'I'll just take a print of that,' says Adrian. 'And would you mind, terribly, filling in this form? As we weren't expecting you, we haven't filled it in ahead of time.' Adrian hands over a transparent plastic biro. The Sheikh looks slightly repulsed. He bends down, picks up his briefcase, takes out a gold fountain pen and proceeds to fill in the form.

Patrick is already waiting, the luggage stacked, ready to follow the Sheikh up in the lift. Dennis, for some purely financial reason, is also in attendance. The Sheikh reaches back into his briefcase and pulls out two

£50 notes. He hands one to me and the other to Adrian. 'Thank you both for your help,' he says. Patrick's eyes are round with astonishment. I feel mine doing the same. Adrian pockets his with professional speed and comes out from behind the desk, ushering Patrick, the Sheikh's two wives and the Sheikh on their way towards the lift.

As the door closes behind the party, Adrian visibly exhales. 'That was a fucking close shave,' he says. 'I'd hate to have bumped him to the Berkeley.'

The cocktail party in the ballroom is coming to a close and groups of inebriated guests are weaving their way through reception on their way out to take a cab. With both Dennis and Patrick dealing with the Sheikh's copious but potentially very lucrative luggage, it is up to me to make sure they don't hang around in reception too long or start to make a nuisance of themselves. I can see a few groups peeling off into the bar. I know Gino won't mind too much, just so long as they are spending cash and not opting for cheap bottles of wine instead of champagne.

A couple of drunk women sit down at Tony's desk and start pretending to use the telephone like it is the most original joke ever staged. Little do they know that we get about six people a week doing the very same thing.

'Excuse me, ladies,' I say with a supposedly

hilarious smile on my face. 'Can you stop that, please?'

'Sorry,' giggles one of them as she gets out of the seat. The other laughs uproariously as they both totter out of the door.

Some of our guests are beginning to arrive back at the hotel after dinner. A couple go back into the bar for some of Gino's expensive nightcaps and another couple go upstairs to finish off the night in our honour bar on the fourth floor.

The honour bar is one of those newfangled modern ideas that tend to be more common in the smaller, cosier hotels. Our honour bar is a new thing, just over a year old, and it's one of Adrian's more revolutionary ideas. You either love it or hate it, and Gino, somewhat unsurprisingly, hates it. He finds the idea that hotel guests would want a small, intimate bar without a barman insulting to say the least. Needless to say, it also deprives him of customers. Although, to be honest, the sort of people who tend to use the honour bar are the sort of people who would perhaps not sit down-stairs shelling out £75 a shot for a glass of whisky. They usually fancy a quieter time rather than the hectic bonhomie of Gino's. Then again, it doesn't stop people from really tucking in as soon as they sit back in the large chintzy sofas and fat armchairs we have up there.

I can tell you one thing for certain: people are pretty dishonourable when it comes to honour bars. Most of the time they fail to write down something – their mixers, their nuts, their third vodka. They will sometimes deliberately write down cheaper brands of wine while serving themselves something expensive. Sometimes it's actually not even intentional: they just get too plastered to remember their room number or exactly how many drinks they have actually had. Gino does occasionally send up a member of the bar staff to check on things. Either Gianfranco or Francesco pops up and down a couple of times during the night to make sure everything is running smoothly, and that no-one has passed out on the sofa. But it's not a popular errand as time out of the bar means time away from tips.

Ironically, the honour bar doesn't make the hotel very much money. With all the thieving and alcohol-induced absent-mindedness that goes on, the place would run at a loss if it weren't for the fact that we added a bit extra on the price of the drinks to compensate. Well, the hotel would never want to be out of pocket, now would it? Still, with all the theft, compensation and covert supervising, it's a wonder a hotel bothers to have an honour bar at all. But rather like jacuzzis in the suites and large heads on the showers, an honour bar is one of those modern things a supposedly modern hotel can no longer do without. It sort of indicates that you are stuck in the Dark Ages if you don't have one. It is also a nod to the new cosmopolitan traveller who expects his hotel to be a home away from home, where his every whim and creature comfort is catered for, including a couple of free vodkas if he needs them.

Ms Austin comes through reception in a long print skirt and pastel shirt, on his way to dinner in the dining room. Both Dennis and Patrick wish him good evening as they all come out of the lift at the same time. The two of them are smiling. Pound signs light up their eyes.

'Fifty quid,' says Dennis as he walks past on his way to Tony's desk. 'That's a nice little earner early in the evening.'

'I know,' says Patrick, his pale face sporting big pink excited patches. 'It can't get any better than that.'

'Oh, it can, mate,' says Dennis. 'Stick around and there's a whole lot more where that came from.'

I find myself feeling the £50 note in my back pocket, thinking perhaps it was worth pulling a double shift after all.

Tony comes through reception, talking on his mobile phone. His navy cashmere overcoat flaps open as he walks. He doesn't pause to speak to any of us; he only dishes out a small businesslike wave. As he walks out of the revolving doors, another young man comes in. He makes his way up to the front desk.

'Room 220,' he says.

'220,' I repeat as I tap in the room number. The room is occupied. 'Is your wife or partner in the room before you, sir?'

'No,' he says. 'I'm on my own. Is there some sort of problem?'

'Um, well, I'm not sure, sir,' I say. 'Could you tell me your name and I'll just check on the computer.'

'Mr Grey,' he says. 'My name is Mr Grey.'

'Right,' I say. I have to say I'm beginning to sweat a bit. Either I've got a sixth sense that something is wrong or I've had way too much caffeine. Both are very possible. 'Mr Grey, you say,' I say as I see that the room has been sold to a Mr McGrath. Fuck. Fuck. Fuck. My heart is now beating really rather fast. My palms are slimy with sweat. This is the bastard whose room I packed up at lunchtime. Jesus Christ, I don't believe it. I'm going to kill Ben when I see him. Why do I have to be on a double? 'Ah,' I say.

'Is there a problem?' he says, leaping down my throat at the earliest opportunity. 'It's the same room I've been in for the past three days.'

'Yes,' I say. 'The room you were supposed to check out of this morning.'

'No I wasn't,' he says, quickly and aggressively.

'Well, according to our records you were.'

'Your records are wrong.'

220

'Yes, well, in your absence, sir, they are all we can go on.'

'What is that supposed to mean?'

'What it means, sir, is—'

'Actually I don't care what it means,' he says, slamming his fist down on the desk. Dennis, still on his mobile, gets out of his chair. 'I demand to go to my room.'

'But that's just it,' I say, trying to sound as un-confrontational as possible. 'It is no longer your room. It is occupied by someone else.'

'What?' he says, taking a step back, like I've thrown a glass of cold water in his face. 'What do you mean someone else is in there?'

'Well, I'm afraid we checked you out,' I say calmly.

'You did bloody what?'

'There's no need to swear, sir.'

'What did you say?' he says, leaning towards the desk, fury flushing across his face.

Shit. Fuck. No. I should not have said that. I'm the person in the wrong here and I am not handling the situation with any great aplomb.

'I'm terribly sorry, sir,' I say. 'I'm afraid that we have sold your room on to someone else as we believed you to be leaving us today.'

'Fine, right,' he says, trying to get to grips with what I am saying. 'So give me another room.'

'Ah,' I say. I can see him bristle. 'There aren't any other rooms.'

'What?' He is now looking so angry I can't get eye contact with him. 'I want to see the manager.'

'He's just left for the evening,' I say.

'What?' He is almost screaming. 'What sort of fucking place are you running here?'

I'm tempted to say the word 'hotel' but decide against it as I sense it might send him through the roof. 'I'm terribly sorry, sir,' I say again. 'I could get you the duty manager but there is nothing I can do. We have obviously made a terrible mistake here, and sadly there is nothing I can do to rectify it.' Mr Grey just stands there dumbfounded. 'We can arrange for you to stay free of charge at the Berkeley tonight, on the hotel, and we will obviously compliment your next stay with us.'

'If you think that for one fucking minute I am ever going to stay here again you have another fucking think coming,' he says. His eyes are now shot with blood as the pressure rises.

'I understand perfectly, sir,' I say. I turn around, go into the back office and return with his packed suitcase.

'You've packed my bags?' he whispers.

'Yes, sir,' I say, half closing my eyes, waiting for the outburst.

'You lot are un-fucking-believable. Call yourself a five-star hotel?' he yells, leaning over the desk. 'Call yourself a fucking luxury establishment? You wouldn't know the meaning of service if it fucking came along and ripped your fucking head off!'

'Yes, sir,' I say.

He bends down, picks up his bag and marches towards the revolving doors.

'Excuse me, sir,' says Dennis. 'I've arranged for a complimentary cab to take you to the Berkeley.'

Mr Grey stops in his tracks and turns to Dennis. 'You can fuck off as well!' he shouts at the top of his voice.

'Yes, sir,' says Dennis. 'Have a good evening, sir.'

Mr Grey scrabbles through the revolving doors, which he unsuccessfully tries to slam in his fury.

'That went well,' says Dennis, with a wink.

'Yup,' I say, exhaling loudly, trying to force out some tension. 'I think I've just cost the hotel over a thousand pounds.'

'And the rest,' says Dennis. 'I don't imagine for one second he's going to hold back when it comes to his mini bar tonight.'

'No. And I also can't imagine us trying to get any money out of him either.'

'Don't think so,' says Dennis.

'Shit,' I say.

'You can say that again,' says Dennis.

'I'd better ring the Berkeley and warn them he is coming.'

'That would be a nice thing to do,' smiles Dennis. 'Rather them than me.'

While I'm speaking to the guy on the front desk at the Berkeley, explaining to him all that has happened, I see Mr Masterson come back into the hotel. His face is all red and jovial and relaxed; he has obviously had a fine dinner at Sheekey's. He makes his way over to Dennis, sits on the corner of his desk and starts to have a chat, which I try to listen to with one ear while training the other on the chap at the Berkeley. Sadly, such multi-tasking is beyond me, so after I put down the phone, I wait for Mr Masterson to disappear into the bar and the grateful arms of Gino before asking Dennis what his conversation was all about.

'He was asking for an "extra pillow",' says Dennis.

'Oh Lord,' I say, looking at my watch. 'It can't be that time already.'

10PM – 11PM

Dennis is quite capable of getting guests 'extra pillows' if he wants to, needs to or has to, but it is not something he particularly advertises. He has a couple of numbers up his sleeve of high-class ladies of the night, but they are only for the most discreet and valued customers. If anyone else other than Mr Masterson had asked Dennis for a prostitute then I'm afraid he would have looked down his rather short, turned-up nose and pretended not to understand. Even if it meant forgoing a backhander. But seeing as it is Mr Masterson, he gets on to it right away.

That is one of the odd things about the Americans. For such a supposedly God-fearing, puritanical nation, they don't half love their whores. I'm not sure whether it's because they normally have lots of money and are far away from home that they go hooker crazy, but they always seem to. Mr Masterson's request on his way back to the bar was as inevitable as his splashing out on ridiculously expensive whisky. The Japanese are the same. They love their whisky and their whores just as much as the Americans.

It is normally, I have to admit, the older guest who pays for sex; the young guys these days aren't so keen. Perhaps it's a generational thing. It's usually the fiftysomething bloke who has his wife and kids at home who goes whore mad in a hotel. He tends to be fat, he smokes a cigar, he's got the company credit card and he's going to spunk some cash.

Out of the Europeans, it's the Germans who are the most keen on prostitutes. The French and the Italians aren't usually that interested, or maybe they just don't have the cash. And the Russians, bizarrely, usually bring their own. They either travel with them, arriving in the hotel with a couple of girls at a time, or they somehow always manage to come back to the hotel in the evening with a Natasha in tow. The English, on the other hand, seem to prefer gay sex. I know it sounds odd, but whenever they get a bit pissed in the bar they start coming on to the staff. We have a couple of regular guests who stay here who are quite keen on their rent boys, and just as long as it's kept quiet and no-one is obvious about what they are doing, we turn a blind eye. What you get up to in your own room is your own business, particularly if you are shelling out two grand a night.

I'm pretty sure Dennis can get you drugs as well. Not smack, but a couple of grams of charlie, speed or a few Es have most certainly slipped through his fingers of an evening – but only if you are rich enough, you spend plenty of your money in the hotel and you tip him handsomely afterwards. That's the thing about those little extras in the concierge service: you have to be the right person asking in the right way, otherwise, I'm afraid, you'll get absolutely nowhere. There are horses for courses, and nowhere more than in the luxury hotel business do double standards apply.

Dennis is muttering and sourcing 'extra pillows' on the telephone. He occasionally laughs heartily at some shared joke. Reception is busy with guests and their friends coming back and forth, to and from the bar. But nowhere is more busy at the moment than the restaurant. This is a silly time, when well-lubricated guests are hopefully going to spend silly money on silly drinks.

I remember one fabulous moment at another place I worked at when the Irish dancer Michael Flatley shelled out £3,500 on a bottle of Château d'Yquem 1921 dessert wine to impress a very trim, large-breasted blonde. The sommelier was doing star jumps in the kitchen so thrilled was he that he'd finally managed to get rid of the stuff. I think it had been sitting in his cellar for over a year. After he'd served the wine, a couple of us minced past just to take a look, to see if they were enjoying it. I don't know how one is supposed to look when drinking over a week's salary with every sip, but as far as I was concerned they didn't look ecstatic enough. Amazingly, they left half the bottle un-drunk at the table. They must have had more interesting things on their mind. You should have seen the race to clear the table afterwards; we all helped ourselves to a slurp of the stuff. And I tell you, it slipped down like ambrosia.

But that's the thing with all these very expensive drinks: you wonder if they are actually worth it. These 1800 brandies we have in the cellar go for over £700 a shot, but half the time I wonder if they are actually what they say they are. How one tells if they are legit or not I have no idea. I'm sure we've bought some dodgy stuff in the past and served it up to the customer all the same. Sometimes guests order these expensive wines and decide, once they open them up, that they don't like them. It can be rather embarrassing. The sommelier has to stand there and tell them that the £1,500 bottle of wine they've ordered is not corked, it's just that they are either too drunk or simply don't have the taste buds to appreciate it. They don't say that, of course, but I have lost count of the number of times I have seen flushed, middle-aged men stand there, sway-ing on the spot, demanding a second opinion.

It is also more than the cellar man's job is worth to let any of this stuff go off, turn or cork. The national debt of a small country is kept in wine in our cellars and every single one of the bottles has to be turned, loved and nurtured. No-one can afford to have even one £5,000 bottle of wine go to waste. It is a huge responsibility.

A middle-aged couple weave their way through reception, pretending not to be drunk. Her skinny stilettos keep slipping on the shiny marble floor while he maintains a firm grip around her waist, trying to keep her perpendicular. She appears plastered enough to nod at a passing potted palm, thinking it some animated object. They look like they've had a good evening.

My night has only really just started, I think, as I stare outside through the revolving doors and watch a taxi pull up outside. The door opens. Patrick stirs to make the effort to open the door of the hotel, and my heart sinks like a stone. Walking towards me, an expectant smile on his face, is a small Japanese businessman. My head falls into my hands as I force myself to stand up. Oh God, here we go.

'Good evening, sir.'

The poor man bows. Little does he know that in a

few minutes' time I'm going to bump him, and he is going to get right back into a cab and be whisked off up the road to the Berkeley. Straight off his sixteen-hour flight, he thinks we have a room for him. I, of course, know better. He pointlessly hands his bags over to Patrick, who puts them in the brass trolley, and gets out his passport. My toes are curling. The man looks exhausted. I go through the motions, pretending to look at Mr Yamamoto's passport, typing his name into the computer, and then I come up with the usual bumping excuse.

'Oh,' I say, pretending to be shocked. 'Oh dear.' They always begin to look concerned at this point. 'Oh, I am so terribly sorry, sir,' I continue. 'It looks like there has been a mistake. We've had some terrible maintenance problems in the hotel today and I'm afraid that your room is no longer available.'

It is always important to pretend to the guest that there *was* a room available at the time of booking, but that a new, unavoidable problem has just surfaced which prevents them from taking it up. In short, it is an uncontrollable act of God that is forcing us to turn them away, rather than Lynette in reservations overbooking the place again.

Mr Yamamoto bows again and takes the rejection in his stride. I tell him there is a place available for him at the Berkeley and he thanks me for my help. Patrick takes his bags back outside for him, Dennis hails him a cab, and I ring the Berkeley to tell them there's another one on the way. That's £60 I've earned so far tonight. For every new guest I send there, the management gives me £20. Tony would be proud of me.

But I do have to say that I feel sorry for the bloke. All that time in the air, only to touch down and find there is no room in the inn. Then again, it is always the single Japanese businessman who gets bumped. Lynette does it on purpose. As soon as she knows she's overbooked, she goes down the list to work out who she can upgrade and who she can bump. If, when you book your hotel room, you say it is some sort of special occasion, you are more likely to be moved into a junior suite. If you book through a travel agent, the result is the same. It is a way of keeping the company sweet and the hotel in its good books. However, the lone traveller, here for one night, is always the first to go – hence the Japanese businessman. Repeat customers are usually accommodated in some way, and a multi-night booking is something to be looked after. The last thing you want to do is lose the hotel money, or affect its yield. So time and again – in fact, every time – it's the Japanese businessman who gets it.

'Goodnight, sir,' says Dennis, giving the bloke a little wave. 'Have a good evening.' His mobile phone goes off again. He answers it all jovial and upbeat. The call is short. 'Shit,' he says as he hangs up. It looks as though 'extra pillows' are hard to find tonight.

The telephone goes on the front desk. It's some drunk calling down from his room, complaining about room service. Apparently the club sandwich he ordered over an hour ago is nowhere to be seen and he can't raise them downstairs in the kitchen. I feel like telling the bloke that I'm not surprised. The kitchen staff are now reaching the absolute end of their tethers. They have done something like 2,000 covers today, including early breakfasts, breakfasts, lunches, teas, pre-theatre dinners, snacks, a selection of canapés for 400 and eats for the bar; the last thing they want to make is some sodding club sandwich for a piss-head who will eat only half of it before falling asleep fully clothed on his bed. However, instead of saying something I'd regret, I inform the drunk that I'll go and investigate.

Walking into the kitchen at this time is like going into the Amazonian rainforest. It is so hot and full of steam, my shirt immediately sticks to my chest. Despite the fact that they are beginning to wind down at the end of another long day, the atmosphere is no less tense and frenetic. Chef is still shouting out last orders, leaning on some knackered commis chef who is in the shit with his sauces. Meanwhile, some peppered beef is sitting on a plate under a heat lamp, slowly giving up the ghost. The same could be said for the staff. Their shiny white faces have a haunted look to them. Under the unforgiving blue strip lighting, the large bags under their eyes look red and raw. They all look colourless, like animals that live under stones and rarely see the light of day – which is actually the case.

The small, dark-haired kitchen porter who still doesn't speak much English despite working here for five years is mopping down the floors with some stinking disinfectant. The chefs are working around him, walking blood and vegetable peelings back onto his supposedly clean floor. A couple of blokes in whites are bleaching the sideboards where they make the starters; there are two more slopping down the larder, and another going at the stockpots – two enormous round barrels that stand side by side, containing carrots, onions, bay leaves, fennel and chicken or beef stock, which are emptied, cleaned, washed and scrubbed every couple of days, the stocks made freshly again from scratch.

The noise is so loud that it is hard to hear oneself shout, let alone think. The crashing of metal against metal, the sound of the high-pressure water sprays cleaning out pans, and Chef's endless barked commands make it impossible for me to ask anyone where the hell the room service bloke is. The small room next to the kitchen where they take the orders is empty and he is nowhere to be seen. Finally, I tap the kitchen porter on the shoulder and he turns around.

'Room service?' I shout, very close to his ear.

He doesn't bother to reply. But he does make a simple smoking gesture with his hand and I understand exactly what he means.

I walk back down the long, dark corridor into the smoking room to find two people in there. The first looks like one of the night cleaners who has turned up early for his shift. He is sitting there in his green over-all smoking a cigarette and reading an Arabic newspaper.

'Good evening,' I say to him.

He looks so shocked actually to be spoken to that he doesn't say anything in reply. He nods the most imperceptible of acknowledgements and gets back to reading his newspaper. Curled up next to him on the bench, and very obviously fast asleep, is the bloke who is supposed to be doing room service. He looks so happy there, snoring gently with a quiet smile on his face, that I am loath to disturb him. It is probably the happiest he has been all day. I bet the drunk has forgotten about his club sandwich by now. Then again he may not have, and it will be only a matter of time before he is down in reception irritating the hell out of me. So I shake the room service bloke gently by the shoulder. He smiles, turns onto his back and stretches out full-length on the bench, like he has forgotten where he is. Then he opens his eyes and sits bolt upright with the shock of seeing me staring down at him.

'Shit, fuck, sorry,' he says. He sounds French. He looks younger sitting up than he did lying down. About twenty.

'Um, room service?' I say, more as a suggestion than a question.

'I know, sorry,' he says.

'Club sandwich,' I say.

'Fuck,' he replies, and slaps his forehead. He is off the bench and out of the room before I can say anything else. I follow him out of the room, only to catch a glimpse of him running down the corridor back to the kitchen.

'Good evening,' I say to the night cleaner as I go to shut the door behind me.

'Good evening,' he very tentatively replies.

Back upstairs, and reception is still busy. Dennis, in my absence, has hopefully been keeping an eye on who is coming in and using the hotel bar.

As regular closing time approaches we often get a rush of late-night drinkers making their way in here. Licensing laws mean that if you are a guest in the hotel you are entitled to drink all night. But to be honest, it depends on what you are drinking or if Gino can be bothered to keep the place open for you. People who aren't guests in the hotel are supposed to be got rid of before 11.30, although often if they are behaving themselves and spending enough we allow them to stay on drinking. In some places, in the more tucked away bars like the Halcyon Hotel in Holland Park, they stay open much later than anywhere else more centrally located. The place was hidden from the police, and because it was in a basement, residents were never disturbed. It used regularly to stay open till dawn. There are also those more determined drinkers who get round the residency law by booking themselves into a room they have no intention of using, just to carry on boozing. These are the sort of guests who make my day, so to speak, as I can charge them for a room I know won't have to be cleaned, and then I can sell it on to an early arrival first thing in the morning. Sadly, the hotel is full, so there'll be no booze bookings tonight.

Dennis looks like he's in a bit of a mood as I walk over to check that everything is OK. I spot Patrick going to use the guests' toilets again. I can't be bothered to tell him off, and I don't really care if a guest spots him in there at this time of night. I don't think it matters. Dennis tells me that the hotel bar is pretty full already with guests left over from the cocktail party in the ballroom. He suggests we could be in for a tough night.

'How's your search for "extra pillows" going?' I ask, trying to tease him.

'Don't ask,' he says, sounding annoyed and devoid of humour. 'I had two women who were supposed to turn up half an hour ago. They're late.'

'Two?' I say. 'Our Texan friend is greedy.'

'I don't think he'll have both of them, it's just to give the man a bit of a choice.'

'How thoughtful.'

'There's no need to be sarcastic,' he says.

'I wasn't,' I say.

'Whatever.'

'Oh my God!' says Patrick, running towards us, his already pale face turned totally white. 'You'd better come with me. I think we should call an ambulance.'

11PM – 12AM

Patrick directs me into the downstairs gents' toilets. Walking into the urinals, it looks like a murder has taken place. There is blood everywhere. Pools of it shine on the white tiled floor; splatters of it flick up the walls in lines and streaks; great gobs of it slide down the sides of one of the basins. And in the middle of it all lies a young man in a pinstripe suit, with his trousers down by his ankles, his penis hanging out and his two front teeth missing.

At first, both Patrick and I think that he's dead, or at least that he's passed out, but it soon becomes apparent through some incomprehensible mumblings that he is still with us. Having ascertained, much to both my and Patrick's relief, that he is still alive, I'm not sure whether to move him or not. There is something deeply undignified about his lying there with his cock out, but I don't want to damage anything. You always hear that you're not supposed to touch people who are injured, but somehow it doesn't seem right.

'Patrick,' I say, as we both stand there staring lamely, 'go and get a blanket from housekeeping. I do think we should cover the guy up a bit.'

'Yes, right, right away,' he stammers, glad to be given something to do.

'The ambulance crew are on their way,' announces Dennis as he rushes into the gents. 'Jesus Christ,' he says, stopping abruptly. He retches into his hands. 'Oh my God,' he says. 'I fucking can't stand the sight of blood. Oh Jesus.' He fans himself. 'The bloke's lips have gone fucking blue.'

I look down and, sure enough, it looks like he's passed out and his lips are turning turquoise.

'Jesus Christ,' I say, leaning over him. 'We're going to have to give him mouth to mouth.'

'Fuck off,' says Dennis. 'I'm getting out of here before I throw up everywhere.' For a supposedly hard man, Dennis doesn't appear to have an iron gut. 'I'll wait outside for the ambulance crew and tell them where to go,' he announces, slamming the door behind him.

I bend down in the pool of blood and cover the man's mashed-up mouth with my hand. I desperately try to remember the first-aid course the hotel made us go on about six months ago, where I sat at the back making paper balls out of my notes. I cover his nose with my mouth and start to blow up it. I look at his chest – it seems to be moving. I do the same thing all over again wondering whether I should also be pounding or massaging his heart. I blow again. He coughs slightly. His lips are looking a whole lot less blue. Then the ambulance crew burst through the urinal doors, dressed in their green jumpsuits and black boots. One of them says something along the lines of 'we'll take over from here'.

I walk out of the toilets in a bit of a daze. That was a bit of a close call. I've no idea whether I did the right thing, or if I've just performed something that was wholly unnecessary. A bit of a crowd has assembled in reception. There is nothing like a drama to gather a group of gawping drunks.

'All right, all right,' says Dennis, having suddenly regained control over his emotions. 'Move along now. Move along. There's nothing to see.' He slowly moves some vodka and tonics and a few flutes of champagne back in the direction of the bar.

It's not long before the ambulance crew bring the young man through reception tucked under a red blanket. He is now clearly conscious, muttering madness as they take him out.

'Is he OK?' I ask one of the paramedics.

'Oh yeah,' he replies, with a seen-it-all-before sort of smile. 'Turns out he slipped in the urinal while taking a piss, knocking himself and his two front teeth out.'

'Oh, right,' I say.

'He was lucky you came along when you did,' he says. 'You gave mouth to mouth, didn't you?'

'Well, a couple of blasts.'

'Things could have been a whole lot worse. He's lucky he's so pissed. He's going to feel it a whole lot more in the morning.'

'Right,' I say.

'You should clean yourself up a bit,' adds the medic, pointing at my trousers which are covered in sticky patches of blood. 'That can't be a good look for the hotel.' He smiles and pats me on the back before walking out of the door.

Jesus Christ, I think I need a cigarette. I can't be bothered to go downstairs to the smoking room, so I wander outside. At this late stage of the evening I don't think anyone is going to mind a few cigarette butts on the pavement. While I stand there, leaning against a pillar outside the hotel, a couple of coppers pull up in a panda car. I suppose they are obliged to follow up any ambulance call-out, especially if it's a luxury hotel. The police and the ambulance crew mix outside the hotel; I presume they are being told that no foul play is expected. One guy looks like he is smiling. I suppose it's not every day you're told that a punter was so pissed that he slipped and brained himself on a urinal. I think if they'd actually seen him, lying in a pool of his own blood, they might find it less amusing.

I stub out my cigarette on the pavement, and as I look up I clock Dennis's two 'extra pillows' slipping into the hotel behind the police. They are easy to spot. Long legs, long hair, short skirts – girls that obviously attractive are rarely seen unescorted, unless they're on the game. I try to follow them into reception but they are so quick off the mark that by the time I've made it through the police presence it appears that the girls are already in the bar.

Dennis is already on his mobile, recounting his passed-out-punter-with-his-cock-out story to his cousin at the Dorchester. He tells it well. Ten minutes in the gestation and it already sounds like one of those un-believable stories he specializes in. I can hear his cousin laughing down the phone as I go past.

I go down into the bowels of the hotel in search of some new trousers. I know there is some cupboard, somewhere, where they keep a supply of black suit trousers because they form the bottom half of both the bellboys' and the waiters' uniforms.

It's very dark down here. I walk past the smoking room, the kitchens and the staff dining rooms. I am in unfamiliar territory now. The hotel opens up like a rabbit warren of corridors and small rooms. It is all badly lit with flickering strip-lights and the place stinks of chlorine, cabbage and stale cigarettes. The smell is so sweet and high it makes you gag if you breathe in too deeply. So I don't. I keep my hand over my mouth, and I walk along, occasionally opening cupboards to see what's inside them. Firstly, I come to a section of dining-room linen, table cloths and napkins piled high; some are plain white, others have those old-fashioned pastel borders on them that I haven't seen for a few years. Further along the corridor are shelves of cleaning equipment, bottles of bleach, yellow plastic containers of Cif, mops, buckets and packet after packet of bright pink rubber gloves. Eventually, I come across one of the night cleaners collecting supplies.

'Evening,' I say. The whites of his eyes blink at me in the dark. 'Do you know where I can find any trousers?' I ask. The man does not reply. He blinks at me again. 'Trousers?' I repeat, scanning his face for some sort of reaction. The bloke obviously doesn't speak any English.

A hotel cleaning job is the refugee's or illegal immigrant's first port of call. Hotels are notorious for employing people while looking the other way when it comes to documentation. They turn a blind eye to doctored passports; they happily employ cleaners with temporary National Insurance numbers. When you apply for a National Insurance number in the UK, you are given a temporary number which starts with 'TN' followed by your date of birth, while they look into your eligibility to work. Most hotel workers have 'TN' numbers and they have been working off them for years. If you have a 'TN' number you are charged an emergency tax rate, but when you are paid minimum wage it barely makes any difference.

It would blow you away if you knew how un-supervised the whole thing is. Hotels pay directly into workers' bank accounts, and see nothing wrong in sending someone's wages into an account under a totally different name. There have been cases where the Home Office has stormed into hotels, on an illegals raid, to find that over half the staff shouldn't be work-ing there and that the names they are using bear no relation to what they're called at all. They then cart off thirty or so people and deport the lot of them. But you can't really blame the hotels for trying. Just so long as people have two hands to clean with, who gives a shit where they are from? Also, there is hardly a queue of people around the block gagging to work those hours, in those conditions, for that amount of money.

Hotels are also good places for people to disappear in. I remember once we had this Colombian chamber-maid who had a temporary National Insurance number and a student visa. Technically, she was only allowed to work twenty hours a week, but she worked a forty-hour week, so we had her on the books as working a twenty-hour week and paid her double. She looked like she did four hours a day but in fact she did a full shift. Anyway, we were visited by these blokes who said they were from the Home Office, and they came asking about her. Fortunately, she wasn't in that day. They said they wanted a photocopy of everyone's passport faxed over, including hers, but they forgot to give us a fax number. We left it alone for a couple of days, did nothing, and they never came back. Mind you, neither did the chambermaid.

The night cleaning staff are not quite as glamorous or exotic. We have Moroccans, Kenyans and a few Iraqi Kurds, but they're mainly Bangladeshis. Forget what I said earlier about the chambermaids; I actually think that the back-of-house guys have the worst job in the hotel. They do an eleven p.m. to seven a.m. shift, during which time they scrub the kitchens, clean all the silver, wipe down all the floors, clean the staff toilets and do all the washing up. And they hate their job. In a business that thrives on tips to top up poor wages, there is no chance of a single spare pound coin coming their way. For not only are they not allowed to interact with the guests, they're not allowed to be seen in any public area at all.

You can understand why morale is low, and they're always slacking off. They will disappear off to sleep anywhere. It is quite extraordinary. The other day I found a bloke squeezed into one of the lockers in the staff room having a kip practically standing up. When I worked at the Savoy I used to have to do these grand tours of all the subterranean passages under the Thames to make sure none of them was asleep on the job. Here it's a bit easier as the hotel is smaller, but there are still loads of places for them to doss down in. There are all sorts of nooks and crannies. It's difficult to keep track of everyone.

The turnover of night cleaners is very high, as is sickness, genuine or not. But the thing is, you can't really blame them. They are in a career cul de sac and there is absolutely no way out of their situation. It is impossible for any of them ever to be promoted to do anything else. They are here to clean, and they could be here for three years or three days – it doesn't make any difference. Still no-one knows their names. They get basic minimum wage and they do the worst jobs. This is a highly abusive industry. The higher you are, the better it gets. But when you are at the bottom, you are nothing.

I bend forward and tug at my trouser leg; the congealed blood and material peel off my knees. The cleaner immediately understands what I am looking for.

He takes me along another corridor and opens up a cupboard full of thin, badly made black trousers. I smile and thank him before he disappears off into the dark. After another five minutes spent riffling through the shelves, I come out with a slightly shiny pair of trousers that look as though they might fit. Walking back along the maze of corridors, I eventually find the kitchen. I poke my head around the door to find it almost entirely empty except for a couple of cleaners slopping down the floor and another couple washing out the industrial mixers and large cooking pots.

The staff locker room is thankfully empty, so I go in there and strip off down to my underwear. The trousers are made of cheap material that starts to itch almost as soon as I get them on. I fold up my own suit trousers and put them in a Sainsbury's bag in my locker. I've still got a photo of my ex-girlfriend in there, I notice. I suppose I should really take it down. I have no idea how I'm going to clean those trousers. I'll send them to the dry cleaner's, I should think, and charge it to the hotel.

On my way back upstairs I bump into the Rentokil man. This place is riddled with vermin and it's his job to hinder their spread and make sure the guests never notice quite how many rats, mice and roaches are just a few yards from their feet.

'Evening,' he says as he approaches, a cage in each

hand. He must be off to bait the traps just outside the kitchens.

It's normally the cleaners' job to keep an eye on the rat-traps to see if we've managed to catch any of the little furry fuckers during the night. But the Rentokil bloke comes once a week, after service when the place is quiet, to check up on their positions, to re-bait the traps and work out if we have any more great infestations. I remember a terrible bedbug plague in a place where I used to work. They'd come in in someone's suitcase and they'd gone right the way through the hotel in a matter of days. You'd be amazed how few guests actually complained. A couple, covered in bites, did come to reception and say something, but we were told to deny all knowledge of them. We just shook our heads and looked worried and rather confused. It seemed to do the trick until we got the problem under control.

But in the big hotels it's almost impossible not to have a vermin problem, mainly because the places are so large and so old, with plenty of areas for them to breed. I mean, I have seen mice dancing along the skirting boards of the dining areas in Claridge's while I was serving afternoon tea. The rats at the Savoy are a nightmare. Situated right by the river, half of the Savoy is underground and runs back underneath the Thames, so the place is crawling with them. It's a problem that they constantly fight to keep under control. There are cockroaches pretty much in every hotel I have ever worked in. It's only good chambermaiding that keeps them out of the bedrooms.

'How are you this evening?' I ask as he comes closer. I don't know the bloke's name but I know that he has been killing vermin here for over five years.

'Busy,' he says, shaking both the cages, 'very busy. We've just caught a big brown rat in the wine cellar.' He smiles. 'So I'm off to re-set the trap.'

'Good.' I smile right back. 'That's excellent.'

'Yeah.' He sniffs. 'Anyway, see you.'

'See you,' I reply, my toes curling slightly when I peer into the cages as he goes past.

'Oh,' he adds, stopping and turning around. 'You'd better get back up there as soon as you can. I think the fire alarm has gone off.'

'Fire alarm?' I query. 'But I can't hear anything down here.'

'I know.' He sniffs again. 'That's no good in the event of a fire, now is it?' he says, walking off in the opposite direction to the nearest exit.

12 AM – 1 AM

I come rushing up the stairs in my itchy, scratchy new trousers that are slightly too tight on the thigh to find Dennis and Andre having a stand-up row in reception. The fire alarm is blaring out at full volume, but no-one seems to be taking a blind bit of notice. Rather like a car alarm in a City street, it inspires curiosity but absolutely no sense of imminent danger and/or panic. I remember even when the Savoy Theatre was actually on fire, it took us a while to persuade the guests to leave their rooms. This time another party of drinkers have walked out of the bar, their beverages still in hand, and are standing around in the foyer with an expectant look on their faces. Not even Patrick, who I thought might be flustering and flapping like a neurotic, seems to be paying the loud siren any attention.

'We've asked you to do something about this before,' I can hear Dennis shouting at Andre. 'It's your fault. Your responsibility. You're duty manager tonight.'

'Fuck you!' says Andre, unwisely giving Dennis a little shove with his white hand. 'I can't keep my eye on everything and everyone all the time.'

'It is your bloody job!' yells Dennis, shoving him rather forcefully right back.

'OK,' I say, approaching at speed. 'Where's the fire? What's going on?'

The screeching noise is enough to put anyone on edge.

'It's a false alarm,' bellows Dennis above the noise. 'And it's all because this little arse—'

The fire alarm suddenly turns itself off. Everything falls silent. Only the scream of 'arse' reverberates around reception. Everyone looks at Dennis. A couple of guests have open mouths.

'Hole,' he finishes weakly. 'This arsehole,' he whispers, with a fat jab of his finger in the general direction of Andre, 'keeps insisting that it is all right to cook a fucking crêpe Suzette underneath a fucking smoke alarm. How many more fucking times? You fucking cretin!'

'Cretin?' asks Andre. 'What is this "cretin"?'

'Arsehole! Idiot! You!' says Dennis, pulling moron faces as he does so. 'Honestly,' he adds, turning towards me. 'I fucking ask you . . .'

'Yes, well,' I say, scratching the side of my neck. 'Well, at least the alarm has stopped.'

'Yeah,' sighs Dennis. 'Thank heavens for fucking small little mercies.'

'We should brace ourselves for the arrival of the Fire Brigade,' I say, looking anxiously outside.

'Shit, you're right,' says Dennis, raising his voice again. 'OK everyone! There is nothing to see here. Everyone back. Back to the bar and enjoy your drinks. Back to the bar, please, everyone, Gino is waiting for you!'

Too right he is, I think. Gino's bound to be pissed off. That's a good ten minutes of prime-time custom that Andre's cost him. It's almost worth coming in to-morrow just to hear the row in the morning meeting.

My heart sinks. Shit. I can hear the noise of the fire engines approaching. There are at least three sirens on their way here. Obviously, no-one from the hotel has telephoned them yet to tell them it's a false alarm. Of course they haven't! It's my bloody job to do it! Oh Lord! Thank God I won't be here at tomorrow's meeting. A lot of shit will go down because of this.

The sirens are getting closer. Fuck. It sounds like there are four of them. That's another two grand we'll be shelling out to the London Fire Brigade this month.

Every time a hotel has a false alarm they end up having to pay out from £750 (for a small hundred-room hotel) a time. You can hardly blame the Fire Brigade. Every hotel call they get they have to treat as potentially an enormous disaster in the making. We have bedrooms of guests to be accounted for; we have dining rooms full of people who've had rather too much wine. You can imagine the hell if the fire were real. So the London Fire Brigade tend to take us seriously. They always send multiple engines and they usually arrive within fifteen minutes of the alarm going off.

They screech around the corner and slam on the brakes. I contemplate running outside, waving my arms, to tell them there's no fire and no need, but then I think I might well look like a traumatized fire-victim escaping the inferno and it would only encourage them. So I stand still and wait for the scenario to unfold.

In a matter of minutes they sprint through the front doors, helmets on, hoses at the ready, looking for the action. A man who looks like he is in charge heads up the first wave. His steps slow down as he takes in the sight of Dennis, Andre, Patrick and me staring at him.

'Oh, right,' he says, grinding to a halt.

'It's a false alarm,' I say, trying not to sound sheepish.

'Oh, OK,' he says, raising his arm behind him, halting the rest of his troops.

'Yes.' I smile. 'Sorry about that,' I add, rather weakly. 'It was a mistake.'

'Right,' nods the fireman. 'We'll have to make an inspection of the building just to make sure.'

'Yes, right, of course,' I say. 'It was a crêpe Suzette in the dining room that started it all off.'

'Right,' he says, staring at me like I'm talking Greek. 'The dining room?' he suggests.

'Yes.' I nod. 'Andre will take you.'

Andre springs into action. The idea of escorting such a handsome man in such a tight navy T-shirt into the dining room, clearly gives him the biggest thrill he's had all evening, or even possibly all week. He sets off with a huge spring in his stride. The reaction to the firemen arriving in the bar is the same: the loud cheer that accompanies their entrance makes it all the way through reception. Well, at least we've made their night. You never know, maybe we'll make back the £2,000 we have to give the Fire Brigade in the bar.

With all the distraction, I almost don't notice the Sheikh walking through reception in his long white robes all on his own. I wonder where he's off to at this time of night. 'Good evening, sir,' I say quickly as he walks out into the street. He doesn't bother to react; he just carries on walking, through the revolving doors and into his black, chauffeur-driven Mercedes.

My telephone goes.

'Reception,' I say.

'Hello,' comes a slightly breathless voice.

'Yes?'

'This is room 233,' he says.

'Right, how can I help you, sir?'

'Can someone go and get me some condoms?' he asks, in a voice that is devoid of embarrassment.

'Condoms?' I say. Dennis pricks up his ears.

'Yeah,' he says. 'A packet of three.'

'Right. Any particular size or make?'

'No . . . um, yes. Um, extra large . . . ribbed.'

'Extra large and ribbed,' I repeat.

Dennis rolls his eyes and opens the left-hand drawer of Tony's desk. It is packed with condoms of various different sorts, but mainly extra large and ribbed, which for some reason is one of the more popular ones on order. Dennis pulls out a packet and waves it at me.

'Right, sir,' I say. 'We'll do our best. But you know—'

'Well, you know, if you have any problems,' he adds suddenly, 'any old condom will do.'

'OK, sir,' I say.

'You bastard!' says Dennis, after I hang up.

'I know.' I smile. 'It's just two minutes ago the whole hotel was supposed to be burning down and all this guy can think of is sex. Anyway, I just hate the idea of people having lots of sex when I clearly am not.'

'Oh, right,' he says, clicking his fingers like he's just remembered something. 'I'd forgotten you'd been dumped.'

'Yeah. From a great height.'

'Happens to the best of us,' he says. 'I hear Gavin is getting divorced.'

'What, deputy manager Gavin?'

'The very same.'

'Oh,' I say, not knowing Gavin that well.

'The same reason as all of us,' continues Dennis. 'Long hours. Apparently he was never home.'

'Tell me about it,' I say.

'Yeah, right,' nods Dennis. 'Do you want to go and get some coffee or something?'

'I might just go and check up on how Gino is doing, if you know what I mean.'

'Yeah, sure,' he says. 'Oi, Patrick!' he yells across reception. 'Take these rubbers to room 233. I hear the bloke's gagging for them.'

I walk into the bar and it is heaving. Gino looks the picture of happiness, doing his cocktail thing; even grumpy old Gianfranco has a smile on his face. The fireman effect seems to have worked and everyone's knocking back the booze. I spot Mr Masterson sitting in the corner, with both hands on his prostitutes' knees. They've got a bottle of Dom Perignon Oenothèque Vintage 1988 (£270 a bottle) between them, but Mr Masterson, to Gino's obvious delight, is on doubles of 1919 Dalwhinnie whisky (at £150 a shot). I'm watching, leaning on the door, thinking about taking another

Pro Plus caffeine pill, when Gino spots me and beckons me over.

'Hello,' he says, coming out to greet me. His lips are smiling, but his eyes are indicating a blonde on a stool. 'I think we might have a problem here.' He puts his arm around my shoulder as he whispers in my ear.

The blonde does indeed look a little the worse for wear. I saw her this morning when I checked her in with her husband, and I know they both had dinner together in the hotel, but for some reason she has been left on her own to drink.

'Good evening, madam,' I say. I always start out polite.

'Oh, hello,' she replies. Her eyes are clouded with alcohol and her white silk shirt is undone a button too far.

'Are you having a good evening?'

'Apart from being left on my own by my shit of a husband, who has gone to some shitty business meeting, I'm fine.' She pauses, then smiles. 'In fact, since you've turned up, things are much improved.'

'That's good, madam,' I reply. It is always best to respond to a flirter, especially a drunk one, as there is no telling what they might do.

She drains her drink and stands up a little unsteadily.

'Are you thinking of calling it a night, madam?' I ask.

'I'm thinking of ordering some coffee in my room,'

she says, with a relaxed smile. 'Will you bring it up to me?'

This is, I have to say, not really my job, but Dennis is in reception and there might possibly be £20 in it. There's no tipper like a pissed tipper. And if I'm here all night I may as well make the most of it.

'Of course,' I say, with a smile. 'I'll be up right away.'

I ring downstairs to the kitchen, wake up the lazy bloke in room service again and order a pot of coffee and some homemade shortbread to be delivered just outside the bar. Gino gives me a shot of vodka while I wait; he doesn't ask me to pay. He mutters something about not having to go through another stock-take in a while. Before long, the room service bloke brings up the tray and I take it up to the blonde's room myself. I knock on the door.

'Come in,' she says.

I walk in, holding the tray, and nearly drop the whole bloody thing. Jesus Christ! She is lying there, stark naked, on the bed. Oh Lord! I don't know where to look. I don't know what to say. I can feel my whole fucking face going bright fucking pink. I've been propositioned by guests before, but nothing like this.

Sex between staff and guests is strictly forbidden, although it does certainly go on. I've never done it myself. It's far too risky, particularly if they're drunk. They might well regret it in the morning, and if you're the guy who's taken advantage of a pissed punter, there's no knowing what might happen. It's not a good look. It is also a sackable offence. So, even though it's difficult to ignore a naked woman, flat on her back, laid out like a starfish, I do just that.

'Where would you like the coffee, madam?' I force myself to ask, just managing to get the words out.

'Over there,' she points, propping herself up on her elbow.

'Right you are then,' I say, putting the tray down on the round table at the foot of the bed. 'Um,' I add, studying the thickness of the shag pile on the floor and clearing my throat, 'will there be anything else?'

'Well,' she says. I keep staring at the floor. 'No.'

'Good evening, then,' I say as I leave the room quickly, closing the door behind me.

Just as I walk a step away from the door, I hear her scream 'Fuck you!' and there is an almighty crash: I presume she has hurled the coffee and the tray against the door. I'm not quite sure what to do. Should I go back into the room and help clear up? Should I tell one of the night staff? I stand there for a second and decide I'm probably the last person she wants to see right now, so I run back down to reception to share what's just happened with Dennis. And while Dennis pisses himself with laughter, I ring up the room service night staff and get one of them to go upstairs to clear up the mess.

The traffic through reception is beginning to calm down. However, it's around now that you really have to start keeping an eye on who is leaving and who, more importantly, is coming into the hotel. Any passing tramp would give his eye-teeth for a nice cosy night in our establishment. They are always trying to slip past us, which is why from now on we keep watch on the door and take regular tours of the hotel, just to check if any of them have managed to find themselves a comfortable fire escape to doss down in. They also have a rather nasty habit of locating the honour bar and relieving it of all its alcohol. I think I might send Dennis on a quick tour of the place when he gets off his mobile phone after telling his long-winded joke at my expense. Dennis is better at dealing with tramps than I am. He's quite tough and unafraid, whereas I always end up feeling sorry for them. I'm always in half a mind to give them their fistful of wine miniatures, only I know it would come out of our wages.

I'm feeling exhausted. The shot of vodka has only gone halfway to reviving me. My legs are warmer and my cheeks feel like they have a bit more colour, but the rest of me feels like it might spontaneously collapse at any minute. I can't believe that Andre set the fire alarm off with a crêpe Suzette. He's been warned about using too much brandy in the past. Adrian is going to be so pissed off tomorrow morning.

I smile. Two firemen come back through the glass doors. Their jackets are open and they have wide smiles on their faces.

'Bloody hell, your bar's a laugh.'

'Yeah. All done then?'

'Yup,' says the other guy. 'We're the last two out. It was definitely the pancake, mate,' he adds. 'That set the whole thing off. The plastic cover's been singed on the smoke sensor and everyone in the dining room saw the blast from the brandy flames.'

'Right.' I nod.

'Everywhere else is fine,' nods the first.

'OK, then,' I say. 'Sorry to get you lot out here for no reason.'

'Not to worry,' says the second one. 'We enjoyed seeing the fit birds in the bar.'

'Good,' I say. 'So it was worth it.'

'Definitely,' says the first, tapping the side of his nose. 'Quality.'

'Goodnight,' I say.

'Night,' they both reply.

I'm about to get Dennis off his mobile phone to go on tramp watch when my telephone goes.

'Hello,' comes a distinctly drunken voice. 'This is room 412.'

'Good evening,' I say.

'Now listen,' he starts. 'I have been calling room

261

service for what seems like ages and I've been transferred to you. I'd like a bottle of champagne.'

'Right, sir,' I say. 'They're probably very busy down there.' I'm going to kill that sleeping bastard.

'OK then,' slurs the voice. 'Right, what I would like is a bottle of your finest champagne.'

'Our finest?' I say. I can hear a girl giggling in the background. This man clearly wouldn't notice if I brought up a bottle of Asti in a bucket.

'Your finest!' he repeats.

'Well, we have bottles of very fine champagne that range from about £270 a bottle to a 1959 Dom Perignon Vintage for £1,450.'

'Oh,' he says, suddenly sounding less expansive. 'A bottle of Veuve Clicquot would be nice.'

'Vintage?'

'No,' he says very quickly.

'That'll be £65,' I say.

'OK,' he says. 'That sounds fine.'

'I'll get one sent up to your room immediately, sir.'

I ponder for a second about doing it myself, but I think I've had enough drunk encounters so I despatch Patrick, telling him that the punter is pissed and he might get a nice tip.

I've always found this time of night rather amusing when it comes to room service. Once people have a few drinks inside them they start ordering the most extraordinary and expensive things. I have lost count of the buckets of caviar that have gone upstairs after midnight only to be found barely touched by the chambermaids in the morning.

I do remember a rather rich Arab guy at the Lanesborough one night who ordered a £5,000 magnum bottle of Château Petrus. It is an amazing wine, and it had been in the wine cellar for bloody ages; it had become a sort of standing joke that the sommelier was itching to sell it. Anyway, he takes it up to the room, opens it with a flourish and serves it like it's liquid gold. He is careful not to waste a single drop. He is thrilled, as he's finally managed to get rid of it, and the management are chuffed that they've got their money back. There are five people in the room and he pours each of them a glass. Then he leaves, only to come back five minutes later, just to make sure that they are enjoying this fantastic and amazing wine. He knocks on the door and expects to find them all in raptures; instead he walks in to find this woman pouring cold Perrier water into his incredible 1947 Château Petrus, destroying the whole point of it. The poor man walked straight out of the room and nearly burst into tears. It was priceless. He was in a bad mood for almost a week.

Dennis finally gets off his telephone.

'Oh, God,' he says, wiping a tear away from his eye.

'They loved your story at the Savoy.' He starts to chuckle. 'Honestly, I haven't had a laugh like that in a while.'

'Well, I'm glad I can be of service,' I say sarcastically.

'Keep your hair on,' he says.

'Would you go and have a look around for tramps?' I ask. 'What with the fire alarm going off and everything, you never know who might have managed to slip past us while we were otherwise occupied.'

'Yeah,' he agrees, getting up from behind his desk. 'You're right. My mate at Charlotte Street has had a few problems already tonight.'

I remember being told a story about Charlotte Street in the run-up to Christmas, about a huge fight going off there.

It's a weird time, the run-up to Christmas; people behave so badly it's amazing. It is a time of total debauchery and madness. People throw up underneath tables and put a napkin on it, hoping we won't notice. They pass out in the street as soon as they leave the place. They piss in plant pots. It is extraordinary.

Anyway, I remember hearing that some film director was in Charlotte Street having dinner and there was someone else sitting on another table who said something to the director and started a bit of an argument. And then, for some reason or another, it all went off. The film director got up and threw the table in the air.

He flew at this guy and head-butted him. And everyone else joined in. One of the Spice Girls was in there, sitting at a table, and she hit her panic alarm button. All four of her security guards piled into the restaurant from their car outside. Everyone else left as quickly as they could, except the chefs who came out (the hotel has an open-plan kitchen) to try to break the fight up. The police were called. The diner who started the whole thing off had his nose broken and there was blood all over the chefs' whites, smashed glasses everywhere. It was like being in a film. It was fantastic.

'So what's happened down there tonight?' I ask Dennis as he walks towards the stairs.

'Oh, a couple of drunks in reception,' he says.

'Oh,' I say, a little disappointed.

1 AM – 2 AM

Dennis disappears off upstairs on tramp watch. I asked him to have a look in the honour bar on his rounds as well, just in case we have a sleeper in there.

Sleepers are another one of those hotel nightmares we have to deal with during the night shift. They turn up everywhere. Slumped in the corridor, curled up on a sofa, leaning against the fire exit doors; guests too drunk to make it to their bedrooms pass out wherever they fancy and lie there dead to the world. It's a mistake to presume that they have keeled over anywhere near the room they are supposed to be staying in. They can be found on any floor and in any area of the hotel. There is usually no rhyme or reason for them being where you find them. I've seen perfectly respectable businessmen lying flat on their backs covered in an explosion of dry-roasted peanuts with their wallets and all their worldly belongings on display for any passing thief. And it's not just the guests. Punters in the bar will take a wrong turning on the way back from the toilet, see a handy sofa and snuggle down for a snooze. Sometimes we don't discover them until the next morning, when they arrive in the dining room, complete with crumpled suit, and rather sheepishly ask for breakfast.

My telephone goes.

'Hello, reception,' I say with as much zing and fizz as I can muster, which is very little.

'Hello,' comes another drunken slur. 'I can't get any porn,' he moans.

'Porn, sir?' I say. 'Oh dear. What sort of porn were you after?'

'Um, on the telly,' he says.

'Right,' I say breezily. 'You have to pay for that, sir.'

'Yeah, I know that,' he says, like I am some sort of moron.

'OK,' I say, trying to control my annoyance. There is something quite fucking irritating about being abused by a pissed porn-seeking punter at 1.15 in the morning. 'Do you have your remote control near you?'

'Yeah,' he says.

'Good. OK now, I'd like you to press the zero on the remote.' I speak very slowly, like I'm talking to a child.

'Yeah,' he says. Then there's a pause and I can hear him looking for it. 'Where is it?'

'At the bottom of the remote,' I say.

'Yeah,' he says. He starts to breathe heavily, he is concentrating that much. 'Got it.'

'Good,' I say again. 'Right, now press it.'

'Yep.'

'And there on the screen you will have a choice of things to watch. Scroll down, make your choice and press the red button.' I say that last bit quickly just to confuse him.

'Hang on, hang on,' he says crossly. The message is clear: never stand between a drunk and his porn. I repeat my instructions. 'Good, right,' he says as he hangs up.

'Thank you!' I say loudly down the phone. 'Tosser.'

A group of three girls with not very many clothes on walk through reception.

'Excuse me,' I say, 'can I help you?'

'Room 450,' says one of them, like it's absolutely none of my business.

'Fourth floor,' I say.

'Yeah, thanks,' says another with heavy teenage sarcasm.

They stand around by the lift, waiting for it to descend. It arrives, makes the sound of a microwave, the doors open and out pops Dennis with the biggest grin on his face I've seen in ages. He lets the ladies into the lift and comes out practically at a jog.

'Jesus Christ,' he says, his face flushed with hilarity, his eyes watering with humour. 'You won't fucking believe what I've just seen.'

'What?' I say.

'Un-fucking-believable,' says Dennis, rolling his eyes. 'The cheek of the girl.'

'What?'

'Honestly,' says Dennis.

'Fucking what?'

'Well,' he starts, 'you know you told me to go and check out the honour bar, right?'

'Yes.'

'Well, I turn up there and guess what I saw?'

'No idea,' I say. 'Absolutely no idea.'

'Two people at it like bloody dogs,' he declares.

'What?' I say, admittedly a little shocked.

'Yeah,' he says. 'He's sitting on the green sofa, his trousers round his ankles, while she's riding him like a rodeo rider, skirt around her armpits, knickers and tights in a pile on the floor. Her backside's bouncing up and down ten to the fucking dozen.'

'Shit,' I say.

'No shit.' He smiles. 'Can you believe it?'

'What did you do?'

'Well, I coughed a couple of times but they didn't

seem to notice. Then I said, "I'm terribly sorry, I'll come back in a couple of minutes." And then – get this – she turns around and says, "Can you make it ten?" '

'No!'

'Too fucking right!'

'What can you say to that?'

'Nothing.' He shrugs. 'So I went back after ten minutes and they were gone.'

'Amazing,' I say, starting to laugh. 'It reminds me of that woman the other week.'

'Shit, yeah,' he says. 'Who could forget her?'

Less than a month ago, when Dennis and I were both on nights again, we had to deal with this woman who was extremely drunk and flirty in the bar. She was fine for a while, if a little leery, but Gino wasn't too chuffed, so I sort of escorted her out of the bar, and she then went to the toilet and completely disappeared. About half an hour later, when Dennis was escorting someone else to their room, he discovered her having sex with another guest on the floor just outside the lift. He tried tactfully to move them on, but they were having none of it. So we decided that as it was late we would leave them to get on with it, as they'd soon get bored and go back to their separate rooms. Then about ten minutes later I spotted her husband coming back into the hotel. Dennis cleverly remembered that his wife was still having sex outside the lift on the third floor, so I took it upon myself to delay the husband while Dennis sprinted up three flights of stairs to de-couple the wife. It was extraordinary. We saved their marriage, and she didn't even bother to thank either of us, or even to tip us when she checked out looking pretty bloody hung over the next day. Some people are so bloody rude. It's amazing.

Another group of young people come through reception. They look half-cut already.

'Excuse me,' I say, 'can I help you?'

'No thanks,' says one of the young men. 'We're going to see a mate who is staying here.'

'Really?'

'Yeah. Room 450.'

'Room 450,' I repeat.

'Yes,' giggles one of the girls. 'It's his birthday.'

'Fine,' I say. I really can't be bothered to argue.

Dennis is back on his mobile, chatting away to one of his relatives, telling them the honour bar shag story. The girl is already asking for fifteen minutes' more time; I guarantee by the end of the night she'll be having sex for a good half an hour. Honestly, I don't know how that bloke gets the energy to chat all the time. Also, I wonder what he and his mates actually talk about when they do meet up, because Dennis has told them every story he's ever known before he sees them. Perhaps they never meet up at all; they just have a relationship down the telephone.

Do you know, half the problem with this job is not the long hours, the rubbish pay and the drunken abuse, but the boredom of it all. Trying to stay awake while your body is craving sleep is a lot bloody harder if you are bored rigid. There really are only so many times I can watch Patrick rub down the brass door plates or polish the luggage trolley. I swear to God every time he uses the bloody thing to take some sod's bags upstairs he comes down and gives it a quick polish. I think he'd shag the thing if he could.

Jesus, I'm beginning to become a little irritable. Poor Patrick. If he wants to rub his trolley down all night, then it's up to him, and I should let him get on with it. I think I might go and check on Gino to see if he needs help getting rid of a few more vodka shots that might be cluttering up the bar.

The smell of cigar smoke is overpowering as I enter the bar. It's a bit quieter now. Most of the hotel guests have gone to bed, leaving behind the hard core and the too-pissed-to-move-from-their-chairs, and, of course, Mr Masterson and his two prostitutes. He seems to be having a whale of a time, sucking on his Trinidad Diplomatic, feeling up his women, the beaming grin on his face visible right the way across the room. One of the girls has certainly had a bit too much champagne. Her red silk chiffon top is slipping so far off her shoulder it looks like her left breast is going to pop out at any moment. She doesn't seem to notice or care; either that or it's part of her seduction technique.

Gianfranco, Alfredo and Francesco are starting to clear up, wiping down the tables, clearing up behind the bar, chucking away half lemons and limes. Gino is out from behind his bar, leaning forward, his hands clasping the back of a chair, talking 'liquid history' or very expensive drinks with a rather well-oiled-looking gentleman whose flushed cheeks match the colour of his socks. Even from here I can tell that Gino is going in for the kill. It's the pseudo-relaxed pose and the terrible jolly smile that give him away. It's only a matter of time before I hear the suggestion that he try the £750-a-shot Napoleon cognac.

'Seven hundred and fifty pounds!' the man splutters. 'It'd better be amazing at that price.'

'How about you, Mr Masterson?' asks Gino, coming across the room, standing equidistant between the two of them. 'Would you like to try a shot? It seems a shame to go down to the cellar and bring out this piece of history if I have only one taker.'

'What?' asks Mr Masterson.

'Would you like to try some of my extra-special Napoleon cognac from 1796?'

'Oh, right, too right I do,' says Mr Masterson, slapping someone else's thigh. 'I remember that from last time. Isn't it over a thousand dollars a shot?'

'That's the one,' says Gino.

'Fabulous,' says Mr Masterson. 'Would my guests like to try some?' he asks the girls.

'Maybe just a bit,' purrs one of them.

'Three glasses,' says Mr Masterson. 'And make them doubles.'

'Right away, Mr Masterson,' says Gino.

He turns around and indicates that Gianfranco should get his arse down to the cellar as quickly as possible. He catches my eye and pretends to ignore me. I know there is no point in bothering Gino when he is in this mood. He's like some sort of tantric snake, luring them in with his hypnotic chatter about history and luxury and the days of yore. I've seen him do this so many times before.

The bottle arrives, and Gino puts it in a special protective basket. He then brings it to the table, blows off the non-existent dust, gently caresses the bottle with his hand and launches into a speech that starts with all the things that have been invented since this cognac was first made and finishes in the year of Catherine the Great's demise. The Americans love it. Gino's final piece of information is the population of America at the time it was made, which always sends them into the stratosphere.

I know for certain that I'm not going to get my shot of vodka at this precise moment, so I may as well go back to reception and bide my time. I still have a long night ahead of me.

Dennis is back on his mobile when I arrive. The reception telephone is ringing.

'Hello, reception,' I say.

'Hello,' comes an irritated and tired voice. 'I can't sleep.'

'I'm sorry to hear that, sir,' I reply, thinking that makes two of us.

'There's a party going on in the next-door room,' he continues. 'Will you sort it out?'

'I'll send someone up right away, sir.'

This happens all the time. Guests book a suite, and before you know it other guests start arriving and you have a party on your hands. I'd thought there were a few too many people going up to 450 but I figured if they don't make that much noise it's not doing anyone any harm. Sadly, it seems I am wrong.

But before I get Dennis off his mobile phone, I make a quick call down to room service just to make sure they're not ordering a fortune's worth of stuff, because believe you me, it makes a difference.

We had a just-married couple who turned up at the Lanesborough, supposedly to start their honeymoon. They had a huge suite, and without telling the hotel they actually had their wedding reception in the room. They had sixty guests and ordered via room service twenty-four bottles of Taittinger (at £49.50 a bottle) and some canapés. It was a full-blown party that went on till five a.m. There were complaints flying in from all over the hotel, but we chose to ignore them. Room service said that as they were ordering so much we should let them carry on, so in the end we moved a couple of people to different rooms and sent them up earplugs. We were as happy as pigs in the proverbial, as we were making a fortune. It's that age-old hotel motto: the more money you spend, the more you can get away with.

Celebrities do it all the time. I suppose if you spend most of your life in hotels then you do end up treating them as a sort of home from home, which is how a lot of the smaller townhouse hotels I've worked in market themselves anyway.

I remember one night at the Covent Garden Hotel when Johnny Depp and Kate Moss had obviously had one of those 'all back to mine' conversations with a whole group of their friends. They'd booked the best suite in the hotel, an amazing room, a massive loft split over two levels. It is stunning. The bed is on the gallery and it overlooks a sitting room/dining room area with fat sofas, so it's comfortable as well as quite stylish. It costs £1,100 a night (including VAT). Anyway, they booked it for a Friday night. They ordered thirty-six bottles of Krug, which of course the hotel didn't have enough of. We went crazy trying to get hold of all this Krug from any open bar, club or hotel all over the West End. They also ordered a whole load of stuff off the room service menu. Slowly but surely all these people began to arrive, and they hosted this fuck-off party that went on all night. They spent a ridiculous amount and ended up with something like a £12,000 bill. It was crazy.

Although judging by Miss Moss's recent thirtieth birthday celebrations at Claridge's in a £4,000-a-night suite, perhaps it was a little tame. That bash seems to have set her back some £20,000, and she drank a loucher Louis Roederer Cristal champagne (the 1994 version goes for £250 a bottle). Guests apparently partied till dawn, Sadie Frost inadvertently showed her bosom to the press, and there were rumours that it descended into a rather wild party.

Unfortunately, this lot in room 450 have only ordered up three bottles of Moët, which is hardly going to keep any of us in any style. So I finally manage to get Dennis off his bloody phone and tell him to get them to keep it down, otherwise we'll throw all of their guests out of the hotel. Dennis agrees and doesn't seem to mind going back upstairs. I suspect he is hoping to find his couple having sex somewhere indiscreet again. Instead, he is down and back in a jiffy.

'Piece of piss.' He sniffs as he walks across reception.

'As soon as I knocked on their door, they shut up. They're a bunch of kids out on Daddy's credit card. They won't cause us any trouble. In fact, after the drama of the first half of the night, I think we're going to be in for a quiet one. I can feel it in my bones.'

Just as Dennis wanders back to his desk, a man in a Prince of Wales check suit zigzags his way through the door towards the desk. 'Looks like I spoke too soon,' says Dennis, with a wink. 'Incoming!' he adds, his hand cupped around his mouth.

'Good evening, can I help you, sir?' I say as the man leans on reception for support.

'The name's Jones, and I have forgotten my room number,' he says. His breath is toxic with alcohol.

'OK, sir.' I smile. This is not a rare occurrence. 'I'll check the computer.'

Mr Jones slumps over the desk. His eyes are red, his suit smells of cigars, his skin is sweating alcohol; he must have been out at some club. I run his name through the computer and come up with nothing.

'You don't seem to be checked in, sir,' I say.

'What?' says Mr Jones, jerking himself awake with a sudden head movement.

'You don't seem to be checked in,' I repeat.

'Of course I'm checked in,' he slurs.

'Well, not according to the computer.'

'Well, look again.'

'I will, sir,' I say. 'But there really isn't any point.'

'What do you mean, there isn't any point? Of course there's a fucking point. I checked in here myself. Six hours ago. Look at the fucking computer again.' Mr Jones is starting to raise his voice and point his finger. The red veins on his nose engorge.

'I was on reception six hours ago, sir, and I'm afraid I do not remember checking you in.'

'I don't care what you *do* or *do not* fucking remember! My name is *Jones*! I am staying here! So give me my fucking *room key*!' Mr Jones is shouting so loud and so close to my face that his acrid breath blow-dries my hair.

'Well, I'm afraid we have no record of you being here,' I say as calmly as I can.

'I don't care if you don't have a *fucking* record of me checking in. I checked in my *fucking* self, *fucking* six hours ago!'

'Are you sure, sir?'

'Are you calling me a *fucking* liar?' He slams his fist on the reception.

Dennis gets out of his chair and starts making his way to reception. For a man who can't stand the sight of blood, he appears foolishly brave.

'Calm down, sir,' he says.

'Calm down?' Mr Jones spins round. 'Who the *fuck* are you?'

'I'm the doorman, sir,' says Dennis.

'Well, you can *fuck off*!' shouts Mr Jones, his hands on his hips. He turns back to face me. Slamming both hands down on reception, he shouts again. 'Give me my *fucking* room.'

'I'm sorry, sir, you don't have a room here,' I explain again.

'I *always* have a *fucking* room at the *fucking* Dorchester!' he yells in my face. 'Every *fucking* month. Almost every time I *fucking* come to London.'

'Well, you may well still have one,' I say. 'Perhaps you should go to the Dorchester and find out.'

'Hm?' says Mr Jones, his body rendered floppy with confusion. 'I'm not at the Dorchester?'

'No, sir,' I say.

'The Dorchester is up the road,' says Dennis, turning Mr Jones gently in the direction of the revolving doors.

'Good,' announces Mr Jones defiantly, on his way out. 'I'm glad, because I'd never stay in this place. It's a fucking *shit hole*!'

'Right you are, Mr Jones,' says Dennis, helping the door revolve. 'Fuck off,' he mutters at the glass, with a little polite wave.

2 AM – 3 AM

Dennis is still doing his little polite wave when the Sheikh comes back into the hotel with a group of about six Gulf guys. They all look somewhat confused by Dennis's greeting, but they swan off in the direction of the bar, their white robes and headdresses flowing on after them.

I smile, wondering how Gino will cope with this. It is quite late for him – he usually likes to be off home at around this time – but the arrival of seven blokes from the oil-rich Gulf states is surely enough to make him put his coat back on the hook and line up his most expensive spirits. Having said that, he may well still be busy as I'm sure I haven't seen Mr Masterson leave the bar with his two prostitutes yet.

'Who are all those guys?' asks Dennis as he sits back

down at Tony's desk and starts playing with the drawers.

'No idea,' I say.

'D'you think they're his mates?'

'No. They didn't look very matey.'

'Businessmen?'

'Possibly.'

'They're always doing business at odd hours, those guys. Their body clocks are wrong,' says Dennis, picking fluff off his own suit. 'They get up at tea time, they eat cream teas for breakfast, they order dinner at three a.m. They're mad.'

He's right. Come August, all the luxury hotels in London are full to the brim with guys from the Gulf states. It's too hot in the Middle East in the summer, so the super-affluent move into the Lanesborough, the Dorchester or the Savoy for the month, taking over suites and sometimes even whole floors. In fact, some places are so keen to keep their Arab clientele happy that they provide indoor barbecue kits for the rooms as well as Arabic room service, where you can order a whole baby lamb. Because the Arabs do like their midnight feasts.

Talking of which, I remember once when I was on nights at another hotel and one of the £2,500 suites rang up for water, or something like that. So I went up with my tray, knocked on the door and walked into the suite to find a dead sheep lying in the middle of the room. It had just been butchered, and there was blood all over the floor and the bathroom walls; the bath was full of blood where they had slit its throat. It was such a horrible and confusing sight that for a second I didn't know if they were going to fuck it or eat it. But I presumed they were going to skin it and eat it. It was all very disturbing. Either way, I didn't hang around to find out. And it wasn't a one-off. Talking to mates in the industry, I heard of more dead sheep in other hotel suites, including the Four Seasons. One thing I have always wondered is how they ever get the sheep in the room in the first place. You would have thought you'd notice a sheep trotting through reception on its way towards the lift, but apparently not. Of all the dead sheep stories I have heard, never once were they spotted coming into the hotel in the first place. It is surely one of life's great mysteries.

'What are you doing?' asks Dennis.

'Nothing,' I say, putting three mints into my mouth at once. And I don't even like mints.

God, I'm bored. And another thing apart from the boredom of the job – the loneliness of it all. If only my girlfriend hadn't dumped me because I was doing too many night shifts, I might give her a call around now. I used to enjoy doing that when we were going out. She'd talk to me in her sleep and forget that we'd ever had a conversation at all the next day. I used to find it amusing. I could tell her things I knew she would never remember. But she got pissed off about being stood up at the last minute all the time. I don't blame her really. I wouldn't put up with it if it weren't my job. So instead I'm sitting here with no-one to call, wondering if I should take another pill. Will it keep me awake, or will it just make my heart race? My eyelids already feel like they've been stapled to the back of my head. I'm a lab-rat experiment for sleep deprivation. The hazards of doing nights are caffeine addiction and lack of sunlight. It's no wonder we all look so goddamn pale.

Dennis is back on his phone again, banging on to another one of his cousins who runs the door at another luxury hotel in town. They're sharing anecdotes, and from the few titbits I can pick up from over here, while obviously pretending not to listen, it seems they've got some showbiz bash on in their ball-room; soap stars and some singers from one of those fake reality TV bands are apparently swanning around like they own the place. Dennis's cousin has just had to stop some bloke from pissing into a plant pot. Dennis is laughing like he's never done that before in his life.

It always amazes me how often guests seem to forget they are staying in a hotel and start treating the place like their own. Not that people piss in plant pots at home, but it is odd how some guests have no respect for the hotel's property at all. It's almost as if they've paid their money, they can do what they want. At one place I worked, they were always breaking into the swimming pool for late-night swims. What did used to make the staff laugh was that they always thought they were being so incredibly original. They'd start up the jacuzzis, take all their clothes off and have their own private pool parties. They'd have orgies and group sex parties in the hot tubs, and all along they'd think they were wild and wacky and fabulous. Like no-one's ever been there and done that before.

Then again, there are a few people who are a little different. I remember one time when Pamela Anderson and Tommy Lee were ingenious, to say the least. They broke into the gym at the Lanesborough, had sex on the exercise bike and went on to use all the other pieces of gym equipment in a manner they were not really designed for. However, unfortunately for them, they were being filmed by the security cameras through the two-way mirror. There to protect the expensive gym equipment from theft, they also recorded every single athletic move for the delight and delectation of the staff the next day.

'I think I might go and check on Gino,' I say, finally swallowing my mints.

'What?' says Dennis, putting his hand over the telephone.

'I think I might go and check on Gino.'

'Fair enough,' says Dennis. 'I'm going to send Patrick off on tramp watch.'

'Oh, good idea,' I say, leaning around the corner to see Patrick looking rather sleepy on his shiny brass trolley. 'He looks like he is about to nod off.'

'Oi, Patrick!' barks Dennis. The boy flinches. 'Get your arse up and check the hotel for tramps, drunks or both.' Patrick is up and off before anyone can say 'you're fired' and he jogs up the first flight of stairs like his balls are on fire. 'Keep an eye out for shaggers in the honour bar!' Dennis yells after him, before returning to his telephone call. 'Sorry about that, mate,' he says. 'What? Didn't I tell you? Going at it like hammer and tongs they were. I saw her arse and everything . . .'

Back in the bar, and the place is thick with cigar smoke. It seems that everyone left in the place is sucking on a Monte Cristo of varying length and thickness. Gianfranco, Alfredo and Francesco look exhausted. Their faces are white, their eyes red-rimmed and their skin looks tacky with old beads of sweat. They are leaning on the bar, their coats tucked under the shelf, waiting for the signal to go home. Around them the bar is immaculate: every glass shines in its place and every silver cocktail shaker is washed, dismembered and laid out to dry on a tea towel. Only Gino is still working the bar for all he's worth. He hands out smiles and bonhomie to anyone who still wants to spend a lot of money on alcohol.

Mr Masterson finally decides to call it a night. He gets unsteadily to his feet, using both his prostitutes for support.

'Gino!' he says, throwing a large hand in the air. 'Come over here, my good man.'

'Yes, Mr Masterson,' says Gino. 'Would you like anything else?'

'I think I've had quite a lot already, Gino, don't you?' He chuckles. Gino joins in. 'Here,' he says, handing over £100. 'Get something nice for your wife.'

'Thank you, Mr Masterson, very kind of you.'

The bar boys snigger. Gino is no closer to having a wife than Victoria Beckham is to having a square meal. Only Mr Masterson doesn't seem to have noticed.

'Excellent,' he says as he weaves his way towards the exit. 'Goodnight, guys,' he says to the Sheikh and his white-robed entourage. They mumble something incomprehensible in return. As he stumbles on towards the bar, he scrabbles about in his pockets, pulls out a wad of cash and proceeds to slip £50 notes into the top pockets of Francesco, Alfredo and Gianfranco's jackets. That brings a bit of colour back to their cheeks. He does the same to me, just because I am standing by the door. I think about saying something, but my earlier smug attitude towards his money has well and truly faded along with the daylight. If the man is drunk and wants to hand out his cash, who am I to argue? So I smile and say thank you, along with the rest of them.

The prostitutes, however, look less than thrilled. The man is clearly too drunk to do it, so it doesn't look like either of them is going to make a full whack tonight. Their date's ability to throw his money about in every direction other than theirs is also clearly getting up their noses.

'Come along now, Mr Masterson,' says one of them. 'One step in front of the other.'

'I am quite capable of walking, woman,' he snaps. 'There is plenty of lead in my pencil yet,' he announces, knowledgeably tapping the side of his nose. 'Thanks to the joys of Viagra.' He laughs, and slaps the other prostitute on the arse. She hoots with delight. 'Now,' he says, grinding to a halt in the corridor. 'Eeny . . . meenie . . . minie . . . mo.' A rather red finger goes back and forth. 'You!' he declares, falling forward a step. 'You're the lucky one.' He hands over a fistful of money to one of the girls without even looking her in the eye. 'Goodnight,' he adds, bowing slightly. The rejected, dark-haired prostitute strops off along the corridor, her high-heeled shoes slapping the marble as she goes. The other girl giggles conspiratorially, takes hold of the drunk's red hand and takes him off in the direction of the lift.

I sigh. The scene depresses me. It's not like I haven't seen it before, or that I won't ever see it again, but somehow tonight it makes me feel down. Maybe it just makes me think – or perhaps, more honestly, it reminds me – that we are all prostitutes in the luxury hotel business. We spend our whole lives fawning around, being nice to arseholes, especially rich arseholes, in the hope that they'll give us a tip. Then again, I think as I feel my top pocket, £50 is £50. It's a hell of a lot more than those guys make downstairs.

Gino gives the bar boys the signal to say that they can go home; he only has the Sheikh's table to deal with and it doesn't seem fair to keep them all on. Anyway, the Sheikh is not being particularly demanding. He is playing cards and slowly working his way through a bottle of 1919 Dalwhinnie whisky with his pals, smoking £175 Davidoff No. 1 Cuban cigars. Gino seems happy: it's all so reassuringly expensive.

Gianfranco, Francesco and Alfredo file out of the bar. I follow them.

'Jesus fuck,' says Gianfranco, stretching his arms in the air as he walks out of earshot. 'That was a bloody shit of a day. I mean, *figlio di putà*.' He shakes his head. 'That stock-taking man.'

'I know.' Alfredo nods. 'Bastard.'

'Who wants a drink?' asks Francesco.

289

'God, I'd love one,' I say, 'but I'm afraid I'm on till seven a.m.'

'You poor bastard,' says Alfredo, putting his arm around my shoulder as we all walk through the glass doors into reception. 'Well,' he adds with a smile, pulling something out from underneath his jacket, 'your need is greater than ours.' He hands me a half-full bottle of tonic water.

'What's that?' I ask.

'Vodka,' he smiles. 'It's a little something I managed to get earlier.'

'Thank you,' I say, trying to hand it back, 'but it's yours.'

'No, man, don't worry,' he says, pushing the bottle back towards me. 'Thanks to Mr American man we can all drink well tonight.'

'Who wants to go to Hombres?' asks Francesco, clearly desperate to let off steam.

'I'm knackered,' Gianfranco replies.

'We're all knackered,' says Francesco. 'Come on! It's only Oxford Street.'

'OK,' says Gianfranco. 'One drink.'

'One drink?' says Alfredo. 'What the fuck is the point of one drink? You may as well have two.'

'OK, two drinks, then,' says Gianfranco.

'Two drinks?' laughs Alfredo. 'What's the point of two . . .'

And the three of them disappear off into the night, leaving me standing in reception with half a bottle of vodka and Dennis still talking on his mobile phone.

I take the bottle into the back office and find a couple of old coffee mugs. Neither of them appears to be too dirty, so I pour some of the warm spirit into each of the mugs. I know I don't have to give Dennis any, but I also know that if he had any alcohol on him he'd do the same for me. I take Dennis over his mug of vodka and he hangs up.

'What's this?' he asks, giving the mug a sniff.

'Vodka,' I say.

'Doesn't smell like it.'

'That's because it's in a coffee mug.'

'Oh, right. Cheers!' he says, downing the whole thing in one. 'Oh!' He sniffs. 'That's much better.' He smiles. 'Thanks, mate.'

'Don't thank me,' I say. 'It was Alfredo.'

'I've always liked those wops behind the bar,' he says. 'Good blokes, all of them.'

'Yeah,' I say, giving my mug a sniff.

'It's better down in one,' he says. 'There's a bit of a coffee aftertaste.'

'Right,' I say, knocking it back. 'You're right. Tastes of Mellow Birds.'

'I hate that coffee,' says Dennis.

'So do I.' I cough. My eyes are watering, but my

throat feels warm and so does my stomach. 'I think I'd better have a look around downstairs, don't you?' I say, feeling suitably fortified.

'Yeah,' agrees Dennis. 'Where's that little shit Patrick? He better not have found somewhere to doss down, the little bastard, otherwise he'll be out on his ear in the morning.'

'I'll keep an eye out,' I say.

'See you in a bit,' he says. 'And thanks for the vodka.'

'Pleasure,' I say.

As I walk back down the stairs and into the depths of the kitchen, I have to admit to being a little scared. There's not much light down here and there is almost no noise. I open each fire door with slightly more trepidation than the last, eventually reaching the kitchen door. It's weird to see the place so quiet. I say hello to the one guy who is still bleaching the kitchen floor; he doesn't reply. I think him a little rude, but it's not until he turns his back entirely to me that I see he is wearing a Walkman.

I walk on. The staff toilets are already clean. The grim, rust-stained bowls are dripping with bright blue liquid, and the bins have been emptied. There are a couple of men sitting and smoking in the staff room, but they stand up and stub out their cigarettes as soon as I walk in. I smile and say good evening, but no-one bothers to respond. They file past and get back to work. After they've gone I check the lockers to see if anyone is asleep. Nothing. I go back and check the storerooms at the back of the kitchen. It's another favourite haunt for slackers. But I suppose word has got out that I'm about and anyone who might have been dossing down is long gone. I'm too tired to check out any of the more out-of-the-way places. The idea of wandering about in the dark trying to catch people out really does not appeal, particularly at this hour of the morning. So I go back upstairs to reception.

'Nothing to report,' I say to Dennis, who is reading one of Tony's pamphlets like he's never seen the thing before.

'Mmm,' he says. 'All quiet here too.'

Patrick finally wanders back down the main stairs. His steps are heavy and he is looking a little drained. 'I have been along every corridor and looked in every doorway and I haven't seen anyone,' he says, sounding exhausted.

'Oh, right,' says Dennis, whose own tramp tour of the hotel takes about ten minutes, and that's including a toilet break near the honour bar. 'Very good,' he says. 'Do you want to go and get yourself some coffee from downstairs? Sounds like you need it.'

'Thank you very much,' says Patrick, and he shuffles off downstairs.

Dennis and I are left in silence. The hotel is quiet.

Occasionally we hear a short volley of male laughter coming from the bar. It's hard to believe that Gino is still in there, serving away, smiling like a maniac with his knife caught in the toaster. Dennis starts to chuckle.

'What?' I say.

'What?' he says right back.

'You started to laugh.'

'I did?'

'Yeah. What were you thinking about?'

'Oh, God.' He smiles. 'That bloke from last week. Do you remember the guy who was so drunk that I had to help him up the stairs?'

'Oh yeah,' I say. 'I remember you telling me about it.'

Poor Dennis almost had to carry a bloke upstairs he was so pissed. Once up in his room, it was apparently chaos. The drunk bloke bent down to take his shoes off, lost his balance and tried to grab hold of the curtain as he fell straight through the French windows and out onto the balcony. The doors shattered, and the curtain rail came down on top of him.

'It was a nightmare,' recalls Dennis with a chuckle. 'The hotel was full and there was nowhere to put him. D'you remember?' I nod and laugh at the same time. 'The guest was fine,' he continues. 'He was lying on the balcony crying with laughter. He thought it was the funniest thing that had ever happened. The room was fucked. The guest didn't care. In fact, he couldn't even speak. He just wanted to go to bed. So in the end we put the curtain rail back up and closed the curtains, and dealt with it the next morning.'

'I remember.' I smile. 'Adrian was bloody furious.'

'Yeah. I bet he ordered a new set of curtains as well as some new French windows on the bloke's bill.'

'You can be sure of that.'

'Yeah.'

'Are you all right there on your own for a moment, Dennis?' I ask, standing up.

'Yeah,' he says, looking at his watch. 'The worst of it should be over by now. It's Nutter Hour next.' He smiles. 'All we need is Dressing Gown Bloke to come down the stairs.'

'Yeah.' I laugh and turn to go to the downstairs toilet. I look up, and my heart sinks. I can see a man in a dressing gown slowly padding down the stairs.

'Oh, hello there,' he says. 'I'm afraid I couldn't sleep. I thought I might come downstairs and join you . . . for a bit of a chat.'

3AM – 4AM

There's nothing that ruins a night shift more than the arrival of a Dressing Gown Man. They are the bane of any sane receptionist's life. They plod down the stairs when you are at your most tired, and often when you least expect it. They then sit there in their bloody slippers and talk you through their turgid lives. I've heard more life stories at three in the morning than any bloody shrink – and at least they get paid to listen to people prattle on about their boring problems, their terrible childhoods, their sticky divorces and their difficult teenage children. I've done it so many times now that I should really consider starting a counselling service.

'Good evening, sir,' I say, when what I really mean is fuck off. 'Can I get you anything? A drink from the bar? The cocktail bar is probably about to close but the honour bar is open.'

'Oh, no,' says Dressing Gown Man, all pious and abstemious. 'I just thought I might sit here for a while, you know, seeing as I can't sleep.'

'Right.' I smile, jaw clamped tight. 'Well, I'm just off to the toilet, but I'm sure Dennis will entertain you.'

'Dennis?' says the man, turning towards Dennis.

'Yes, that's right,' says Dennis, standing up and giving me a discreet finger with his left hand under the desk.

'Good,' says Dressing Gown Man, sitting down on the yellow chintz sofa next to Dennis's desk. He sits back and crosses his legs, giving me a quick flash of his bollocks as he does so. I do wish people would put underpants on when they come down to bore us with their insomnia. 'Well, I'm Terence, but my good friends call me Terry.'

'Right, Terence,' says Dennis. 'How long are you staying with us, then?'

'Oh, I've been here a couple of nights already.'

'Oh. Did you manage to sleep all right the other nights?' Dennis asks this in such a way that if you didn't know him any better you'd think he actually cared.

'Last night was all right,' shares Terence, 'but I have to admit that Wednesday night I was tossing and turning a bit.'

'Oh, dreadful,' says Dennis. 'There is nothing worse, is there, than tossing all night, in bed, on yer own?'

I snort, and bite the skin between my thumb and forefinger to stop myself from laughing. I decide it is better to leave the lobby quick sharp, before I collapse into a fit of laughter and take Dennis down with me. As soon as I am through the glass doors I let out a howl, and walk off giggling to myself.

Downstairs, the staff urinals, despite being recently cleaned, are as unsavoury as usual. There's a constant dripping of some tap, or cistern, that no-one ever remembers to repair, accompanied by a cloying smell of urine, damp and old cigarettes. There's water and possibly piss all over the floor as well as graffiti in about seven different languages, which I presume all say something like 'Hell', or 'Get me the hell out of here'. It is not the sort of place you want to dawdle in. I can't face using one of the urinals so I open one of the cubicle doors whose locks have never worked since I have been here. I find one of the cleaners sitting down in there, his head leaning against the wall, fast asleep. He's wearing a pair of bright yellow rubber gloves and he's carrying a J-cloth, both of which are sitting neatly on his lap. He is dark-skinned, but perhaps a little pale to be a Bangladeshi. If I lean in and listen above the dripping water, I can hear him snoring. He looks relaxed. His mouth curls upwards underneath his moustache. I cough. He wakes with such a start that he leaps off the toilet seat, dropping his J-cloth on the floor.

'Oh my God, oh my God, oh my God,' he repeats, panic-stricken, like I'm about to hit him or fire him, I can't work out which. 'Please sir, please sir,' he begs, his yellow hands flapping.

'Calm down,' I say, stepping back out of the cubicle. 'Calm down, mate. I only wanted a pee.'

'Sorry, sorry,' he says, looking and sounding confused. I'm not sure if he can understand English.

'I only wanted to use the toilet,' I say very slowly.

'I understand you,' he says, equally slowly.

'You do?'

'Yes, sir.'

'There really is no need to call me sir,' I say.

'OK, sir,' he says.

'Where are you from?'

'Iraq.'

'Oh.'

'I'm from the north.'

'Oh,' I say again as I look him up and down. 'How long have you been here?'

'In the hotel?'

'Yes.'

'Three months. But I work days in another hotel in Bayswater.'

'Oh, right.'

'It is a three star,' he adds.

'Right.' I nod. 'How long have you been in the UK?'

'Eighteen months. I was a doctor before.'

'A doctor,' I say, sounding surprised.

'Yes.' He nods. 'But now I clean and change beds. I'm not complaining,' he adds quickly.

'Yes, well, I'm sure not.'

'No,' he confirms.

'Good.' I smile. 'Not long to go now till the end of your shift.'

'No,' he says.

'Then back home to your wife.'

'She's still in Iraq.'

'Oh.'

'Goodnight,' he says as he walks past me and out the door.

'Good evening,' I say, 'um . . .' And then I stop as I realize I didn't catch his name.

Halfway back upstairs and I can sense that Dennis is about to keel over with boredom. I can hear the monotone of Terence's voice, punctuated by Dennis's curt responses: 'Really? . . . Really? . . . Is that right? . . . Really?' I can't believe Terence actually thinks he's listening.

'Ah ha,' Dennis says as I come through the doors, 'there you are!' He gets out of his chair, relief writ large all over his face. 'I think I'd better pop off to the toilet myself.'

'Oh, oh, right,' says Terence. 'Take as long as you want, Dennis.' He pats the yellow chintz sofa. 'I'm not going anywhere.'

'Oh, right,' says Dennis as he walks towards me. 'You shit,' he whispers quietly in my ear as he goes.

'All right there, Terence?' I say as I go back behind the desk.

'Oh, fine,' he says, mincing his buttocks into the sofa cushions. 'He's very nice, your doorman.'

'Yeah,' I say. 'He's been with us for years.'

'So he said.'

'Good.' I look down at the desk like I'm very busy indeed.

Just as Terence inhales, ready to strike up another conversation, the Sheikh comes into reception, accompanied by his card-playing entourage. Their arrival through the glass doors finally makes Terence put a sock in it. The Sheikh kisses each and every one of his friends/colleagues/employees on both cheeks and escorts them to the front of the hotel. Patrick rushes forward and opens the door. The Sheikh waves them goodbye and hands Patrick a £10 note before turning to walk back towards the lift.

'Goodnight, sir,' I say as he walks past.

'Goodnight,' he replies.

'I hope you had a good evening.'

'Very pleasant,' he says, getting into the lift. 'A nice early night.' He smiles and looks at his gold watch.

'Sleep well,' I say as the doors close.

Before Terence can pick up his conversational baton once more and launch into 101 questions about who the Sheikh is, where he comes from and how long he's here for – which I can see he is itching to do, and I mean that quite literally – my telephone goes.

'Hello, reception.'

'Oh, hello,' comes a very chirpy voice. 'I'm terribly sorry to bother you . . .' he starts.

'Yes?'

'But I have stayed in your hotel before . . .'

'Yes?'

'And I was wondering if you could help me.'

'Um, if I can, I will,' I say, wondering where this conversation is going.

'Good,' he says. 'Right. I've got this corn on the cob and I was wondering how I should cook it.'

'I'm sorry?'

'Well, I've got this corn on the cob, and I was wondering how I should cook it,' he repeats.

'Corn on the cob?'

'Yeah, that's right, corn on the cob.'

'Oh,' I say.

'I mean, should I pan fry it? People are doing a lot of that these days, aren't they?'

'Sorry,' I say. 'When did you say that you stayed here?'

'Oh, right,' says the man. 'God.' He exhales loudly. 'That would be a couple of years ago now. I took my wife away for the weekend. We're divorced now. Hence the call, I suppose.'

'Oh, right,' I say. 'Well, I wouldn't pan fry it.'

'You wouldn't?'

'No. I'm afraid I'm a bit traditional when it comes to corn on the cob. I'd boil it, cover it in butter and pepper and eat it with my fingers.'

Terence is looking at me like I have gone mad. Even Patrick is managing to look quizzical through his fatigue.

'Interesting,' says the man, sounding impressed. 'That sounds like a very good idea.'

'Thank you.'

'No, thank *you*,' he says. 'You've helped me no end.'

'Good. Just as a matter of interest, you sound a bit far away, where are you calling from?'

'New York,' he says. 'Good evening, and thanks.'

'Good evening,' I say, hanging up.

'That sounds like a weird phone call,' says Terence.

'Not really,' I say, looking down at my desk again. I'm not actually lying. We get the odd culinary telephone call every now and then from guests past. However, they are usually ringing up to ask about some dish that was made in the kitchen here that they are trying to re-create. Gino also gets an awful lot of cocktail calls – people, drunk and sober, asking him how to make a chocatini or a raspberry martini. We've even had other restaurants call up and say they have a table of six demanding White Russians or something, the way we make them here – could we give them the recipe? More often than not we tell them where to get off – if they want one of our White Russians they should come here – but everyone else we try to help. Even the mad hostesses who ring up during their own dinner parties and ask for the recipe for a béchamel sauce or a champagne sabayon. I have talked so many not so domestic goddesses through making hollandaise sauce I could make it in my sleep. But it is all part of the service. Making people feel part of the hotel family.

Gino comes through the glass doors, navy coat on, cashmere scarf wrapped around his neck. He does his fake-stagger exhausted walk towards the front desk and flops his head forward.

'Good night?' I ask.

'Exhausting,' he says.

'Oh well,' I say.

'But . . .' He lifts his face and a triumphant smile beams from it. 'But I made over eight hundred in tips and managed to shift one bottle of that 1919 Dalwhinnie and half a bottle of the 1796 Napoleon cognac.'

'Jesus,' I say.

'No,' he replies, 'Mr Masterson, the Sheikh and his friends from the Gulf.'

'Well, you'll sleep well tonight.'

'Well, I was going to have a couple of drinks to celebrate. Do you know where the others have gone?'

'Oh, shit,' I say. 'I'm sorry, I wasn't listening. Hombres or Samantha's.'

'At least I shall enjoy looking.' He grins. 'Goodnight,' he adds, pulling his collar up. 'See you tomorrow.'

'I hope not,' I say.

'See you anyway,' he says, heading for the door.

Dennis comes in through the glass doors and Terence shifts expectantly in his seat.

'Back so soon,' I say.

'Yeah, well,' sniffs Dennis, 'I thought I'd check the kitchen for kippers while I was down there and I found three of them asleep in the store cupboards at the back,' he says. 'Scared the life out of them, I did. I told them to get some coffee and get back to work. You still here, Terence?'

'Oh yes,' says Terence. 'Don't think I'll sleep for a little while yet.'

Dennis sits back down at his desk and takes out some folder that has Tony's theatre tickets in it. He picks up a pen and makes as if he is very busy. Terence's gaze wanders around the lobby, looking up at the enormous chandelier and over at the various pot plants we have dotted around the place. He looks over at my desk, checking out the tropical flower arrangement.

'Those are fairly amazing,' he says. 'I wonder where—'

Thankfully, my telephone rings. I put my hand in the air. 'I'm sorry,' I mouth, 'I have to take this. Reception?'

'Oh, hello,' comes this very quiet female voice. 'You've got to help me.'

'Of course, madam,' I whisper back. 'What can I do?'

'There's a man outside my room,' she says. 'He's knocking on my door. I think he wants to break in.'

'Don't answer the door,' I say.

'I have no intention of doing that,' she hisses. 'But will you send someone up? Get the police, anyone. Make him go away.'

'Right, madam, absolutely,' I say. 'I'm on my way.'

'Hurry up,' she says. 'Please. Room 306.'

'I'm on my way.' I put down the phone. 'I'm sorry,' I tell Terence. 'There's a bit of an emergency on the third floor. Dennis,' I say as I leap out from behind the desk, 'some woman is saying there's a pervert outside her bedroom door, so I'm going up.'

'OK,' he says. 'Do you want me to come as well?'

'I'll call you if I need you.'

'OK,' he says as I rush through the glass doors and sprint up the front stairs. It's so much quicker than waiting for the lift.

Six flights of stairs later I arrive on the third floor, completely out of breath. I must stop smoking, I think, as I walk along the corridor towards room 306. You can't fight perverts if you're knackered when you get there. It's quite dark walking along these corridors late at night. All the hall lights have been turned down so that bright lights don't seep under guests' doors. My imagination is working overtime. I have an image of this huge hairy bloke dressed in black and wearing leather driving gloves waiting for me. Instead, as I turn the corner, I'm greeted by a sight that could only be described as a slightly larger version of Gollum from *Lord of the Rings*.

'Jesus,' I say as I see him.

'Oh, thank God,' says the small, naked man, frantically trying to cover his genitals with his hands. 'Thank God you are here,' he says again, his large eyes imploring me. 'I've locked myself out of my room and I can't get back in.'

'Sorry?' I say. I have to admit that I am a little stunned. This small, naked man is not what I was expecting.

'I got up in the middle of the night for a pee, I walked out the wrong door, and before I realized my mistake the door closed behind me. And now, no matter how hard I knock, my wife won't wake up.'

'Oh, right,' I say, the whole situation making itself clear. 'What's your room number?'

'308,' he says.

'I'm afraid, sir, you have been knocking on the wrong door, which might explain why your wife would not wake up. You see, you have been frightening the lady who is sleeping next door to you.'

'Oh Lord,' he says. One of his hands reaches for his mouth. He immediately regrets it. 'Oh Lord, what a business.'

'Don't worry, sir,' I say, reaching for my passcard. 'You get to bed, sir, and I'll explain the situation to the lady next door.'

I let him into his bedroom and try to talk to the woman next door. It's a good three minutes before she will open her door. And when she does, the poor thing is so distressed that she bursts into tears and puts her arms around me. It transpires that the naked man has been knocking on her door for the last half an hour and she has been getting more and more frightened and increasingly desperate. I tell her that if anything worries her again she should call immediately; I then suggest she gets herself a brandy from the mini bar to help her unwind a little more. She smiles. I think she thinks she now looks a little foolish, but you can hardly blame her for panicking.

Back downstairs, Dennis is still talking to Terence. No amount of pretending to look busy is going to put this man off his chatting.

'All right, then?' asks Dennis as I come out of the lift.

'Fine,' I say. 'The pervert turns out to be a naked man locked out of his room.'

'Oh, right,' says Dennis. 'One of those.'

'Except,' I add, 'he was knocking on the wrong door, trying to get in.'

'Shit,' says Dennis. 'I bet that scared the living daylights out of the person next door.'

'Yeah,' I say. 'She was a little shaken up.'

'I bet that sort of thing happens all the time,' says Terence with a laugh.

'No, not really,' says Dennis. 'That sort of thing is actually quite rare.'

'Oh,' says Terence. 'How very interesting.'

'Mmm,' says Dennis, picking up a booklet on walking in the Peak District.

Terence gets out of his seat and smooths down his dressing gown. Dennis is looking at him out of the corner of his eye, his body tensing with expectation as Terence moves in the direction of the stairs. I'm watching him as well. I can sense that we are both willing him to go upstairs, desperate for him to fuck off and leave us in peace. Terence has his hands in his pockets as he looks one of the pot plants up and down. He is moving closer to the stairs. Go on! Go on! Off you go! Neither Dennis nor I is really breathing, fearful that our very movement might peak his interest and bring him back down to our end of reception again. Then Patrick moves. The twat.

'Would any of you mind if I go and get myself a cup of coffee from downstairs?' he asks.

'No,' says Dennis, his head lolling to one side.

'Oh, coffee,' says Terence, turning round and rubbing his hands together. 'That sounds like a good idea.'

'I'm afraid it's only staff coffee, for members of the staff,' says Dennis quickly.

'Oh,' says Terence, sounding disappointed.

'It doesn't taste very nice,' adds Dennis, in an attempt to sound polite. 'If you do want some coffee, you'll have to go back to your room, order it from room service and take it up there.'

'Yes,' I add, somewhat unconsciously. 'Go back to your room and have it there.'

'Oh, I don't think I fancy it that much after all,' says Terence, sitting back down on his sofa. 'It might stop me from going back to sleep.'

My telephone goes again, and for some reason I think it must be the weeping woman from number 306.

'Are you all right?' I ask immediately without thinking.

'Not really,' says a male voice.

'Oh, I'm sorry,' I say. 'I thought you were someone else.'

'I can be someone else if you want,' he says.

'No, don't worry. How can I help you?'

'Oh,' he says, 'you can really help me.'

'Good.'

'Oh, in fact, you could really, really help me.'

'Sir?'

'Mmm?' I think I can hear the sound of him wanking in the background. 'Would you come up here and finish me off?' he asks.

'What?'

'Come up and blow me,' he says.

'No, sir, I don't think I can.'

'I'll pay you.'

'No.'

'Please.'

'No, sir, I'm afraid that is not possible.'

'Please.'

'No.'

'Is there anyone else in the hotel who would blow me for money?'

'No, sir,' I say, 'and I'm afraid I am going to have to put the phone down right now.'

4 AM – 5 AM

Perverts are always calling up in the middle of the night asking for blowjobs or full sex. It is one of the hazards of doing the late shift that you have to deal with those sorts of calls. That is one of the reasons why the management don't particularly like putting women on the desk on their own (although they do) as they tend to get quite a lot of abuse. Drunk men calling up and demanding blowjobs from the front-of-house staff is not that unusual. The waiters and barmen get pro-positioned all the time. Some are offered money to make late-night visits to bedrooms, and I have known a couple of guys who have actually gone and done it. But it's a very dangerous game to play. Then again, maybe it's the danger that makes it so appealing.

That's not to say that female guests aren't equally

predatory. The coffee-throwing woman who went after me tonight is not a rarity. Waiters and bar staff are getting goosed and asked up to the rooms all the time. I did hear a story recently from a mate of mine who is working in New York about a businesswoman who asked for butler service for the weekend and then spent the entire three days fucking him. I wonder if he charged her for extras.

But it's the calls from outside the hotel that can some-times be very upsetting. We get all sorts phoning us, not only former guests who want to be talked through a recipe or two. We used to have a heavy breather who I think must have been watching the hotel, or perhaps lived nearby and walked past to check to see who was on reception, because he would only call when one of the girls was at the desk on her own. He'd say things like 'I can see you' and describe what the girls were wearing before wanking himself off down the phone. We did get the police involved but there is very little they can do in that sort of situation.

We also get depressives and potential suicides on the phone. It's dreadful, often heart-breaking stuff. I suppose they call because they know whatever the time of day someone will answer the telephone, and they just need to talk to somebody. We do have the number of the Samaritans at hand, but often they just want to chat. Last week I had some bloke on the phone who was threatening to kill himself, and it was enough to give me nightmares. Which it did, for at least a couple of days afterwards. He was drunk and rambling, saying that he was going to take these pills. It's one of those things, you know: you want to help but you don't know where to begin. I made him tell me about his girlfriend who had walked out on him, taking his child. Eventually I got him to give me his address, and Dennis called the police. I don't know what happened to the bloke – we don't tend to be kept in the loop – but Dennis assures me he wouldn't have topped himself. Dennis says that if a man really wants to kill himself he goes ahead and does it right away; he doesn't call anyone or tell people that he is going to take pills. If he does that he has no intention of seeing the thing through. Women, on the other hand, according to Dennis, take pills when they know someone will be coming home. They are often more attention-seeking than men. I'm not sure if he's right, but I do like to think that I managed to stop the bloke from killing himself. It makes me sleep better that way.

Talking of sleep, I can't believe Terence is still sitting on the yellow sofa. He appears to be one of our more determined dressing gown men.

'Have you ever thought about taking pills to help you sleep, Terence?' I ask for want of something to say to him.

'Funny you should ask that,' says Terence, leaning forward, opening his legs. I try to keep eye contact with the man for fear of what may now be on display.

'Really?' I ask.

'Yes,' he says. 'I took a couple of them earlier and they didn't seem to make a blind bit of difference.'

'Oh,' I say, nodding.

'Very interesting,' says Dennis.

'Isn't it?' says Terence. 'Then again, I find they don't often work. I'm just one of those people who clearly doesn't need much sleep.'

'Mmm,' says Dennis.

'Margaret Thatcher used to survive on four hours a night, you know,' adds Terence.

'That would explain a lot,' says Dennis.

Terence laughs.

While he is laughing with unnecessary exuberance at Dennis's amazingly quick wit, a large white van pulls up outside the hotel. Dennis is immediately up out of his chair and clicking his fingers at Patrick to follow suit. The morning newspapers have arrived, and the two of them go out to meet the deliveryman to help him in with the bundles. Dennis always seems to like this job. He stands for a good ten minutes outside with the bloke while Patrick struggles back and forth with the heavy piles of newspapers. I think perhaps it's because this van does all the luxury hotels at once and

Dennis likes to be the first with the gossip, picking up any titbits he can. He is laughing, joking, chatting and blowing on his hands. Neither of the two men pay any attention to Patrick; they turn around to acknowledge him only after the job is over. Dennis pats the delivery-man on the back and comes back inside.

'Jesus Christ, it's like brass monkeys out there,' he says, still blowing on his hands. 'Apparently they've had quite a party tonight at Claridge's. There are pissed posh people in black tie littered all over Mayfair searching for cabs. Jeff there' – he points outside where the newspaper van had pulled up – 'he says he thinks it was some film party or something; he swears he saw a couple of stars reeling their way up the street. Let's get a few papers out to see if it's in them.'

'You're not really supposed to read those before we hand them round to the guests,' I say.

'Fuck it,' says Dennis, bending down with a pair of scissors at the ready. 'None of them will notice.'

With the arrival of the newspapers detracting attention away from him, Terence decides to call it a night.

'I can't believe it's almost morning,' he says, looking at the newspapers. 'I think I'd better just lie down, even if I don't actually manage to sleep.'

'Yes, OK then,' says Dennis.

'Goodnight,' he says.

'Goodnight,' I reply.

'Don't work too hard,' he says with a small smile, before getting into the lift.

'We won't,' says Dennis as the lift door closes. 'Thank God for that.'

'Oh, I know,' I say. 'I thought he'd never go.'

'I don't know what you're complaining about,' says Dennis. 'You didn't have to listen to his whole bloody life story.'

'I did a bit.'

'Fuck off you did. You pissed off on any and every bloody errand you could think of so as not to have to talk to the dull bastard. Honestly. Next time I'm on nights with you and we get another dressing gown bore, you're going to have to talk to him. He was driving me mad.'

'He wasn't that bad,' says Patrick, almost out of earshot.

'What?' says Dennis, his head turning swiftly in Patrick's direction.

'He wasn't that bad,' he says again.

'Yes, he was. He was a tosser,' says Dennis. 'Anyway, why aren't you polishing shoes?'

'Oh,' says Patrick.

'Yes, "oh",' says Dennis, imitating him. 'Shouldn't you be off around the hotel picking up shoes to polish by now? Or are you forgetting how to do your job?'

'No, sir,' says Patrick.

'Yes, sir,' says Dennis, nodding towards the stairs. 'And hurry up about it. People will be wanting those soon. Get to it. Now!'

Patrick rushes off up the stairs. Truth be known, he is actually really rather late to be collecting shoes at this time: he should have been standing there, brushing away, for an hour at least by now. Fortunately for him it's Saturday, so there won't be that many pairs of shoes waiting to be done; there won't be any demanding City boys desperate to get their shoes back for their seven a.m. breakfast meeting. If it were a week-day morning, I have to say, Patrick would be in some serious shit right now. I just hope there are no guests with early planes to catch.

It is looking distinctly lighter outside now, but I still have quite a way to go before I can even think about going home. I am so tired now that I'm actually finding it hard to concentrate, and there is a metallic taste in my mouth. The lights are too bright and I am beginning to feel really quite cold. I get some more Pro Plus out of my pocket and try to swallow them without any water. Jesus, they taste bitter. I really hope they'll do the trick. It's too early in the morning for me to be feeling this tired and this shit. Perhaps I should move around a bit.

Dennis is going through the morning papers looking for the Claridge's party story to see if there were indeed any celebrities at the soirée, or milling around afterwards on the streets of Mayfair. Patrick comes downstairs, his arms loaded with pairs of shoes in felt drawstring bags. He has seven pairs in all – all of which, so he says, belong to Mr Masterson. He lays them out in his area near the luggage trolley and both Dennis and I come over to have a look.

'Well, they aren't designer,' says Patrick, holding them up. 'I've never heard of Lobb, have you?'

'They're all handmade especially for him,' says Dennis, picking up one of the shoes and examining it at close range. 'This is some very expensive footwear, my son. Look and learn, Patrick, look and learn.' He smiles. 'And don't fuck it up.'

'No, sir,' says Patrick, sniffing the leather. 'They smell great.'

'Yeah, well,' says Dennis, 'there's no need to go that far, mate. Did you get the breakfast hangers while you were up there?'

'You never said,' stammers Patrick, suddenly looking pink and sweaty. 'Honestly, had you asked me . . .'

'I'll go,' I say. 'Dennis, mate, I could do with the walk. I'm falling asleep here.'

'All right,' says Dennis. 'Next time,' he adds to Patrick, 'try and do a couple of jobs at once. You'll find you might save yourself some time.'

I set off round the hotel collecting breakfast hangers.

It should normally be a room service job, but for some reason in this place it falls to front of house. One of the things that always makes me laugh about breakfast hangers is you're always told you have to leave them out on the doors before 11.30 p.m. But we never come and collect them until around 4.30 a.m. We're far too busy with drunks and prostitutes even to think about collecting before then. Just so long as you get your hanger out before dawn, I guarantee you'll get your breakfast.

It's the weekend, so there'll be many more breakfast slips than during the week. During the week, most of the business guys are up and out for meetings before seven a.m. so they rarely manage to eat before they go. But come Saturday there's nothing a weekender likes more than a big fat fry-up, or some scrambled eggs and champagne.

It's always a bit eerie walking along the corridors at this time of night. It's dark and quiet, and the only thing that stops you from thinking that the place is empty is the constant snoring that guides you along each floor. You wouldn't believe the different snoring pitches there are – high lady snores, the deeper baritone male, and what can only be described as some sort of low-growling marsh dweller who manages to vibrate the paintings in the corridor as well as the bedroom door.

On my way back down the stairs, my hands full of

breakfast hangers, I can hear some scratching along a corridor on the fourth floor. I stand still, my ears straining, trying to hear it above the snores. My toes curl in my shoes. I stare into the darkness, wondering what vile piece of vermin has been missed by the man from Rentokil. My catering trousers are really itching, but I have no time to worry about that as I sidle my way along to the end of the corridor.

The honour bar lights are on. From the amount of loud rattling going on, the rat sounds like it must be enormous. As I turn the corner, I hear the noise of a fridge door opening and I am greeted with the image of a tramp who is standing, backside facing me, with his head in the mini bar, rootling around for alcohol.

'Oi!' I shout, striding into the bar like I am all authoritative and in charge. 'What the hell are you doing?'

The tramp leaps out of his skin and whacks his head on the fridge door. Judging by the collection of empties that are lined up on the side, it looks like he's been in here for some time, knocking back the booze.

'Oh shit,' he slurs, clearly trying to focus on me. He is definitely the worse for wear. 'I was just . . .' He stops. He knows he has been caught with his hands in the fridge, so there is little use in trying to argue his way out of this situation. He holds his tatty, fingerless gloved hands up in the air, like we are in some sort of shoot-out. 'I'll come quietly,' he says. 'Only please don't call the police.'

'Come on,' I say, grabbing the back of his coat. There is a rattle of glass. 'What have you got in your pockets?'

'Oh, nothing,' he says.

'Empty them,' I say.

'You can't make me do that,' he protests.

'Well, it's either me or the police,' I say.

'OK then,' he says, shoving his hands into his pockets and pulling out a whole load of Bombay Sapphire miniatures. He has loads of them: six in his right pocket and a whole fistful in his left. He places them all on the side.

'Anything else?' I say.

'Nothing,' he says.

'How about your inside pockets?'

'Well . . .'

'Come on,' I say. 'Do you really want me to call the police? Because I am very happy to do that.'

'No,' he says, swaying slightly as he pulls open his coat to reveal a small clutch of Penhaligon bottles.

'Shampoo?' I ask. 'What do you want shampoo for?'

'I don't know.' He shrugs. 'The cupboard door was open so I helped myself.'

'Oh,' I say as he puts all the small plastic bottles and three small soaps back on the side. 'What is it with the Bombay Sapphire?'

'I like it,' he says. 'It's my favourite drink.'

'Right. Can I just say, you look a bit familiar.'

'Right.' He nods, looking at the floor.

'You've been here before.'

'A couple of times.'

'This week.'

'Possibly.'

'Have you taken Bombay Sapphire with you every time you've been here?'

'Might have done,' he replies, sounding like a teenager.

'Well, I think you have,' I say.

'Think what you want.'

'I will.'

'You can't fucking prove anything.'

'I can,' I say. 'I found you in here with your hands in the fridge and your pockets full of booze. What more proof do I need?'

'That doesn't prove anything,' he insists.

'It does,' I say. Then I stop myself. What the hell am I doing? Why am I bothering to try to reason with a tramp at 4.45 a.m. in an honour bar? This does have to be one of the more surreal aspects of the job. 'Right, come on,' I say.

'Come on where?'

'Out.'

'Oh, come on,' he moans.

'No, out,' I say. 'You can't stay here. Come on.'

He doesn't bother to kick up a fuss. He turns around and pockets two small bottles of Bombay Sapphire gin before accompanying me towards the lift. I decide not to say anything; Tony will be so pleased to have his Sapphire thief stopped he won't mind a couple more miniatures missing. We travel down in silence in the lift. It grows progressively less fragrant the longer we stand in this confined space together. When the doors finally open on the ground floor I am relieved to get into some fresh air. After that short trip part of me wishes I had given him the Penhaligon shampoo as well before sending him on his way.

'Shit,' says Dennis as we come into reception. 'It's not you again is it, Spike?' Dennis rolls his eyes. 'How many more bloody times do we have to throw you out of here before you know that you are not allowed in here? Mmm? How many?' Dennis seems to have this amazing ability to make a tramp appear sheepish. Spike shuffles along, looking at the floor. 'Don't worry, mate,' Dennis says to me. 'I'll take Spike from here.' Dennis walks up to Spike, puts his arm around his shoulder and escorts him to the door. 'Come along now, Spike. Next time I'll call the police. Honestly, mate, I will, and I'm not kidding.'

I watch as Dennis takes Spike outside. He is not rude or unpleasant to him; in fact, as the two of them talk outside on the street, I see Dennis reach into his pocket, pull out a note and hand it over. He then slaps Spike on his back, sending him on his way.

'Did you just give Spike some money?' I ask as Dennis comes back in to sit down at his desk.

'What? Me?' he says, acting all shocked. 'What do you take me for?'

'Oh,' I say. I know the bloke is lying.

Dennis and I sit in silence. All I can hear is a brushing sound coming from Patrick's corner. He is still hard at work polishing shoes. My stomach starts to rumble. I really fancy having something to eat. The breakfast chefs should be here any minute, I think, as I lean on my desk. I could really murder a bacon sandwich. I could go down and pester the blokes doing the all-night room service, making chicken salads, club sandwiches and burgers, but quite frankly I always think that none of those guys can really cook. Half of them could burn water.

Instead I take them down the breakfast hangers and by the time I come back up I have completed the list of people I would actually kill for a bacon sandwich, my ex-girlfriend being right at the top. The breakfast chefs come in through the door. The two of them arrive together. They both look thin and cold as they walk into reception.

'Morning,' says one of them.

'Is it?' says Dennis.

'As far as I'm concerned it is,' says the other.

'How long before you've got some bacon on the go?' asks Dennis, reading my mind.

'Yes,' I say, 'how long?'

'Five or ten,' says the taller of the two.

'Fantastic,' says Dennis, rubbing his hands together. 'We'll be down in a second.'

It's not really these guys' jobs to cook breakfast for us, but they do it all the same. They are supposed to get everything ready for the big breakfast push at about eight a.m. They are supposed to par-cook all the sausages and bacon so all they have to do is reheat the ingredients to get the breakfasts out on time.

My mouth is filling with saliva. I'll eat my hand soon if I'm not careful. I had no idea I was that hungry. It's the chefs' arrival that sets everyone off, like Pavlov's dogs.

The telephone goes.

'Hello, reception.'

'Why are we here?' comes this weird female voice.

'I'm sorry,' I say.

'Why are we here? Who are we?' she says.

'I'm sorry, I have no idea,' I say, and hang up.

'Who was that?' asks Dennis.

'Oh, that nutter woman who has been staying here for a couple days locked in her room,' I reply, thinking about bacon. 'She was asking all sorts of shit.'

'Oh,' says Dennis.

The phone goes again.

'Hello,' I say.

'You hung up on me,' she says.

'Um, sorry,' I say, not feeling at all sorry.

'No-one hangs up on me,' she says. 'No-one. I'm coming down.' She hangs up.

'Oh shit,' I say to Dennis. 'The nutter woman is on her way down.'

5AM – 6AM

Dennis and I sit and watch the lift, waiting for the mad woman to come down. I suppose it's a bit unfair of me to call her mad, but she has been in the hotel for three days now and no-one, apart from the guys serving room service, has seen her.

We do get guests who book in occasionally for a bit of splendid isolation, but they are usually men and they are usually on some drug binge – rich junkies who want to take their heroin in peace, or cokeheads who have a three-day party with fellow cocaine takers and then leave looking like they've been exhumed. I remember a group of new Russian boys who came here and booked themselves into three suites. They had about three unfeasibly pretty dolly birds with them and bags of cocaine. They closed the bedroom curtains and did not leave the hotel all weekend. They ordered something like thirty bottles of Cristal champagne and almost nothing to eat. When they left on the Sunday, I contemplated calling an ambulance, they looked so ill.

Dennis and I still have our eyes on the lift as it counts down the floors. The bell rings, it arrives on the ground floor, and the doors open. We brace ourselves. Nothing. The woman is nowhere to be seen. Dennis sits back in his seat and I put another foul-tasting mint in my mouth.

'She's changed her mind,' I suggest, watching the lift doors close.

'Looks like it,' says Dennis.

'That's a relief,' I say.

'Mmm,' he says.

'Do you think the bacon is ready yet? My stomach is so hungry it's eating itself.'

'Um,' says Dennis, looking at his watch, 'give it a couple of minutes.'

I start scratching again. The sooner I get home, the sooner I can get out of these trousers. I wonder if the man who knocked himself out on the urinal is OK. Perhaps one of us should ring the hospital and find out.

'Do you think Urinal Man is OK?' I ask Dennis.

'What? Yeah, I'm sure,' he says. 'We would have heard something otherwise.'

'Yeah,' I say, 'you're right. How are you doing with

329

the shoes there, Patrick?' I ask, leaning my head forward over the desk.

'Only one more left,' he says, waving a shiny shoe in my direction. 'Then that's it.'

'You'd better show them to me before you take them up,' says Dennis.

'Are you suggesting that I don't know how to shine shoes?' asks Patrick, sounding a touch offended.

'No,' says Dennis. 'It's just that we have standards, that's all.'

'Yeah, right,' laughs Patrick.

Their conversation is interrupted by the sound of a sort of singing on the stairs: 'Da da da da da da, New York! New York!' We turn and look up the stairs as the mad woman comes down one step at a time, high kicking like a showgirl. She is wearing her complimentary towelling dressing gown but it's hanging open at the front and underneath she is stark naked. 'Da da da da da da,' she sings. 'Da da da da da da.' She kicks again. 'Da da da da da, New York! New York!' Both Dennis and I are so shocked we can't move. Patrick carries on brushing his shoe, his face trained on the woman, his mouth wide open. The woman doesn't look like she can actually see anyone or, indeed, where she is going. She stares in front of her, her head held high, eyes shining in a demonic fashion. She looks like she is lost in the world of show. Her face is sheet white, the bags under her eyes are dark red, and her very bleached blonde hair is standing on end. It would actually be funny if it weren't so disturbing.

She continues on down the stairs still singing 'New York, New York' and kicking her legs. She has me locked in her sights, like I am the only member of her very private audience. She swings her naked hips and takes off an imaginary glove, like a stripper in a nightclub. Flicking it around her head, she throws it at me. She seems disappointed that I don't rush to catch it. 'New York, New York!' she sings, and then, in one swift action, she whips her dressing gown off. She stands totally naked in front of me and says, 'There, that got your attention, didn't it?'

The lift bell goes and a suited man comes out. He doesn't notice the woman at first, he is too busy fiddling with his tie. When he does, he stops dead in his tracks and stares. She ignores him, or doesn't notice him; either way she doesn't even flinch.

'Morning, sir,' I say as he stands there.

'Morning,' he says, rather quietly.

'Checking out?'

'Um, yes,' he says. 'Room 14.'

'14,' I repeat, trying to sound normal. 'Right away.'

The woman doesn't seem at all perturbed at the increase in the size of her audience. She carries on swaying from side to side, staring at me, singing 'New York,

New York' softly under her breath. Her dressing gown is gathered around her feet like a puddle of water.

'How will you be paying, sir?' I ask.

'What?' he says, staring at the naked dancing woman. 'Oh, right,' he adds, gathering his thoughts. 'Visa.'

'Visa,' I repeat.

'Yes,' he says, rattling around the inside top pocket of his suit.

'Anything from the mini bar, sir?' I ask.

'Um, yes,' he says. 'A bottle of red wine.'

'Just the one?'

'Yes.'

'No nuts or anything?'

'No.'

'Right, sir, that's £385.70.'

'Good,' he says as he hands over the card.

'Would you like to check the bill?'

'No,' he says slowly. 'I have a plane to catch.'

'Right, of course.'

I go into the back office and run his card through the machine. I can feel the mad woman's stare boring into my back. I can still hear her muttered rendition of 'New York, New York' behind me.

'Good stay, sir?' I hear Dennis trying to make pleasant conversation.

'Yes, thank you.'

'First time?' Dennis carries on valiantly.

'What? No,' says the man. 'Third.'

'Third,' says Dennis, sounding impressed. 'I think I'd call sir a regular.'

'Yes,' says the man, looking relieved as I come out of the office bearing his credit-card slip to sign. He scribbles his signature, picks up his bag and makes a dash for the door.

'Do you want your receipt, sir?' I ask.

'No,' he calls back. 'You keep it.'

'Can I get you a cab?'

'No, thank you,' he says as he hurls himself through the revolving doors.

'OK,' I say in a breezy voice. 'Dennis,' I continue, maintaining the same tone of voice, 'I think you'd better call the police or an ambulance or something.'

'Do you know,' says Dennis, sounding just as jolly, 'I might just try that nine-nine-nine service.'

'You do that.' I smile. 'Right away.'

I walk slowly around the desk, keeping eye contact with the naked dancing woman through the tropical flower display. I keep an inane smile on my face as I nod along to her tuneless singing. I approach her with caution, and very slowly I bend down to pick up her dressing gown. She points at me like some provocative showgirl. I slowly stand up and put the dressing gown around her shoulders in an attempt to claw back some of her dignity, but she starts to scream at the top of her voice. She turns around and tries to pull the towelling off her back.

'GET IT OFF ME! GET IT OFF ME! GET IT OFF ME!' she yells. Her voice is deep and demonic. She sounds possessed.

Dennis looks shocked as he talks on the telephone. 'D'you hear that?' he says. 'I have a feeling this is serious. Some sort of drug-induced psychosis.'

I back off, holding my hands in the air. This woman is really quite scary. I actually don't want to have anything to do with her. In fact, if she wants to sing show tunes while stark naked in reception, who am I to interfere?

'Well, that's good,' says Dennis in a sing-song voice. 'They'll be round in a couple of minutes.'

'Just a couple?' I say.

'Oh yes,' he says back.

'In the meantime?'

'In the meantime, let's enjoy the show.'

'OK,' I say, my voice sounding high and tight.

The mad woman is now bored of staring at me and seems to be more interested in the chandelier above her head. She starts to dance in a circle, staring skywards, snaking her arms around her swaying body. I don't know what she's singing any more; it sounds like a song of her own composition. Dennis and I look at each other across the room. He shrugs and does one of those circular crazy gestures at his temple. I am just relieved that she has found another audience.

The police are as good as their word: they arrive within a few minutes. They approach the naked woman quite carefully, moving forward tentatively. Not that she is noticing a thing. She keeps staring up at the ceiling doing her Queen of Sheba dance.

'Excuse me, hello, excuse me,' says the policewoman. 'How long has she been like this?' she asks me.

'About ten minutes,' I say, 'but she has been in her room on her own for three days now.'

'Three days?' asks the policewoman.

'Yes,' I say.

The policewoman picks up the dressing gown and makes to put it on the woman's back.

'I wouldn't do that if I were you,' I say.

Too late. The policewoman places the dressing gown on the woman's shoulders and all hell breaks loose. She screams and screams. We really can't have her here any more – she's going to start waking up the other guests. She starts to roll around on the floor, patting her arms and back like the dressing gown has set fire to her skin.

'I think we should take her,' says the policewoman. 'Get her to hospital to see what drugs she has been taking.'

'That would be good,' says Dennis. 'We do have a hotel to run.'

'Do you know what her name is?' asks the policewoman.

'Um,' I say, 'I could find out.' I look on the register and come up with Claire Parker. 'Claire Parker,' I say.

'OK, Claire,' says the policewoman. 'Me and my colleague here are going to help you.'

Claire doesn't even appear to recognize her own name; she carries on spinning around naked in the middle of reception. Then, through the front door comes a policeman carrying what looks like a white straitjacket. Jesus, they look frightening. It is one of my room 101 fears to be taken away in one of those. In fact, I'm afraid I can't look; all I can do is listen to her scream as she is wrestled to the ground. I can hear her flailing around on the floor while three people pin her down and strap her into the jacket. I know there is no other way of getting her out of here and getting her help, but it doesn't make it any more palatable. By the time I feel able to turn round they have her all strapped in and they are dragging her out towards the van. She's still shouting and screaming and swearing at the top of her voice. Her slim white legs are still trying to run away, but she is going nowhere.

As she goes out through the revolving doors, another guest is on his way in, straight off a plane from somewhere. His face looks a picture of shock and horror.

'My God,' he says as he dumps his bags at reception, 'what happened to her?'

'She refused to pay the bill,' declares Dennis from the other side of the room. 'We do that to all our guests.'

'Oh,' says the guest, looking confused.

'Don't worry.' I smile reassuringly. 'He's only joking. What is your name, please, sir?'

I check in a rather confused and disturbed Mr Armstrong. You can tell he's asking himself if he really wants to stay here for a whole week. When I also tell him that he'll have to wait for his room as it has yet to be made up, he looks like he is about to walk straight back out of the hotel. But then I remind him he should have made a pre-reg booking if he expected to be allowed to check in this early, and he shuts up and walks rather slowly into the dining room, to wait until they start serving breakfast. It normally begins at seven a.m. at the weekend, but I said I'd go downstairs into the kitchen to see if they can make an exception.

Downstairs, the kitchen is buzzing with a bit more life. The cookers are on, there's the smash and rattle of activity and the chatter of conversation, and all the while the smell of frying bacon competes with chlorine. The two chefs seem to have a lot more than bacon and sausages on the go: they've already made a pile of toast and a vat of scrambled eggs by the time I get in there.

Just as I start to negotiate a full English breakfast for

the tired Mr Armstrong in the hotel dining room, the head chef turns up. He's very early. There must be a wedding or something on today. I've worked with him before. His name is Matthew, and he's a temperamental old bastard. I start to explain the situation and he brushes me away with a wave of his hand, pretending that he can't hear above the noise of the kitchen.

'Please,' I find myself saying, 'it would really make our life so much easier.'

'I'm not here to make your life easier,' he declares. 'Rules are rules and they're not allowed to be broken. The guests don't get their breakfasts until seven a.m. He'll just have to wait.'

I'm so tired and pissed off that I march straight out of the kitchen. Then I turn round and give him the finger. He pretends not to notice, but I know he's seen me. Even then it doesn't make me feel any better. I walk into the staff dining room, thinking I might make myself and Dennis a bacon sandwich. There are about seven Bangladeshi cleaners in there, chatting away to one another while eating some sort of curry dish the kitchen makes especially – or should I say reheats especially – for them. They ignore me as I go up to the hot plate and look through the stainless steel trays. There are a few rashers of bacon in a bowl. They are still bright pink, and the fat is barely cooked. They must have been frying for about a minute at most.

There is also some white bread in a pile that was toasted a while back; it's now stretchy and springy like a trampoline. I butter the toast and make two sandwiches, making sure that I cover Dennis's in brown sauce. I've made enough sandwiches for him not to make the mistake of leaving the stuff off ever again. Helping myself to a couple of paper plates, I turn around to leave the dining room. On my way out I bump into the Iraqi doctor I spoke to earlier. I smile. He looks the other way, and neither of us speaks.

Back upstairs, Dennis is on his desk phone. He's on hold for one of the airlines. It's his job at about this time in the morning to ring and check to see if any flights are delayed or if any have come in early so that we can work out who to expect for an early check-in. It's not so vital on a Saturday morning, but in the middle of the week when we have rooms to vacate, others to clean and businessmen on their way from Heathrow, these vital minutes, or half-hours, can make all the difference between keeping a New Yorker waiting in reception and getting him straight up to his room.

Dennis gets off the phone. 'There's snow in Washington,' he says, 'and some fog in Paris, but apart from that all the flights appear to be on time.'

'Right,' I say.

What Dennis is forgetting is that I don't really care. I've one hour left and I'm just desperate to get through it with the minimum amount of fuss and effort. I am even rather hoping that after my bacon sandwich I might grab a quick forty winks on the desk. What's good enough for that lazy shit Ben is good enough for me.

'Those bacon?' asks Dennis as he walks towards the desk.

'Yup,' I say. 'And brown sauce, just how you like it.'

'You'll make someone a great wife one day,' says Dennis as he follows me into the back office to eat his breakfast.

It wouldn't look good for either of us to be caught eating in reception, but then that's why, I always think, they gave us the back room. We're always popping in and out of there to eat a sandwich or a bag of crisps, which goes some way towards explaining why the place stinks so much. Dennis eats his sandwich in about three mouthfuls. He's a man who is clearly too busy to chew. I take a bit more time, savouring every single distinctly inorganic mouthful. But when I'm only halfway through someone rings the reception bell. I come through the door to be confronted by the woman who threw a pot of coffee at the door after I wouldn't have sex with her. She's standing there with her husband.

'Good morning,' I say.

'Good morning,' she says, looking down into her handbag like nothing ever happened. She does at least have the decency to blush.

6AM – 7AM

I check out the coffee-hurler and her husband with the minimum of fuss. The weird thing is, looking at her in the pale purple light of dawn, she's a lot more attractive than the night-time version of herself, and I kind of wish I had slept with her. She has a pretty turned-up nose, large lips that curl up at the corners and lots of thick blonde hair, and she does sheepish very well indeed. I notice, as I hand back her credit card, that her name is Ciara. That's always been one of my favourite names. Next time, I think, as I watch her walk away . . . Jesus, I must be tired if I'm even thinking this way.

Dennis is back on his mobile phone again, telling another relative of his the story about the naked woman singing in reception. He's telling it like it's a joke. It sounds much better in the telling than it did in the witnessing. I can hear the person on the other end of the telephone hooting with laughter. I do like Dennis; nothing ever really seems to touch him.

A couple of the kitchen staff and a few of the chambermaids are already coming into the hotel for early breakfasts. Some of them come from miles away. They leave home early so that public transport doesn't make them late, then make the most of their spare time by having a spot of breakfast.

Mr Armstrong comes out into reception. The man looks tired, hungry and a little pissed off. I have to admit that in my quest for my own bacon sandwich I had rather forgotten that he was sitting there, waiting to be served.

'Any idea when I might get some food?' he asks.

'Any minute now.' I smile.

'Right,' he says, not sounding at all convinced. 'There isn't even anyone serving in the dining room,' he adds. 'I haven't spotted a waiter in the half hour I have been sitting in there. Just a cup of coffee, something.' He sounds more desperate than pissed off.

'I'd go back and sit in the dining room, sir,' I say. 'I'll send someone in to take your order and bring you a pot of coffee.'

'Please,' he says. 'And hurry up about it.'

'Right away, sir,' I say as breezily as twenty-four hours standing perpendicular will let me.

I call down to room service in the kitchen. It takes an age for someone to answer the phone. I ask them to bring a pot of coffee into the dining room and to get one of the breakfast waiters to take Mr Armstrong's order. For some reason I have to make this request three times. Either the bloke on the other end doesn't understand English, or he is being deliberately obstinate.

I've just about had enough of this job, this night, this life. I have less than an hour to go and I swear to God I am counting down the minutes. I keep looking at the clock on the switchboard. In fact, I have been doing it so much over the past ten minutes or so that I am going to have to ration myself, otherwise the clock doesn't appear to be moving at all.

Dennis is still chatting away on his mobile. I think that next time I do a shift with him I'm going to ask him to switch it off. Patrick suddenly stops his polishing, announces that he has finished doing the shoes and walks over to Dennis to show him. Frankly, I thought he'd done them all a while ago, but apparently not. From over here, Dennis looks impressed. He holds each shoe up to the light, checking to see if the soles and the heels are clean. He pats Patrick on the back, gives him the thumbs up and sends him on his way to Mr Masterson's suite. Patrick looks pleased with himself as he stands by the lift. His pale skin has a bit of colour to it. It's amazing what praise does to a lad's complexion.

My phone goes.

'Reception,' I say.

It's one of the room service boys, and he's outside old Mrs Robertson's room with her morning tea, except she's not answering the door. He's been knocking on her door for the past couple of minutes and he can't hear anything. I explain that it's not odd that he can't hear anything, because neither can she. But I do also feel that it is a little strange. Mrs Robertson has had her cup of tea delivered to her room at 6.15 a.m. every day since she moved in here two and a half years ago. It is one of the hotel routines; it sort of marks the beginning of the day. Mrs Robertson gets her tea, and we all change shifts. It's odd that she's not answering. I offer to phone and see if I can wake her. I dial the number and wait for a long while before hanging up. Her television can't be on; she must be able to hear it. I have an odd sensation in my stomach and I don't like the way I am feeling.

I tell Dennis that I am off upstairs to check on something and he seems to register. All the way up in the lift I have butterflies in my stomach, and I am beginning to feel sick. I arrive on the top floor and walk to the end of the corridor where I find the young lad with Mrs Robertson's morning tea, now getting cold as he stands anxiously outside her door.

'Have you tried knocking again?' I ask.

'Many times,' he replies, his face looking white and strained. 'I have brought her morning tea almost every day for the past year,' he continues, 'and she always answers the door.'

We look at each other. I glimpse a terrified yet resigned look in his eyes. We both know what we will find once I open the door.

'Mrs Robertson,' I shout hopefully, hammering on the door again. He joins in, his fists banging away, sounding even more desperate than mine. 'I think perhaps I should open the door,' I suggest, reaching into my pocket for my passcard. The young man recoils. He takes two steps back and shakes his head. His eyes start to shine, and I can see he is about to cry. 'I'll go in first,' I say. 'You don't have to come in.' He doesn't say anything. He stands with his back to the corridor wall, firmly holding on to his tray.

I open the door to her bedroom and walk in. The curtains are closed and it is still dark inside. The air is very still indeed. The bedroom smells of mothballs, lavender and the sweet, high aroma of talc, but it feels like there is no oxygen at all. I walk over to the other side of the room and draw the curtains. I also open the window. I read somewhere that when someone dies you should always do that; it releases the spirit or something. I turn round towards the bed and see Mrs Robertson lying there. She is flat on her back, the bedding pulled up tight around her neck, her thin hands still holding on to the sheets. The woman is definitely dead. I can tell from here. I don't need to put a mirror in front of her face to check if she's still breathing. I walk over to take a closer look. Her eyes are firmly shut and her mouth is the slightest bit open, but her face looks hollow. She looks tiny, all skin and bone. She wasn't exactly enormous when alive, but in death she looks half the size. They say the soul weighs twenty-one grams. Well, hers must have been a hell of a lot heavier than that.

I hear the room service boy come in behind me. He walks slowly towards the bed and squeaks when he sees the body. He stands there with his hands over his mouth. He starts to shake, and a silent tear runs down his cheek. It must be the first time he has seen a dead body. This is my third.

You'd be amazed how many people die in hotels. I'm sure they must be second only to hospitals for corpses. Hotel deaths fall into two separate categories: there are some who have every intention of dying here when they check in, and there are others, of course, who do it by mistake. Take Mrs Robertson, for example. Both she and the staff always knew that she would die here. After her husband passed on she chose this hotel as the place where she wanted to end her days. There are other guests who do the same. Hotels are a popular choice for people who want to commit suicide. You can see why. You book yourself into a room and no-one will disturb you for days at a time, unless you want them to. It sounds odd, but I sometimes think committing suicide in a hotel is a way of sparing the family. The discovery of the body, the clean-up and the aftermath are all dealt with by strangers. The family doesn't have to be involved at all.

Then, of course, there are the people who die by mistake through drug overdoses, heart attacks and sexual misadventure, by choking on their vomit or even falling over when drunk, like the man in the urinals earlier on tonight. I have only come across one heart attack victim so far: he'd taken too much cocaine while sleeping with a prostitute and died on the job. Half the guys working in the hotel couldn't think of a better way to go. However, if they'd seen the body they might have changed their minds. It was not a pretty sight.

Mrs Robertson is my second death by natural causes. The other was another old man in a hotel I worked in before. It was a bit of a nightmare, actually. He wasn't the nicest of blokes and, if I'm being honest, the hotel didn't notice for a couple of days. He wasn't a long-termer. He'd booked in for a short stay, and we'd all rather taken a bit of a dislike to him. So when he didn't answer his door for breakfast, it was just left outside. As was breakfast again the next day. It was only during the afternoon of the second day that someone thought it a little odd that no-one had seen sight nor sound of the bloke, and to be honest the chambermaids wanted to get in to clean the room. So I was despatched to try to raise him. He was as stiff as a board when I got in there and had obviously been dead for quite a while. We called the police and an ambulance crew, and informed all the relevant people. But when the ambulance crew turned up to take him away, there was a bit of a problem. We had a wedding blocking the whole of reception and the ambulance couldn't get anywhere near the front of the hotel, so we had to bring him down the back stairs and out through the kitchens. I know you shouldn't laugh at the dead, but for some reason it was very funny. We wrapped him up in a blanket and hauled him down the stairs. One of my old mates dropped him as we came through the kitchen and we all cried with laughter. God knows what Health and Safety would have said. I suppose you really had to be there in order to find it funny. But take it from me, it was.

Anyway, Mrs Robertson is obviously a little different. I really liked the old dear. She was sweet and elegant and lovely to everyone, tipping 10p for every cup of tea she had. The room service bloke standing next to me, with his nose running, obviously agrees. I call down to reception to tell Dennis the sad news, and for once he doesn't have very much to say. He goes all monosyllabic on me and tells me to cover the body, come back downstairs and let him call the emergency services.

I walk back over to Mrs Robertson's bed and pull on the sheets. The room service bloke starts crossing himself and muttering prayers in some foreign language while I cover Mrs Robertson's face. We both then leave the room, closing the door behind us. He bends down to pick up her tray of cold tea and we travel down in the lift in silence.

Dennis seems to have got everything organized by the time we get to reception. He looks at me with a serious face as I walk back in.

'All right, mate?' he asks.

'Yeah.' I nod. 'It's not my first.'

'Oh, right,' he says. 'That's OK then.'

'Yeah,' I say again. 'But it's the only one I really knew and liked.'

'Yeah,' he says. 'She was a nice old bird.'

For some reason, his referring to Mrs Robertson as an 'old bird' annoys me. But I don't say anything. Instead, I walk into the back room to be on my own for a second, to try to get the image of her hollow face out of my head. I stand with my nose pressed against the window, clouding up the glass.

Through the fog, I can see the night staff leaving. The

cleaners have changed out of their overalls, and suddenly they look like individuals. They are leaving in groups of two or three at a time, chatting away. They look animated and alive, unlike the sad ciphers I see every night scrubbing the floors. There is also a steady stream of chambermaids and kitchen staff turning up for work. Their heads are down and their collars are up against the wind. They are all going straight into the staff dining room for their free breakfasts.

The telephone in the office suddenly goes. I jump a bit – I must be exhausted. I answer it, and it's some music PR in a panic on her mobile at Heathrow. She has got a band arriving from America and wants to know if we can put them and their entourage up in the hotel. She mumbles something about the lead singer not wanting to go to the hotel the record company has booked. I tell her that unfortunately the hotel is full and we can't help her.

I'm not lying, but I might well have said the same thing even if we'd had room. Hotels are not big fans of entourages. Financially, we like them as we always overcharge for the rooms. If you want eight rooms on the same floor, we tend to sting you for it, but only because we have to compensate ourselves for the trouble. I remember Mike Tyson at the Grosvenor House Hotel hanging someone out of the window by his feet. The hotel security couldn't do anything about it because Tyson had come with his own beefcake. It's a scene we can do without. Having said that, the Lanesborough was jumping with joy when Michael Jackson booked the whole of one floor. And then, of course, they charged him again when it came to the extras.

I come back out into reception and Dennis tells me that the police and the ambulance crew have gone upstairs. Not that any foul play is expected, but they have to go and make sure.

Someone calls down and asks me to prepare his bill. I start the printout and notice that he is yet another man who has been hitting the porn lines. He's spent £487.30. I sigh. I really hope that Liz gets here soon before he comes down and starts arguing about it. I'm not in the mood. In fact, I am absolutely knackered. I can't believe I have made it to the end of my shift. I look at the reception clock; I only have five minutes left. Dennis still has another hour to go, but he's already tidying up his papers and getting ready to leave.

At last, I see Liz walking through the rain towards the hotel, her body and brolly bent against the wind. My shoulders collapse slightly with the release of tension. Adrenalin pours out of my body so fast I feel like a rag doll. I am suddenly mugged by my own tiredness. I feel weak and sick, and I can barely see in front of me.

'Oh dear,' says Liz as she wafts back into reception, her blonde hair blown, her face made up, her body well slept in and her skin smelling strongly of perfume. 'You look terrible.'

'Do I?' I reply, thinking you don't look that goddamn super yourself.

'Tricky night?' she asks sarcastically.

'Not really.' I smile, picking up my thin overcoat. 'Nothing I couldn't handle. In fact, I might go so far as to say that it was really quite banal.'

'Oh, right,' she says, putting her coat in the back room and shaking out her umbrella, a tight smile on her lip-lined mouth. 'Anything I should know about?'

'Nothing, really,' I say nonchalantly. 'I think some men will be appearing in a minute,' I add, 'bringing a dead body down the front stairs.'

'Yeah, right,' she says, picking up her ballpoint pen and clicking it efficiently. 'Goodnight.'

'Night,' I say, buttoning up my coat as I walk towards the door.

I'm only really putting one foot in front of the other in the hope that I will actually make it home. Come Monday morning I'll be back at my desk to do the whole thing all over again.